"WASSA MATTER MATE, SOMEBODY 'ITCHYER?"

A Suburban Childhood

TONY BETTS

First published in Great Britain in 2001
by Pen Press Publishers Limited
39-41 North Road, Islington
London N7 9DP

Copyright © Tony Betts 2001

British Library Cataloguing-in-Publication Data.
A catalogue record for this book is available
from the British Library.

ISBN 1 900796 24 4

Cover design: Catrina Sherlock
Photograph of Harewood Road (1935) from 'Isleworth - 2nd Selection' by Tempus ©Mary Brown, reproduced with kind permission

For My Wife Irene

and all the relatives, friends,
neighbours, and acquaintances
who made those days memorable

ACKNOWLEDGEMENTS

Special thanks to: Pauline Betts; Nellie Betts; Sylvia Betts;
John Mundell; Evelyn Horne; Mike Curwen; Brian Howard;
Brenda (Morrison) Harling; Brian Bidgood;Shirley Brown;
L. Peter Cooper; Elisabeth (Pegg) Moon; Olive (Jukes) Taylor;
Jill (Martin) Turner; Mary and Kevin Brown; A.G. 'Phil' Harris;
Cicely D.(Webb) Fox; Dorothy (Saunders) Jackson;
Thelma (Scales) and Ian Hutton-Penman; Ernie and Eileen Hole;
Fareham Borough Library; the BBC Written Archives Centre,
Reading; Isleworth Town School staff especially Beryl Small and
Pauline Grahame; Andrea Cameron and the Hounslow & District
History Society and Hounslow Library Heritage Services;
Whitstable Library.

'Wind In The Willows' by H. Fraser-Simson -
Published by I.M.P. Ltd.
'Miner's Dream' words and music by Will Godwin and Leo Dryden
c1891, reproduced by permission of E.M.I. Music Publishing Ltd.
'The Elf and the Dormouse' by Oliver Herford (1863-1935) -
Published by Doubleday (New York) = Random House Inc.
'The March Wind' by E. H. Henderson,
'Book of a Thousand Poems' by Evans Bros 1951-
Rights now with Harper Collins Publishers Ltd.
'Jingle, Jangle, Jingle' by F. Loesser and J. J. Lily -
Published by B.M.G. Music Publishers.
'Duck's Ditty' from 'The Wind In The Willows' by Kenneth Grahame
copyright The University Chest, Oxford, reproduced by
permission of Curtis Brown Ltd., London
'Odd Ode' by Cyril Fletcher - Rights held by C. Fletcher.

The photograph of Harewood Road (1935) is reproduced by kind
permission of Mary and Kevin Brown. It appeared in the excellent
complementary Archive Photographs series of books on Isleworth,
now published by Tempus.

FOREWORD

Primarily this is a story of childhood, in the London suburbs, during the period 1939 to 1946. It centres on Isleworth, nine miles west of London's Hyde Park Corner, but touches little upon the more visible and famous edifices, or civic and other events, which are all well-documented elsewhere. Rather it is a child's experience of life at home and away, on schooldays, holidays and washdays, during war and peacetime, with an intimate view of street and bedroom, park and playground, alleyway and bushes, recapturing the flavour of primary school, reliving the anxieties and mistakes, and the pleasure of being entertained, and of being engrossed in books and toys, reflecting enjoyment and endurance, and seeing events and surroundings being absorbed into a child's ever-expanding horizon.

It is, of course, also about me, and about my family, which is why I found it necessary to devote a few pages to explaining just who they all are, and how we came to Isleworth - a journey that will have echoes in many other families.

Essentially it revolves around people. Apart from family and a few friends, most of them have, alas, long vanished from my life and probably from Isleworth too, but they are not forgotten. Everybody's recollection of an event is, of course, slightly different, but whether the occasion was joyous, tedious, distressing, or an apparent conflict, from this distance, all can be seen as part of the great learning process that in the end makes us what we are.

I am grateful for the privilege of having encountered all those people, and many others who are not even mentioned in these pages, and this is my tribute to them.

CONTENTS

Illustrations

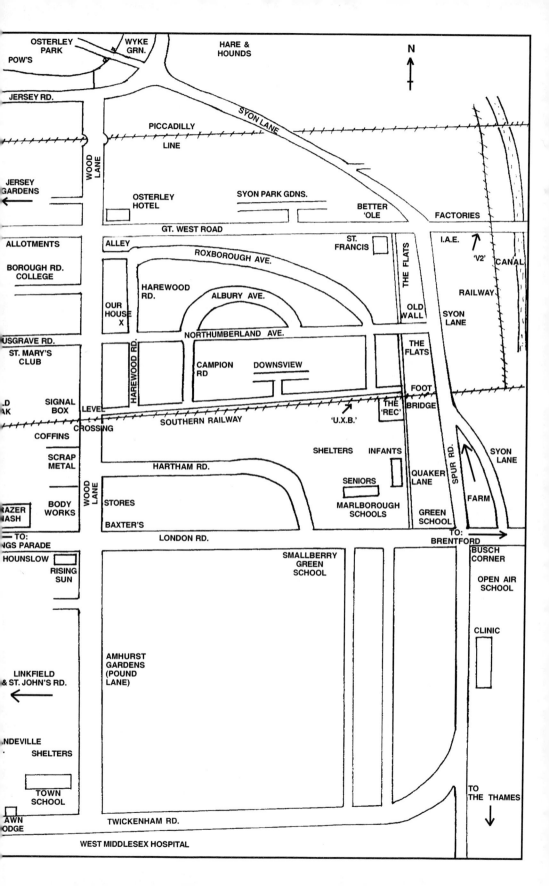

CHAPTER ONE

WHO?

'Wassa matter mate, somebody 'itchyer?' The round, friendly face loomed large over the low fence that enclosed our front garden. Startled, I mumbled a negative response and watched as the boy grinned and rocketed off to join his pals on their raucous progress down the road to school.

I was four; tear-stained after some trivial domestic upset, and this was my first conscious encounter with the world that lay outside the control of our family. I was favourably impressed. Somebody out there cared!

Walking back through the open side entrance to the kitchen door, I found my mother at the sink, and told her what had been said. Quite to my surprise, she laughed and laughed, until I joined in. Perhaps it was the incongruity of the phrase, now delivered by a well-spoken innocent, but whatever the reason, it remained a 'Huge Joke'. I had discovered that humour might lie, unsuspected, in ordinary, everyday things.

There is no doubt that a sense of humour helped to sustain us through the Second World War, which was then imminent. But who were we, and how did we come to be in Isleworth?

Queen Victoria had not long been crowned when Thomas Betts walked away from the dire poverty of agricultural labour in the late 1830s, while he was still a teenager. He had already lost his parents, his grandparents and his guardian uncle, John Betts, when he determined to seek better fortune in London. Penniless, he made his way from Hadleigh in Suffolk to Marylebone, a journey of some seventy miles, and there he met up with Alfred Eperon, and established a house painting business.

By 1844, Thomas was able to call himself a 'journeyman' house painter. In the same year he married Alfred's young sister Charlotte. It was, however, another eight years before their first and only child, Frederick, my grandfather, was born.

In what seemed like a cruel repetition of history, both Thomas and Charlotte died while Frederick was a young boy, and his guardian, Uncle Alfred, died a few short years later. Frederick went to stay with Alfred's sister Sarah, who lived in Paddington with her two daughters and her husband John Rouse, a French polisher from Isleworth.

Frederick also became a house painter - perhaps he was just old enough to have learnt the rudiments from his Uncle Alfred, and to inherit whatever equipment there was. Anyway, he managed to earn a living, and then from the late 1870s until his retirement he was one of the army of contract decorators working for William Whiteley of Westbourne Grove.

Around 1880, Frederick became acquainted with Alfred Baker and his wife Fanny, who lived in Kensington, and he married Alfred's sister Ellen. At about the same time, William Greenwood, a railway worker, married Emma, another of Alfred's sisters, and they emigrated to raise their family in South Africa.

The three families, Baker, Betts and Greenwood, remained in touch for some eighty years. The Greenwood descendants returned to England in the 1970s and are still in contact with the Betts family. The Bakers have for the moment, alas, been 'lost', and the reasons for that are as follows.

Alf and Fanny Baker had three sons, Pash (christened Alfred), George and Len, and they moved from Kensington to Hammersmith around 1896. Pash, a regular soldier who served in the Boer War and the Great War, married and eventually settled in Barnehurst, Bexley Heath, but he and his wife died in the 1960s without issue. George went to America around 1910 'to join a circus and become a lion tamer', but although we know he might have adopted the name of George Betts, there is no record of him in the circus personnel lists and he has not been heard of since. Len married and took his wife and two boys to Canada around 1920, and they too vanished from our lives.

Meanwhile, my grandparents Frederick and Ellen Betts initially set up home in Portnall Road, Paddington, and over a period of twenty years or so produced ten children. The contract decorating work was spasmodic in the 1890s and thereafter, and the family was poor enough to have to resort to 'moonlight flits' to dodge the landlord. In this manner, and mostly at night, they progressed westward up the Harrow Road, finally settling in Harlesden.

Charles, my father, left school at twelve and joined a local Harlesden man making bicycles. They went on to make motorcycles and maintain motor cars, and so Charles learnt to drive. By 1912 he was a hire car driver.

When the First World War came, he volunteered to fight, and was naturally placed in Motor Transport, which became the Army Service Corps. He was trained near St Alban's, and then, along with nine brothers and cousins, he served his time in France. He emerged unscathed, but it was a traumatic experience. Two of the Greenwood boys from South Africa were killed on the Somme, and Father's brother Alfred Betts was lost at Passchendaele.

After the war, Father got a job as chauffeur to the directors of J Lyons & Company, based at Cadby Hall in Hammersmith. He met my Mother, Nellie Savage of Enfield, while she was working as a despatch clerk in a Lyons restaurant in Shaftesbury Avenue, and they married in 1924.

Nellie's family had moved to rural Enfield from Kennington in 1887, having also previously lived in Camberwell and Walworth for many years. She was the youngest but one of ten brothers and sisters, two of whom died in infancy. It was said that Nellie's grandfather, William Savage senior, performed in the early South London halls with handbells and accordion, and so Nellie and two of her brothers inherited a natural musical talent.

Largely as a result of geography, my Mother's family were less well known to us than Father's. Enfield, where Grandma Savage remained until her death in 1946, was considered a difficult and expensive journey from Isleworth, and we made it only three or four times. During the Second World War, one also had to take account of the Government's admonishment: 'Is your journey really necessary?'.

I did meet Aunt Alice, who was over six feet tall, and lived with Grandma Savage. We also visited Uncle Tom, who had a very successful men's outfitters and drapery business, and Uncle Charlie, who managed Howard's cycle shop in Enfield. The rest of the Savage family were scattered, and today there are many more descendants in Australia than in England.

Not surprisingly, visitors from Enfield to our house in Isleworth were also quite rare, but they included Uncle Charlie and his wife Alice, and Mother's sister Aunt Alice, who came once, and their cousin, Bill Powis, who kept a couple of butcher's shops, one at Hounslow West, and one on the Staines Road near Wellington Road in Hounslow.

Father's family were nearer to us, and at that time perhaps more inclined to be in touch. Aunty Win (Cook) lived at Hayes with her large and lively family, and we often visited them by bus. The others we saw occasionally - Aunt Rose (Jermy) at Wembley, Uncle Harry at Greenford, Uncle Wilf at Harrow, and Uncle George at Uxbridge. George was a small man who loved animals and had a reputation for being fearless, and indeed he had earned the Distinguished Conduct Medal during the Great War in an incident involving a burning ammunition train, and had more recently thrashed a bigger man for ill-treating a dog.

Grandma Betts, who survived until 1950, went to live first with Rose, then with Win. The family home in Drayton Road, Harlesden, was still occupied by Uncle Fred, whose wife had died in 1917, and his unmarried sister, Aunt Em, and it remained in the Betts family until Em died in 1971.

Aunt Em was the emissary who travelled round to the various relatives carrying word of this and that, circulating photographs and writing to those she could not reach otherwise. This was a good thing, in that it kept everyone in the picture, but it backfired now and then when stories were given a bit of a slant in the telling, and somebody's feathers got ruffled. As a result, the reception she got was at times a little prickly, but Em, conscious of her duty to the family, continued her rounds undaunted, and no lasting harm was done. Uncle Fred remained a widower, content to live quietly with his sister, but evidently had a bright side and was known to the Cook family as a man who enjoyed a pint and a football match - he supported QPR. However, Father's impression was of a man who had been a regular in the Middlesex Infantry in the rough, tough days at the turn of the century, a 'bouncer' at a Portsmouth dance hall pre-1910, and eventually a rent collector. He was also the man who knocked down my grandfather and put a stop to his drunken bullying of the family at home.

The only time I met Uncle Fred was when he came to our house, and I found him a tall, lean, dour man of few words. When I was introduced, Fred turned to Father and said 'He's lanky, isn't he?', then the two brothers stayed shut in the back room talking until Fred left. He died not long after, and the close conversation may have had something to do with the money he left hidden in the wall of the house at Harlesden, to be shared out between the remaining brothers and sisters.

A few times we made an expedition to Barnehurst to see Pash and Nell Baker, the last remnant of that family in England. They were very welcoming and homely, and in contrast to the impression left by Uncle Fred, it was much more difficult to imagine the genial pipe-slippers-and-cardigan Pash as the smart, tough, dashing sergeant of the Hussars, whom Father so much admired.

When my parents Nellie and Charles married, she was genteel and extremely shy, whereas Charles was already an experienced man of the world, with the horrors of the Great War and family loss behind him. He was also something of an extrovert who had entertained with his singing, and even made a brief but not too successful appearance on the stage at the Shepherds Bush Empire ('We got the bird, and my chum ran off the stage, leaving me to finish the act on my own!') They lived in a flat at 16 Sterndale Road, Shepherds Bush, and Dennis was born in a nursing home near there in 1925. Then in 1929, Father obtained a mortgage and they moved to a newly built house in

Harewood Road, Isleworth. Pauline was born in an Ealing nursing home that same year.

I was born at West Middlesex Hospital in 1935, much too late to meet my grandfathers, who had both died some years earlier, and just too late to be a 'Jubilee Baby' (it was another fifty years before I acquired one of the celebratory mugs that were awarded to qualifiers). The youngest member of the family, Sylvia, was born in 1942, in the middle of the war, at Harewood Road.

We all grew up in the same house and garden, becoming familiar with the same surroundings, sharing and handing on our toys and books, and following each other through the local primary schools.

Dennis went to Isleworth Town School Infants and Juniors, but then, owing to illness, he did not take the scholarship. He went on to Marlborough Senior, which was a mixed school until Smallberry Green School for boys was opened. At fourteen, he successfully transferred to the Twickenham Technical College, where he became school captain, and at one time held six athletics records. Pauline started at the Town School Infants, then attended the newly opened Marlborough Infants, and returned to the Town School Juniors, where she passed her scholarship to the Green School. She later trained at Whitelands College, and became a well-known and respected local primary school teacher.

I too went to the Marlborough Infants, then the Town School Juniors, but the continuity did not end there. Long-serving teachers like Miss Saunders (Mrs Jackson) at the Marlborough Infants, and Miss Keene (Mrs Redgrove), Miss Pegg (Mrs Moon), Miss Webb (Mrs Fox) and Mrs Nicolson at the Town School Juniors knew three out of four of us, and Mr Brown was headmaster of the Town School for us all, from 1930 to 1954.

What follows is mostly comprised of what I remember about being a child: living in the West London suburb of Isleworth, Middlesex from the late 1930s through the mid-1940s; being at school during the war; sampling victory; and returning to peacetime.

THE BETTS FAMILY - SOME ROOTS AND BRANCHES

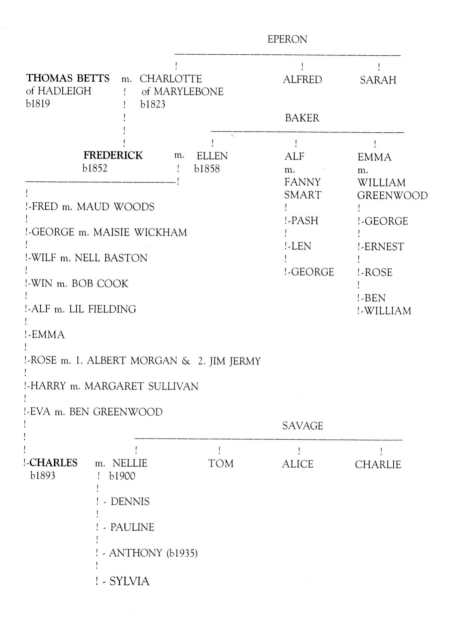

```
                                              EPERON
                              _____
                                   !                    !              !
THOMAS BETTS    m.  CHARLOTTE                        ALFRED          SARAH
of HADLEIGH     !   of MARYLEBONE
b1819           !   b1823
                !                                       BAKER
                !                         _____
                !               !                       !              !
     FREDERICK     m.  ELLEN                          ALF            EMMA
       b1852       !   b1858                          m.             m.
_____!                                 FANNY          WILLIAM
!                                                    SMART          GREENWOOD
!-FRED m. MAUD WOODS                                 !              !
!                                                    !-PASH         !-GEORGE
!-GEORGE m. MAISIE WICKHAM                           !              !
!                                                    !-LEN          !-ERNEST
!-WILF m. NELL BASTON                                !              !
!                                                    !-GEORGE       !-ROSE
!-WIN m. BOB COOK                                                   !
!                                                                   !-BEN
!-ALF m. LIL FIELDING                                               !-WILLIAM
!
!-EMMA
!
!-ROSE m. 1. ALBERT MORGAN & 2. JIM JERMY
!
!-HARRY m. MARGARET SULLIVAN
!
!-EVA m. BEN GREENWOOD
!                                           SAVAGE
!                              _____
!                    !              !              !              !
!-CHARLES    m.  NELLIE          TOM           ALICE          CHARLIE
  b1893      !   b1900
             !
             ! - DENNIS
             !
             ! - PAULINE
             !
             ! - ANTHONY (b1935)
             !
             ! - SYLVIA
```

Chapter Two

Our Road

Fear and fascination kept me clinging to our front fence as I watched from the safety of the garden while my big brother and a number of other boys from our road fought a rival gang from Northumberland Avenue and beyond, ostensibly as cowboys and Indians. My alarm increased as more and more boys were 'captured' and tied with rope to trees and lamp-posts. It was evidently not as threatening as I thought, because at teatime everyone was released and scampered home, but they seemed to take their play very seriously. I never again saw children actually securely trussing up their prisoners, but in those pre-school days, the territory outside our fence seemed a hugely exciting place.

Harewood Road, Isleworth, is at the western edge of the Allen estate, and Mr Herbert Allen, the estate builder, lived in a house on the Great West Road, by St Francis Church. The purchase of the land he acquired for development in the 1920s, and its subsequent resale in individual plots, involved a number of local worthies, including one Albert Musgrave, who had a nearby road named in his honour. The land itself, however, was comprised of orchards which had been owned by the Duke of Northumberland, a fact which was reflected in the names given to the estate roads. The orchards had been crossed by Quaker Lane, which originally led up from the London Road, then turned north-west a little above the present junction with

Northumberland Avenue, to lead to Wood Lane Farm. The Farm used to occupy a site on the west side of Wood Lane, where the Great West Road was cut through.

Our estate was bounded by Quaker Lane to the east, Wood Lane to the west, the recently opened Great West Road to the north, and the London and South Western railway, later the Southern Railway, to the south. A curious relic of earlier estates was the stretch of very old high wall at the Syon Lane end of Northumberland Avenue. It had several stone alcoves like blank windows, and near the red telephone kiosk with its thoughtfully located wooden seat to accommodate queuing callers, there was an inset drinking fountain, and an engraved stone, long vanished; the inscription stated that the wall was built in 1722 by a Mr Jodrell, who owned a property there. Nearby, on the other side of Syon Lane, there once stood Syon Hill House, the property of the Duke of Marlborough. It was this former presence that resulted in the naming of the Marlborough Infants and Senior Schools, which were built on part of that estate's fruit-growing land.

Our front garden was enclosed, and the gate kept shut, so that was for a long time the boundary that defined the extent of my exploratory wanderings. My earliest recollection of 'life beyond the fence' is of walking at the top of our road with my dad, who was holding the leather reins I was wearing. Wags may suggest I was eighteen at the time, but in fact I was about two years old. Also at about that age, I remember being taken for walks to Syon Lane and stopping at the junction with Spur Road to look down onto a small farmyard, where one could buy vegetables. A little later a deep impression was created by a walk to Kidd's Mill, in what we called 'Old Isleworth'. I was uncomfortable with the tall, deserted building and its many small windows, and even more disturbed upon being lifted up to look down at the enclosed mill pond far below, with its rushing, roaring, foamy waters. I found it a sinister place.

It may be coincidence, but I am always reminded of that first sight of the mill pond when, from time to time, I have an unpleasant recurring dream in which I am trying to find a way out of deep, dark waters, alongside a man-made wall with massive iron girders rising vertically into the gloom above, which I know is roofed over.

The atmosphere of our road was on the whole pleasant, with its amply-spaced, well-ordered brick houses, cultivated front gardens, and decorative trees, but it had very different moods, determined by the seasons and the weather. There were extreme days in July and August, when the scorching early afternoon sun shone directly up the empty and silent road, as if the population had decided of one accord to turn its back on such a dry, dusty, barren spot, and it was left to the windows to watch over the baking, shimmering surface. When we had a summer afternoon thunderstorm, we would often open the front door and watch as the lightning flashed and the rain fell like stair rods, bouncing up off the path and pavement to create a miniature flood which gurgled down the drains in the road, and we would breathe in the freshness of it all and wait, hoping for the rainbow which frequently appeared beyond the houses opposite, over in the eastern sky above London.

In contrast, autumn mist and fog or winter's gloom made our house seem more inviting than the road, which was still our playground, whatever the weather. During the winter of 1944, we had a heavy fall of snow, and on the path up to our front door it measured over a foot deep. It was even deeper on the pavement where it had drifted against the garden walls, and all the local children were out until twilight, playing with snowballs, snowmen and sledges, until reluctantly responding to the teatime call and going in to suffer the agony of taking off the sopping woollen gloves and defrosting mauve fingers in warm water.

The next door neighbours on both sides had been there since the houses were built, as had most of the residents. On our south side, Lennie Hills lived with his mother and father. They were an unconventional, happy-go-lucky household, with no high regard for material things. Mrs Hills was small and cheery with a strong Gloucester accent. Her London-born husband, taller but equally cheerful, had white hair 'from being gassed in the Great War'. He called me 'sunshine', which always made me feel good, and no matter how often my ball went over the fence, it was always returned, and in good part.

They kept chickens in a coop and run at the bottom of the

garden, and I liked to hear them clucking and crooning through the fence. The rooster could be heard early in the morning, and it was a familiar and welcome herald of daylight, although it never prevented us from going back to sleep. Now and then Mr Hills would kill a chicken for their dinner, and I used to see the birds hanging upside down from the linepost, still struggling and flapping despite their broken necks. Once, when I was watching over the fence (I used to stand on the garden roller, or on our little step ladder), a lively one got away and, with its neck lolling, ran off around the garden with Mr Hills in pursuit.

They would sometimes pass us a few eggs over the fence, warm from the nest, to supplement our wartime ration. Their son, Lennie, was in the REME during the war, later rising to the rank of Regimental Sergeant Major, and one day we were astonished to receive a stamped addressed coconut from Sierra Leone, where he was stationed for a while. It was a rare treat, as coconuts were not available in the shops.

Only once did our chimney catch fire, and quite alarming it was too, with such a roaring noise inside the house, and sparks and the 'wrong' smoke showing above the roof, until it went out of its own accord when we blocked off the through-draught. The Hills' house, however, achieved something of a reputation for the number of times they managed to set fire to the chimney, which usually engulfed the neighbourhood in choking, smelly black smoke and soot. As a first indication, we would hear the surrounding windows being banged shut, and we would join neighbours in a scramble to bring in any washing from the line before going out the front to await the fire engine.

The Hillses remained cheerful and unperturbed by the resulting mess. In fact when Lennie was home, there were hot summer days when they themselves were responsible for creating as much mess and hilarious chaos. They could be heard shouting and shrieking as they chased each other through house and garden with buckets of water, which were jettisoned in the general direction of any moving target, including the dog. I thought it all tremendous fun, although Mother remained rather strait-laced and slightly uncomfortable about it. However, it was viewed as their way, which was unlike ours but not a matter for complaint.

The house next-door and above ours, the other half of our semi, belonged to the Scales family. Mr Scales was a taxi driver, but his big red Austin Twelve was put up on brick blocks in the garage for the duration of the War, to preserve the tyres while he fought the Germans in a tank regiment. Mrs Scales was often out at the front gate, just as I was, and she would sweep her path and polish her brass number plate and chat to passing neighbours. She would talk to me and to Judy, her black Scottie dog, which would trot up and down the path, barking occasionally when she felt like some attention, or if she found a passer-by more irritating than usual. I was always made very welcome and frequently went into their house and garden, which was naturally more interesting than ours. They had birdbaths, and fir trees to hide behind, and a fish pond, and gnomes. Indoors, my eye was always taken with the print of The Laughing Cavalier beside the fireplace, while I waited in secret hopes that the polished wood and silver biscuit barrel would be opened.

Sometimes one of the Scales' nieces would be visiting - Audrey, five years older than me, pretty and dignified, or Heather, about the same age as Audrey, vivacious and full of fun. In one misadventure with Audrey, I accompanied her on a long walk with Thelma, the new Scales baby, in her pram, but on our return we found we had lost Thelma's cuddly toy. I went indoors and handed over my toy dog Patch as a replacement, but within a week I broke the unwritten rules and retrieved it. Perhaps I had an inkling of the new baby sister who was to complete our family, although I failed to give a satisfactory explanation at the time.

Heather was at boarding school, and regaled us with tales of the dorm, featuring midnight feasts and 'squashy spiders', and scary accounts of walking at night through the creepy Vineyard on visits to her grandmother in Richmond.

The Harrises lived next-door-but-one at number 49, along with a lively small black mongrel called Rags. Mr Harris was a ship's carpenter and away most of the time. He had been on the SS Medina when it was torpedoed off the coast of Devon in 1917, and so their house was called 'Medina', proclaimed by a brass name plate on the front gate. Their son Alfred was later universally known as Phil, after the great American vocalist Phil Harris, who had a smash hit with his song 'The Darktown Poker Club'. He was my brother Dennis's best friend for years, as they grew up together, and we regarded Phil as something of a genius, because he could draw, make wonderful working models with meccano, play the ocarina, and play 'Nola' on the piano. Since both he and Dennis occupied a back bedroom, and there was just the Hills' house in between, if one wanted to exchange a quick word, he would step into the garden or just lean out of the window and whistle like a curlew to attract the other's attention.

Other neighbours further up or down the road came to be recognised by their characteristics, or by features of their property. Old Mrs Shepherd over the road had a velvet palm tree in her front garden, and also boasted the Council's big metal sand bin backing onto her fence.

Up the road were the Willises. 'Very smart, the Willises,' pronounced Father. He was referring to their modern clothes, and the fact that they both had good office jobs. Mrs Willis caused all the curtains to move when she became the first lady we saw wearing 'the New Look' in 1947.

Further up was Mrs Lewis - 'Auntie Loonis' was the joyous approximation uttered by little Thelma next door, and it stayed with us. As well as having a son with the unexplained but indisputably masculine name of Feller, she also owned a sizeable parrot, which lived in a cage near the window of her front room. With a certain amount of ceremony, Mrs Scales took me in to see it ('He won't hurt you, dear'), and almost immediately I arrived back on the street, nursing a pecked finger and clutching a compensatory biscuit. I resolved to show no further concern over the welfare of caged birds, as they evidently lacked both appreciation and respect.

The Lasletts, also from up the road, were a pleasant couple who had no children, and at weekends they would dress in checked shirts and corduroy shorts and pass by on their tandem, giving a cheery wave despite the fact that Mr Laslett had only one arm.

13

Another nice couple were the Hawkinses. They always spoke to me, but he would suddenly and unaccountably break into a loping run, which we did not then know was probably the onset of Parkinson's disease.

There were residents that one rarely seemed to see, like the Vintons. He was rumoured to be a former tandem cycle racer, which even then seemed an unusual, if not old-fashioned, claim.

'Mum,' I would say, 'haven't the Vintons got any children?'

'No, dear.'

'Why, Mum?'

'Because they go out to work, dear.'

The logic seemed reasonable, but I found exceptions.

'Mum, does Mrs Rose go out to work?'

'No, dear.'

'Why haven't they got any children, then?'

'They're too old, dear.'

From the top of the road, Mr Tilbury, tall and blind, would tap his way along with white stick and dark glasses, doing his rounds as a piano tuner. Sometimes I would say hello, and at other times I would stay still and quiet to see if he knew I was there, which he usually did.

Piano lessons were given by Mrs Freeman, two doors up. She owned a thoroughly unpleasant, yapping Yorkshire terrier called Midge, and a sadly silent and somewhat doleful henpecked husband. Mr Freeman was only ever seen as he cycled slowly to and from his job with the Water Board, his drooping moustache and overlarge boots emphasising what one felt must be a depressing existence. Children round about who went for lessons complained about Mrs Freeman's waspish tongue, and the constant use of the ruler upon the knuckles of erring fingers. She did, however, have saving graces, as she succeeded in teaching even some of the more recalcitrant to read a little and knock out a tune, and helped some pupils reach a high standard. She also put on some passable concerts, featuring singers as well as pianists. The last one I attended was with my pal Mike Curwen, at the school hall in St John's Road. We were unwisely given seats in the middle near the front and, being of a certain age, were so reduced to hysterics by the facial antics and free-wheeling eyebrows of her prize baritone that we had to leave prematurely, staggering off into the sober air of St John's Road, reeling and clutching our aching stomachs, to the puzzled amusement of passers-by.

A little way up the road, old Mrs Westlake and her daughter Iris owned Rusty, an elderly dog which posed no threat to humans but roamed the locality, like most dogs then, and indulged in the dangerous game of chasing and barking furiously at passing cars. The locals expected it, but it tended to startle and upset strangers, who would observe Rusty suddenly bounding and barking alongside their cars as they accelerated, and the next minute standing stock still in the middle of the road watching them foolishly speed away when there was no longer any cause.

On the corner of Northumberland Avenue that was visible from our house lived Mr Price the plumber ('Aptly named,' said Father, who felt that all tradesmen overcharged). Robin Price was the same age as me, and I played with him and his younger sister Ann, until one day they said they were going to Australia, and to my astonishment, they did. They were the first emigrants I had known, although some of Mother's family had already established themselves in Australia by 1930.

Orientation naturally centred on our house, which was in the top half of Harewood Road. 'Down the road' meant going to the local shops, or in Father's case, going to the Rising Sun on the London Road. 'Up the road' implied going to the Osterley Hotel on the Great West Road. We would go 'round' to the telephone box by Quaker Lane, or to the pillar box (post box) in Northumberland Avenue, but anywhere else was just plain 'to'. That is, except Hayes; we went 'over' to Hayes to visit our relatives, the Cook family.

I was taken on occasional visits to the houses of Father's local friends, most of whom were regulars at the Rising Sun or the Osterley Hotel or, as in Father's case, both - which is not to say that they did not visit the Iron Bridge, the Rose & Crown, the Coach & Horses, and the Hare & Hounds. There was Alfie 'Ughes (to reflect Father's accent) who lived on the London Road and worked for the Middlesex Builders Supplies; old Fred Lockyer who maintained an incredibly productive vegetable garden with amazing marrows, backing onto the railway in Parkwood Road; Pat Rodgers who became chief accountant with J Arthur Rank in New Oxford Street and lived in Wood Lane; Frank Landolt of Northumberland Avenue who worked on the newspapers in Fleet Street; and many more besides. But the closest friend was Arthur Thurlow, who lived with his wife and sons Bob and John in the lower half of Harewood Road.

The Thurlows were my godparents. They kept chickens in the back garden which, in contrast to ours, had a low paling fence that enabled me to see what was going on in the surrounding gardens. Their house was full of dark wood furniture and smelt pleasantly of furniture polish. Mrs Thurlow was a jolly lady from Chester, while Mr Thurlow, a Londoner, was a dignified man of the world with a great sense of humour. Like Father, he was an 'old soldier', and though slight in build, he had a grip of iron. Like my grandfather, he had worked for William Whiteley, but he left to become an independent bespoke tailor and dress hire agent, working from home.

He opened his first shop in Odeon Parade, Isleworth, around 1950, and to celebrate the occasion arranged for Peter Brough, the 'Archie Andrews' ventriloquist and star of radio's 'Educating Archie', to appear on stage at the Odeon. The Broughs were also connected to the cloth trade, as Peter Brough had originally worked in the 'materials' department at Selfridges, and his father had given up ventriloquism on stage to keep in steady employment at William Whiteleys.

In time, Mr Thurlow moved his business to premises in Lampton Road, and thence to the vicinity of Hounslow Southern station, where his son John continued the business.

Mr Thurlow was instrumental in getting Father to join the Freemasons, which was to widen his circle of friends considerably. However, the rest of us were not too clear about the benefits at the time, because Father's principles prevented him from doing anything except giving to the cause what little he had. One of the last things that Mr Thurlow said to me was :'You know what would please your dad more than anything in the world would be to ask him to introduce you into the Masons.'

16

I never did. It seemed to have no relevance to the way I looked at life.

Cigarette addiction took its toll, and after gradually losing his voice, Mr Thurlow was gone; but I found that a man of such character is often recalled.

When we needed medical attention, we placed ourselves in the hands of Dr Ewart. He was a large, red-faced, energetic, ex rugby-playing, Scot, who wore horn-rimmed spectacles and always had his stethoscope at the ready. Like most folk then, we did not have a telephone, and if Dr Ewart had to be asked to visit the house, either somebody had to go to the telephone box along Northumberland Avenue, at the entrance to Quaker Lane, or walk down to his surgery in St John's Road. His arrival would be signalled by a rat-tatting on the front door that could not be ignored, his voice would boom on the stairs, then he would be in the room looking keenly at you and seeing straight through any pretence. A quick examination, and he was gone.

At his dingy, cramped surgery, they would be queuing into the street, but somehow he got through it all with gruff, good humour. I saw another side of him once, when a man trying to get off work with a bad back limped into the surgery, but was spotted afterwards walking briskly down the steps. Dr Ewart went out after him as if he were going to score a try for Scotland, and returned holding the unwarranted certificate.

He was the epitome of the family doctor, and when he died suddenly we had no doubt it was largely due to overwork.

The first funeral I remember was that of one of the elderly residents from up the top of the road. Mother went round closing all the curtains at the front of the house 'as a mark of respect '. I watched the proceedings through a crack in the curtains, but the procession of black cars gave me little indication of what it meant when people said that 'old Mrs Wassname had passed away '.

I do not remember seeing any weddings. They did take place, because Kathy Taunton, who lived with her aunt, old Miss Shepherd opposite, suddenly became Mrs Wilkinson, Jessie Webb became Mrs Counsell, and Iris Westlake became Mrs Cheyney. This last change exposed me early on to the question of how to correctly address people outside the family.

I noticed that Father called other men by their first names, but in the fashion of her upbringing, Mother avoided over-familiarity and always used title and surname. In contrast, Mrs Scales knew everyone by their first name, though in deference to Mother's preference, she and my Mother always addressed each other as 'Mrs so-and-so'. In similar vein, when Mrs Scales' daughter Thelma came along, nearly everyone became 'Aunty' or 'Uncle', except, of course, my Mother and Father. I was slightly confused by this, and after being in the informal atmosphere of Mrs Scales' house when 'Iris' popped in for a chat, it seemed natural to me, when she next passed by, to say, 'Hello, Iris'. She stood in front of me, put her face close to mine, and said, 'You will not call me Iris, you will call me Mrs Cheyney.' The message got through, and I was thereafter more inclined to err on the formal side when addressing people.

From around the age of four until I went to school, I was often at the fence, watching the 'passing show'. There were few private cars in our area in the 1930s and early 40s, and consequently there were quite a lot of passers-by, on foot and on bicycles. In the morning there were men and young people going to work, then children going to school, and later the housewives going shopping. Sometimes a butcher-boy would cycle indolently past, whistling as he rode the heavy black machine with the shop name plate suspended from the cross bar, and the square iron tray over the front wheel, delivering a choice cut to some better-off or incapacitated customer.

Then there were the regular delivery men. The Cliffords' milkman came to us from Hounslow each morning with his horse and cart, and there were other carts too, like the various coalmen: Hill, Taylor, Johnson, Beattie and Charrington, Branson the greengrocer from Syon Lane, and Johnson the greengrocer from Brentford Bridge. There were vans like Chapman the baker, and an occasional sighting of the distinctive green Harrods van, or Carter Paterson's railway parcel waggon. For years I thought the driver, an elderly man dressed in uniform, with 'bad' feet set at ten to three, was 'Mr Paterson, the carter'.

A few times I saw a horse lose its footing and fall down in the shafts. There was much noise and fuss, with the tradesman holding its head and shouting encouragement, and it was a pathetic sight to behold the animal plunging and scrabbling to get a purchase on the icy road, although it was probably more stressful than physically harmful.

With those tradesmen who came directly to our house, there was all the excitement of the disruption to daily routine, the alien conversation, the invasion of our ground. The postman with his big canvas sack was friendly enough, and sometimes entrusted the letters to me. The coalman, with his horse and cart, was more interesting, as he brought with him the noise and dirt that everyone else had a horror of. He was covered in black dust, from his old cap with the long backflap, right down to his boots. His eyes and teeth shone white out of a coal-blackened face, and his voice was gravelly hoarse:

'One hundredweight Welsh Nuts, Missus?'

'Yes please, coalman.'

'Round the side?'

'Yes please.'

He carried the full sack on his shoulder and shot the contents expertly, with a rattling roar and a cloud of dust, into our wooden coal-shed. I always followed him and stood too close to the shed, because I wanted to see and hear, and inhale the fumey smell. As he left with the empty sacks folded under his arm, I followed him out again, so that I could shut the gate and say 'Cheerio', making the most of his visit.

At the beginning of the war, our 'national' bread was delivered by Chapman's from Old Isleworth, but they were unfortunate enough to be bombed out, and we changed to Chibnall's, an old established firm in Hammersmith. They ingeniously beat the fuel shortage by using 'rickshaws', pulled along by the delivery man, who stood between the shafts - a great novelty to behold. How they coped with the hills and the ice and snow is a mystery. Another mystery was why the price of bread in those days seemed to always include an odd number of farthings, leaving everyone foraging for change.

Rowles the sweep was an annual visitor, usually in May. I welcomed the diversion, but Mother dreaded the aftermath. The living room chimney was his main target, and the preparations seemed extensive, with furniture being taken out, and everything covered in bedsheets. I usually watched through the French windows from outside, and ran down the back garden time and again so as not to miss the magic of the moment when the brush appeared above the chimney pot. Despite all the precautions, in those days before vacuum cleaners, it took a lot of dusting, washing and carpet sweeping to remove the residual covering of soot and return things to normal. But whenever the pale winter afternoon sun shone into the back room, it always revealed, on dark wood, red tiles and blackened iron, the thin covering of dust we lived with.

Other visitors to the street were the muffin man, who rang a handbell as he walked along Northumberland Avenue carrying his wares on a large tray, and the Walls ice-cream man, who pedalled a tricycle with a large white cabinet on the front, bearing the familiar slogan 'Stop me and buy one'. He would ring his cycle bell to call the children. We had no pennies to spare, so I just used to watch, but on one exceptional occasion Lennie Hills from next door, who was much older than me, looked over the fence and said, 'Hello, Tony, would you like an ice?' This was unexpected and quite without precedent; I stammered a 'Yes please' and watched as he returned from the queue of half-a-dozen with a triangular strawberry water ice. The memory of the delicious flavour lingers to this day, but it was not long afterwards that the product was to disappear forever with the outbreak of war, followed, perhaps, by a subsequent change in processing and in public tastes.

Sometimes the knife-sharpener would appear, with the green painted Heath-Robinson contraption that he could sit at to use pedal power while grinding the blades. Then there was the 'ex-serviceman' who came periodically to the door with his suitcase of brushes, and sometimes an old crone of a gypsy would call, squinting fiercely and demanding that we buy wooden clothes pegs or lucky white heather. When we did not, she would go off muttering and casting baleful backward glances, which made me uneasy, although

I had faith in the security of our fence and my well-rehearsed escape route through the side entrance and into the kitchen.

The dust cart came every Monday, with its roll-up-and-over side doors and the raucous team of men who wrenched every possible decibel out of the galvanised metal dustbins, throwing off the lids, crashing the bin contents into the cart, and banging the bin lid back on with a final slam of the gate on their way out. In contrast, the ragged and hunched old roadsweeper would pass almost unnoticed, pushing his silver galvanised-metal barrow, stopping to sweep the kerb and pick up odds and ends, and giving only a mumbled response to those who wished him good morning. The rag-and-bone man was another lone figure, sitting up on his cart pulled along by a tired old sway-backed horse. His approach and departure route could be tracked out of sight by the mournful cry of 'Rag bone!', which the lads later translated into an authentic-sounding but nonsensical 'Nyea-bob!'

A very smart vehicle was the Gas Light and Coke Company's green fuel lorry, with side chains to keep the full sacks secure; but most impressive of all the outfits was the road menders'. The men worked with broom and shovel, but in addition, not only did they have the magnificent and stately green, black and gold steamroller, they also had a tar lorry pulled by two massive shire horses in splendid full leather harness, stamping and snorting and jingling their brasses as they waited for action, while we watched the scene and drank in the rich smell and fumes of the boiling tar spreading thickly and stickily along the road.

Other than at Christmas time, there was little music in the local streets. Sometimes an 'ex-serviceman' would be singing at the kerbside near the shops in Hounslow, and on an isolated occasion one summer's evening, as we walked back from a 'treat' at the Hare & Hounds, we encountered a drum and fife band marching up Wood Lane, probably from some local fete.

I did once see a barrel organ at the Broadway in Hounslow, attended by an old man turning the handle, with the indispensable monkey in a red jacket perched on top of the instrument. The correct name would be barrel piano, but we always called it a barrel organ. Mother was careful to point out that this should not be confused with the real street organ or hurdy gurdy, which she also remembered and liked, but which sounded entirely different and had disappeared from the streets long before my time. She loved the sound of a barrel organ, and seemingly in her young days they were often in the streets of Enfield. I too became fond of the sound, which I discovered has a dual effect. On the one hand, its strident, remorselessly repetitive airs and *arpeggios* suggest a devil-may-care kind of gaiety, but on the other hand, those tinny tunes and that torrent of sound can induce pathos and evoke images of the struggle for survival on the cold, foggy, poverty-stricken, gaslit streets of Victorian London.

It was as a result of accompanying Mother on her frequent shopping trips that I got to know the area 'down the bottom' and beyond. For our local shopping, Mother went to Wood Lane Stores at the bottom of the hill, or to King's Parade on the London Road.

Wood Lane Stores consisted of a greengrocer, a grocery, and Mr Loughram the butcher, so it sometimes took a while to complete the shopping there. One day I was standing outside waiting for Mother, watching the comings and goings, when I suddenly received a severe blow on the back and was knocked to the ground. A bulldog, owned by the scrap metal man whose premises were opposite, was habitually left in the front seat of his Hudson Terraplane car parked by the kerb, but this time the window had been left open, and I had evidently strayed too close. I lay on the ground, winded and nonplussed, with this most un-British of bulldogs standing over me, until some of the assembled housewives shooed it away and I got up and was dusted down. The owner was sent for, and predictably he said , 'I can't understand it, he's never done anything like this before.'

When Mother emerged from the shop a few minutes later, I was standing where she had left me, but despite finding me somewhat the worse for wear, she laughingly refused to believe my explanation and, with all witnesses having left the scene, I was unable to substantiate my bizarre story. I knew, however, and the bulldog knew, and for years whenever I went past we used to glare at each other through the windscreen.

Right on the corner of Wood Lane and London Road was Baxter's, the newsagent, confectioner and tobacconist. In fact, this was known as Baxter's Corner. We got our newspapers here, and on the rare occasions when we could afford a treat, our sweets, chocolate and fizzy drinks. It was here too that we came for our Easter eggs, fireworks, ice-cream from the big Walls cabinet, and birthday and Christmas cards. The shop was long-established, as witnessed by the mellow wood-and-glass door and its smooth-worn wooden handle. The step too was worn, and when you went in the bell over the door clanged loudly. Across the lino-covered floor was the big wooden counter, and on and around it every space was filled with papers, comics, wooden crates of soft drink, cartons and huge jars of sweets, small toys, marbles, packets of foreign stamps for collectors, big ledgers for the newspaper rounds, and of course the shelves behind the counter were full to the ceiling with cigarettes, tobacco, pipes, matches and more sweets. Times were hard, and many tried, but canny old Mr Baxter was equal to all the tricks attempted by scallywags wont to try and escape with more than they were paying for.

At least once a week we walked to King's Parade on the London Road, and sometimes on the way we would call in on Mr Figg, the shoe repairer in Linkfield Road. He was always busy hammering, caulking or sticking, and the air of the cosy little shop was heavy with the overpowering smell of leather. Taking shoes for repair and collecting them again became one of my more regular jobs. If we went directly to King's Parade, we would walk down College Road, and near the bottom of the hill, as we passed the side wall of 'Myfyrion', 454, London Road, and reached their front garden, we would almost invariably be sent two feet in the air by the deliberately startling, deafening barking of the diminutive but irascible resident pekinese, which I believed had a megaphone installed behind the wall. Its frenzy was always quickly quelled by the housemaid, and I suspected from her proximity that she had had more than a hand in setting us up as regular victims.

Recovering our nerve, we would walk on to visit Platts Stores (the grocer), Watkins the chemist, Lillyman the butcher, the United Dairies shop, Easter the greengrocer, and thence perhaps to Turner's

Stores, the hardware shop in St John's Road, where the assistant, a pretty brunette with her hair in a fashionable roll, bore an intriguing resemblance to film star Dorothy Lamour. Each of these shops had its own distinctive smell, familiar and not unpleasant. Platts smelt of biscuits, cheese, butter and bacon, Turner's of paraffin, creosote and string.

The London Road Post Office was another regular port of call, and we were later always mindful that this was the scene of the tragic accident in which young Laurie Mitchener from Albury Avenue was killed by a GPO van. The inside, with its high, echoing ceiling and nose-high, polished brown wooden counter, I got to know well when I began using my scarce birthday and Christmas money to invest in National Savings Stamps, or to make a deposit into my Post Office Savings Account. These proved to be short-term investments, as I got no regular pocket money and had to raid my capital to buy anything. Nevertheless, by the time I was twelve, I had accumulated the grand sum of thirteen pounds: an average of just over a pound a year!

Mother had to make a weekly expedition to Hounslow for other necessities like clothes or for cheaper food, or to pay the gas or electricity bill, or the rates at the Council Offices. This meant a ride on the 657 trolleybus, which had replaced the trams in 1935, travelling from the Rising Sun to Kingsley Road bus garage, or as far as The Bell at the end of the High Street. Most often we went into Worlds Stores or Home and Colonial for groceries, and Woolworths for household goods, and only visited the various shoe and clothes shops if we had to buy, as there was no time to spare for browsing. My favourite shop was Treble's at Lampton Corner, because they had an 'overhead railway' for despatching cash and receipts to and from the till. The assistant would pull down and unscrew the little pot on the overhead wire, put in the bill and cash, pull a lever and set it off on its whirring journey across the shop. As mysteriously, it would come whirring back with the receipt and change, and all the while other assistants were sending and receiving. How I would have loved to have that little toy at home!

Going shopping and looking at the world over the front fence were significant activities during my early childhood, but the pre-war and pre-school era of the 1930s was encapsulated for me in a moment when I was playing on the lawn in our back garden, a high line of washing reflecting the bright summer sun. Against the blue sky a shining silver bi-plane flew slowly past, with its engine buzzing softly and a great, coloured advertising streamer trailing behind. I watched, captivated, and time stood still.

CHAPTER THREE

OUR HOUSE. . .

"There's no place like home." That most unoriginal of sayings was often expressed and firmly believed in by Father and Mother, and we all felt it, especially in the dark days of war. My home, in childhood, seemed pleasant and safe, despite the air raids. It embraced the family, and life was centred on our house and garden.

The house was a typical two-reception, three-bedroom semi-detached, bay-windowed, brick and tile dwelling on a plot of one hundred feet by forty. It was in the process of being built when Sid Reynolds, a colleague of Father's at Cadby Hall, moved into Roxborough Avenue and recommended the estate. Father put down the deposit, and when he and Mother moved in at the end of the summer of 1929, he felt that at last he had succeeded in life. This was not just because it proved to be a good investment, with the price rising from £750 to over a £100, 000 in sixty years; it was also because he had worked his own way up from being a member of a large family living in poverty, and in rented accommodation, enduring the insecurity and transient life that was the lot of those who could not earn enough money to pay the landlord every week. So, at the age of thirty-six, having fought for his country and survived the Great War, and then got himself a steady job, he felt that buying this property as a home for his family accomplished his essential objective. It was his 'Great Achievement'.

Over the porch was the name plate, 'Berry Narbor', after the Devon village near Ilfracombe where Mother and Father had stayed on their honeymoon.

The layout of the house was conventional, but the furnishing and decor were such a mixture of quality, colour and styles that, while relating to an overall theme of 'brown-ness', they gave the not altogether untrue impression that each component might have been donated by somebody who had not seen the rest of the items. In fact, this was not uncommon in those times, and it had more to do with practical necessity and the scarcity of money than any lack of taste. But once installed, lifelong preservation orders went out on everything. We were locked into the philosophy of the three Ms: make do, maintain and mend.

Passing through the yale-locked front door, one was faced with a hallway leading to the kitchen, with the stairs on the left. The plentiful woodwork was stained brown and varnished, and on the walls there was brown 'Lincrusta' (anaglypta) paper up to the chair rail, with dull yellowing cream paper above. By the front door, there was a large Edwardian mahogany and tile hall stand. This well-utilised staging point, which had a central mirror for last minute adjustments to hair and headgear, was largely hidden by coats loaded onto hooks, topped by Father's caps and trilbies, the whole being underpinned by a lidded mahogany box for gloves and clothes brush. On each side of the box was an umbrella stand, in one of which resided Father's elegant polished mahogany walking stick with rounded top and brass ferrule.

Off the hall was the larder, with its cool atmosphere and various long-standing occupants, like the white enamel bread bin, the wooden breadboard, the large round wicker basket used for fruit gathering, and the sweet tin, which had once held Jacob's biscuits. From time to time the larder was invaded by mice or ants. Then the food and most other things would have to be evacuated, followed by the strategic placing of cheese-laden traps or trails of borax powder. Like the outcome of any hunt, the morning inspection of the traps was always exciting, but I was disappointed by the grubby, lifeless victims, because they were not a bit like Teddy Tail, the newspaper cartoon mouse.

Also in the hall was the 'cupboard under the stairs'. While this was the storage place for the mop, brushes, dustpan and Ewbank carpet sweeper, it housed our playthings too - books, magazines, board games, and the toybox, which was a sizeable wooden crate containing a large, mixed selection from balls to building bricks, and Plasticine to painting palettes. Of course, the cupboard was also an obvious but nonetheless favoured place for hiding, playing or sulking in, or for pouncing from.

The kitchen was the centre of activity, and mainly Mother's province, although in my early years I spent a lot of time loitering round the sink, asking 'Why, Mum?' The questions are long since forgotten, but in later years I often wished there was still such a place, inhabited by someone in whose knowledge and wisdom I could have the same absolute belief.

The late 1920's design and equipment was very basic, but a great improvement over the dark, damp kitchens and sculleries of yore. (Father, who was all too familiar with such things, pronounced the word 'scollery', and likewise would look at grey skies and speak of a 'doll' day - the remnants of a Victorian Paddington accent). There was a New World gas cooker with an oven, a wooden dresser labelled 'Kitchenette' with cupboards and drawers, a sink with a wooden draining board, and a gas-heated copper, which served the dual purpose of boiling the washing once a week and boiling the Christmas pudding once a year.

On top of the dresser Mother kept a light cane, culled from the garden, but in my time at least, it was only ever used as the mildest of threats when the laughter at the dinner table got out of hand.

The most interesting kitchen gadget was the Spong mincer, which was dismantled for storage, and had to be reassembled and screwed to the side of the dresser for use. We had minced meat at least once a week, and I was enthusiastic about doing the mincing, although I never liked eating the result. Most of our food was good and wholesome, but sometimes Mother's knowledge or creativity and the limitation of available ingredients took us no further than plain mince or cottage pie, both of which, as a child, I found too strong in flavour, and as unappetising as the cold lamb we regularly faced on Mondays. I never had any such reservations about pork, bacon or rabbit, nor our daily porridge, pies and rice puddings, nor the suet puddings, all homemade and liable to be referred to as 'plum duff' by Father, but which were mixed or topped with fruit, jam, sultanas, rhubarb, chocolate or ginger, and always served with custard.

The kitchen was light, with a glazed back door, and windows overlooking the back garden; but for warmth it depended on the afternoon sunshine or the gas stove being on for Mother's cooking, so in the winter we made use of a portable Valor paraffin stove that stood in the corner.

Adjoining the kitchen was the living room, although it was always called the dining room. This was where the family ate, rested, played, talked, listened to the radio, read, thawed out, dried off, convalesced, and waited for things to happen. The focal points were the open coal fire with back boiler for heating the water, and the radio in Father's corner between the fireplace and the French windows.

The living room had the benefit of the same colour scheme as the hall, which was achieved by using the same brown and cream paper and brown stained woodwork. It had then been easy to blend in the brown armchairs, the dark oak gate-leg table with its brown woollen cover, the brown curtains over the French windows, the brownish bronze fender set, and the brown furnishing of various chairs. Also complementary to this was the brown frame of a large print of some unremembered incident in the Crimean War, showing red-tunicked, pith-helmeted troops marching in a valley, and entitled 'Drums of the Fore and Aft'. For this latter decoration, we were indebted to Uncle Pash Baker, late of the Hussars.

There were two armchairs in brown moquette with brown velvet cushions, and a 'bed chair', stoutly made of wood with canvas struts. This served as quite a comfortable armchair, but by pulling on the wooden knob at the front and letting down the back rest, it could be transformed into a single bed with high and unforgiving wooden sides. The transformation action was lethal, and operation was confined to the over-sixteens, but the sleeper's bruised arms were testimony to the fact that the chair always won in the end. A curious adjunct to this chair was that under the cushions could be found, neatly folded, a full-sized, very heavy, blue-backed and white-woollen-chequered horse blanket of superior quality, 'jolly good for picnics on the grass'. This was a gift from Aunt Rose, who ran a boarding house in Marylebone for sporting gentry and respectable personalities of the stage, some of whom were wont to depart without all their personal effects, though whether by accident or in payment of outstanding accounts was never clear. Whatever the explanation, the large case of colourful South American butterflies in the back bedroom also came from the same source.

The dining table occupied one wall, and had to be pulled out and extended for meals, as well as for writing, games, jigsaws, homework (the brown woollen cloth had a permanent Stephens' blue-black ink stain in one corner), the sewing machine, and any 'running repairs' to clothes, radio or toys. On Tuesdays, it was covered with an old blanket and used for the ironing, which meant heating flat irons on the fire, and plucking them off in turn with an iron holder, homemade of thickly padded material. There were three irons of different sizes, and we had a triangular-shaped stand made of iron with a wooden handle, upon which the iron rested while clothes were folded or laid out.

Before and after the ironing, the washing would be left to dry or air round the fire on the wooden three-sided clothes horse. This cut off the fire, making the room rather miserable, and greatly reduced my play area, so Mondays and Tuesdays were not my favourite days.

I was similarly restricted when the 'housework' was in progress downstairs. Dusting, moving furniture and carpet sweeping were in direct conflict with my indoor play, and as Pauline took to doing these tasks to help Mother, usually on a Saturday morning, territorial disputes were inevitable. However, I found that Pauline was credited with being 'good', whereas I was in the way, and no help at all, so I just had to accept that housework was a necessary evil.

In Mother's corner of the dining room, opposite the window and to the right of the fire, was her armchair, alongside which was the sewing workbox, a wooden stool with a lidded box which Dennis made while he was at Twickenham Technical College.

On the opposite side of the fireplace, Father would take control of the fire, the radio and the current newspaper, which he kept on his lap or down the side of his chair. He 'possessed' his paper, be it the Daily Express, Sunday Dispatch, Evening News or Standard, and devoured it from front page headline and circulation figures to back page sport and the printer's address, and only reluctantly did he let it go to somebody else for a quick read. He had his selected pipe ('the old gun') beside him, his spills within reach, and on the wall a pipe rack, which was eventually replaced by one I made at the County School. Standing beside him was the tall, slender (brown) cabinet which contained the remains (that might come in handy one day) of an obsolete wireless it had once housed, and which was now surmounted by the current model. This was at first a set with valves as big as electric light bulbs, housed in a large, polished (brown) cabinet, with a setting sun artistically fretted on the front. Subsequently, this was replaced by a wireless in a smaller, rectangular (brown) cabinet, bearing the emblem 'GEC '.

The fireplace was of red tiles, nearly matching the red linoleum, furnished with black metal hobs and hood. The hood had a 'damper', which puzzled me, as it was only used for quite the opposite. There was a fender set across the front of the fireplace, and on the wall on either side of the fire a dark oak surround led up to two mantelpieces, with a mirror in between. The lower mantelpiece held an ashtray, spill barrel and other oddments, while the high over-mantel featured two unremarkable black vases flanking a (brown) cuckoo clock in the form of a castle. The cuckoo emerged from the turret to perform its plaintive song upon the hour. It was also known that this irrepressible bird could be forced against its will to chirrup at other unscheduled times by opening the back and working the twin bellows - 'revenge with music' - a surreptitious treat reserved for visiting pals on those occasions when adults were safely out of earshot.

The fireside furniture consisted of the usual companion set, comprising tongs, poker, brush and shovel, suspended from a neatly engineered stand, and this was complementary to the fender, at each end of which was a matching, solidly made box with a varnished lid. In winter, these boxes provided a coveted cosy seat almost on top of the fire. Use of this perch was permitted for making toast, or for thawing out after coming in from extreme cold, but a body so placed caused a drop of about ten degrees for everybody else on that side of the room, so the privilege was necessarily curtailed.

Mother's fender box was in fact an outpost of Father's territory. It contained a mixture of small items that could not be thrown away, but were not yet ready to be consigned to the shed, which was the halfway house to being thrown away. There was an old silver tobacco tin, round and smooth with a hinged airtight lid, and full of nails, several proprietary tobacco tins containing screws, washers, clips and rawlplugs, a hammer, a screwdriver and pliers, the halfpennies for playing shove ha'penny, various radio spares, and a magnificent silvered metal sphinx that had once graced the front of an Armstrong Siddeley car. This might have looked well as an ornament, but it remained out of sight as a heavy, awkward object with two projecting bolts in the base, and ultimately it vanished before anyone had the vision to adapt it. The box at Father's end contained coal, and he was the sole architect and 'draughtsman' of the fire, as well as being an inveterate stoker and poker. When he was dissatisfied with the performance in the grate, and tongs, poker and damper had been tried to no avail, then a double page of the Daily Express would be recruited to the fray and skilfully positioned across the opening above the grate to funnel and increase the draught. Behind the paper the desultory plumes of smoke would either suddenly explode into a blaze that sent a yellow and blue flame through the centre of the pages, provoking an exclamation from Father and causing him to ram the burning tatters hastily into the chimney, or there would be a deepening, cold silence from within, broken by impatient rustlings as the paper was adjusted to block any gaps, and finally a total withdrawal to acknowledge temporary defeat. This action often brought a fugitive cloud of smoke and soot into the room, accompanied by Father's terse commentary 'Oh, Lord! Blessed fire - here, give us another sheet of paper.' And with bulldog persistence the process would be repeated until successful. Father's expertise in these matters was never challenged. It was recognised as a sensitive subject, and we were all content that his wrath should remain directed at the sullen and unresponsive grate.

Failure in the fireplace could be frustrating, but whatever the provocation, there was no swearing at home, and transgressors outside were rather looked down upon. I later discovered that Father considered swearing within earshot of women or children highly offensive, but in purely male company of the right sort it was all right to let go one or two mild expletives.

Cleaning out and relaying the fire next day was one of the chores that Mother disliked, and one of the few I did not mind too much, as I got old enough to do things. The ash had to be shovelled and emptied into the dustpan, and then taken out to the dustbin, newspaper had to be rolled and turned into loose balls or rings which were placed in the bottom of the grate with one or two projecting ends for 'fuses'. Finely chopped wood had to be laid criss-cross on the paper, then some small coal on top of that, ready for the hit-and-miss business of lighting the fire. Keeping a supply of chopped wood ready became another of my jobs, for which we kept a stock of branches and old box wood outside, with the chopping block and axe. There were always logs too, for the front room fire. These were not usually bought, although a log cart would come round occasionally; rather, they were accumulated either from our garden or from one of the neighbours.

Coal smoke and tobacco smoke combined over time to give the brown theme of the dining room a yellow tinge, which in winter contributed to the cosy mellowness, but in summer was surprisingly less noticeable. In contrast to this, the front room, usually referred to as the 'drawing' room, had a bright, cool aura. This was because it faced east, the lincruster was painted green to complement the green fireplace tiles, the curtains were green (inside the blackout), and the wallpaper above the chair rail was light-coloured with a pale green pattern.

Despite the brightness, the drawing room could be a cosy room in winter, although we rarely 'withdrew' into it except at Christmastime or when relatives came to dinner or tea. In the event of visitors, the table had to be carried through from the back room, until we eventually acquired a second-hand (brown) mahogany draw-leaf table and our options were accordingly enhanced.

One of the main items of drawing room furniture was the (brown) moquette sofa, which filled the window bay. We called it a couch, and it matched the two armchairs in the dining room. The couch had a drop arm operated by a lever, but the arm could not then sustain much weight, and was rarely dropped except for someone in convalescent repose, or someone else in unseen, forbidden, childish experimentation. Like the armchairs, the couch had hungry gaps all round the seat cushions, and the canvas bottoms at times built up quite a collection of coins, combs, crumbs and confectionery.

Along the wall behind the door was a good quality (brown) mahogany sideboard with circular mirror above, and ample covered space below, where I spent many hours playing with toys, looking at books, and 'hiding'. A very early recollection I have is of playing an infinitely repetitive game I invented using our woolly ball, which I would deliberately roll out of reach under the sideboard, and complain to Pauline 'Ball-ball gone unner nare Paul-paul.' Fortunately, I outgrew the game, but as a Huge Joke it lives on.

Near the window stood the elegant, black, Edwardian plant stand, with curved legs, slim struts and fine brass chains, in which our disdainful aspidistra brittled, curled, and quietly pined for the propriety of a palm court. Opposite the window, on the far side of the room, was the prized upright piano, by Schultz of Berlin, resplendent in its good quality, solid, shiny black case, but showing signs of age and Teutonic resentment through its stiff and uncooperative yellowing keys, although Mother could still coax a tune out of it.

The floor was covered in the same blue and white linoleum that was laid in the hall, but in the middle of the room was a red patterned carpet, accepted and installed for warmth rather than colour, a tendency that was repeated when it was replaced by one of an overall brown pattern.

By way of contrast, the fireplace was made of green tiles, but was otherwise similar to the one in the dining room, with a dark wood surround and mantelpieces, and a mirror in the centre. Having no back boiler, the grate was different, being simply open with an arched chimney covering, and this lent itself to creating large blazing fires of coal and logs which were such an integral part of our Christmas delights.

The bronzed fireside fender set here also had a companion set and two matching boxes with upholstered lids, in one of which we kept coal or sometimes logs, and in the other there were magazines. The latter were mostly the glossy but bland National Geographic, but there were some rather more inspiring Wide World true adventure magazines, and colourful colonial ones called The Times of India, brought back in the 1920s by Mr Scales next door, full of eye-widening illustrations of tiger hunting and wild elephants in conflict with railway trains. There was, too, a humorous trifle entitled The Passing Show, a paper magazine donated by the Thurlows, and full of flappers and vacuous young 'Algernons' as the butt of jokes in the manner of Punch. I was often drawn to these pages without ever needing to grasp the punchlines.

In front of the fire, we kept the white, fluffy and very real sheepskin rug that Pauline had brought back from Wales in 1938. She had been taken by Uncle Harry's wife, Margaret Sullivan, on the train for a short holiday at Tony Refail, where Margaret had been born, and from this adventure she also treasured the traditional Welsh lady jug souvenir that stood on her dressing table.

Wilson's 'Great War' books occupied a whole corner of the room. While my Father served in France, his father, evidently aware that his sons were participating in history in the making, paid out an ill-afforded sixpence a week to buy the magazines, and we had all thirteen volumes. However, as they were not bound, but remained as a very large pile of magazines, they were largely unexplored, just picked up for a quick browse of the profuse illustrations in idle moments.

On the walls were two paintings of sailing boats on the Norfolk Broads - gold-framed, and golden hued, and rendered unusual by the artist having twice successfully captured that magical moment when the fading evening light and the rising mist combine to reduce a graceful ship to a featureless smudge on the horizon.

In the hall was a large but only slightly more detailed version of a similar subject, this time with the boat firmly captive in the foreground, but perhaps painted with some haste before it was entirely swallowed by the waterside ooze. This painting was flanked by two black-framed prints of Dutch interiors, after van de Hooch, in which the square-tiled floors could plainly be seen to be the source of inspiration for our patterned linoleum.

The pictures were all second-hand, and probably gifts, but their presence at least indicated a desire for culture, even if satisfying actual personal taste in such matters was a luxury which at that time was still beyond our means.

Upstairs, Mother and Father occupied the front bedroom, and the two back bedrooms were shared by us children, in various arrangements over the years as we grew up or were away from home - Dennis and I doing our National Service, and Pauline at teacher training college.

During my first years I slept in the front bedroom, in the drop-sided iron cot, as did Pauline before me and Sylvia after. Dennis was already four when they moved in, so his experience was different. The cot was high-sided and painted, with transfer pictures of nursery rhymes round the sides. Once in, there was no getting out, but there was also no ignoring the noise that could be made by the incumbent standing up and rattling the drop side, although the request for a drink of water must have seemed a little tame after such a racket.

I used 'the rattler' to summon any sympathiser when I had nightmares, which seemed tiresomely frequent. Once I awoke to find I could only see coloured patterns above me, but normal vision returned when Mother arrived. A persistent night illusion was that, upon waking in the gloom, all the furniture, which was just visible, appeared to have shrunk, and could not be restored to its proper size by blinking. This stayed with me until I was nine or ten years old.

I remember standing in the cot at dusk on a summer evening, and watching through the window with Dennis and Pauline as the lamplighter came on his bicycle and used a very long pole to switch on the street lamp outside Mrs Freeman's house, next door but one. This later gave a particular poignancy to Tobias and Simon's 1947 hit song 'The Old Lamplighter (of long, long ago)'.

The furniture in this front bedroom comprised a nice (brown) matching suite consisting of wardrobe, dressing table and washstand with marble top. There were a couple of chairs, one an ancient Victorian nursing chair, which was upholstered in soft leather but had no arms, and the other a bedside chair.

In the wardrobe, the special items that always got my attention were Mother's fox fur and a large blue cardboard box. The fox fur had been bought at Pearson's of Enfield, during Mother's independent wage-earning days, but although they were still being worn in the 1940s, she rarely used it, and its only value then seemed to be as a special diversion for me to play with on the bed while some upstairs chore was in progress. The blue box contained the ingenious 'Escalado' table-top horse racing game, whereby lead horses and jockeys were urged along a track by vibration resulting from turning a handle attached to a cog. It belonged to Father, and there must have been some story attached to it, simply because it was never mentioned. In any event, the handle and cog were broken, and so one way and another the game was never brought out until I was old enough to be able to mend it myself and set it up on the dining room table, where my pal Mike Curwen and I had hours of fun placing bets and losing a fortune in matchsticks.

The dressing table had Mother's bits and pieces set out on top, including various small ornaments, and despite the fact that she was not at all keen on dogs, there was a set of black wooden Scotties in three sizes, a china terrier, and an elegant greyhound, as well as other Goss-style items. Father did not approve of the use of make-up, and so Mother did not have any; perhaps as a reward, she retained a good complexion into her nineties. Overall there was a distinctive and pleasant smell, from a mixture of lavender bags, mothballs, 'Lily Of The Valley' perfume, and bars of toilet soap, including one in the form of a sitting black cat (Mother did not like cats either).

There was a wash basin and jug on the washstand, although these were only used in the event of somebody being confined to bed, unlike the (matching) ceramic chamberpot, which was liable to be used at night despite the fact that the lavatory was right outside the door. At a young age I was a regular user of the pot at night, and Father would always ask, in the language of his childhood,

'Droppies or business?', hoping it would not be the latter, because that did entail going out to the lavatory, and the philosophy was that at all costs the children in the other rooms should not be disturbed.

The focal point in winter was the gas fire, which roared out its friendly, cosy warmth and glow on cold dark mornings and evenings, and provided a soft light while we got dressed or undressed. Every other room upstairs would be icy cold, and the gas fire was a great luxury. It was put to good use when someone was unwell, and also on Christmas morning, when our tradition, like that of many families, was to invade Mum and Dad's bedroom with our presents while they had a cup of tea in bed.

On some rare weekend mornings, Father would have an extra half hour in bed, and when I was three or four I would crawl in with him, and he would remind me that 'From Wimbledon to Wombledon is fourteen miles, from Wombledon to Wimbledon is fourteen miles ', and I would persuade him to tell me the story of Mr and Mrs Squiggly-wiggly Worm and their Squiggly-wiggly children, a tale which did not have a strong or consistent plot, and was nothing more than a sure route to my being tickled until I fled. I also enjoyed holding out my hand while he walked his fingers on it and up my arm to the rhyme 'Walkie round the garden, like a teddy bear, one step, two step, tickley under there!', 'there' being my all too sensitive armpit.

A feature of the room which I did not learn until much later, was that by standing on a chair in the southern corner of the bay window and looking through the transom, on a clear day you could see the northern tip of 'the Downs' - only the Surrey Downs, of course. Hardly an agent's selling point, rather a secret of the house that was known only to the privileged.

The larger of the two back bedrooms contained the airing cupboard with its hot water tank, so with the door ajar, this was another favoured spot in which to dress or undress in winter. With so little heating in the house, it was very cold in winter, and we used to waken to find thick ice formed in patterns on the inside of the bedroom windows, and Mother used to say Jack Frost had been to visit us during the night. Towels had to be spread on the window sills to soak up the water as the ice melted. There was a coal fireplace in this bedroom, but the only time I recall it being used was when Dennis was confined to bed with a strained groin, which he 'won' through over-exertion during athletic training at school.

From this rear window there was a pleasant view of the tree-filled back gardens, and in the distance, of the decorative square tower on the roof of Borough Road College, which always caught the last of the setting sun in summer. In late August, we could reach out of the window and pick the delicious, soft ripe Czar plums off the branches of the 'bedroom tree' that grew nearest the house.

The trees were an attraction and host to many birds, especially starlings, sparrows, chaffinches, tits, blackbirds, and thrushes, and recognising them and their song was a feature of daily life, and at night too. There was a dead plum tree by the shed, which was used as a perch by a tawny owl, giving the autumnal too-whit, to be followed by the answering to-whoo of her mate. On winter nights we would sometimes hear the screech of the barn owl which was thought to inhabit the old oak in St Mary's sports field.

When I slept in the large back bedroom, I was not usually awake for the dawn chorus, but would gradually gather my senses to the incessant chirrup of the sparrows, which perched on the gutter and on branches just outside the window, and which seemed to be late risers like me. Later in the morning, the territory would be taken over by starlings, 'the gangsters' of the birdworld, especially in winter, when their whistling and quarrelsome squawks provided a background that I always associate with the reading of books in bed, from occasions when I was unwell.

For some years, I shared that bedroom with Dennis, and his possessions predominated. Apart from the bed and a couple of bedside chairs, the only other furniture was a dressing table, and this was mostly full of Dennis's things. In the small top drawer, he kept an assortment of interesting relics from his boyhood - pens, pencils, tie pins, a convex torch glass for magnifying, old diaries, a boy scout's woggle, army badges, dismantled watches, a couple of mouth organs, and a small firework, a banger, called a 'Boy Scout

Rouser'. The firework remained there intact throughout the War, and I looked forward to the day when I could discover what fireworks were like in action, which did not happen until the approach to VE day in May 1945, when fireworks were once more on sale after the lifting of wartime restrictions.

More of Dennis's things were stored on top of the airing cupboard - his stamp album, cigarette cards, boxing gloves, tennis racket, cricket bat - and books. The books became of greater interest as I grew older. I particularly liked the two Ovaltine-financed athletics coaching books, featuring Jesse Owens, Dennis's hero from the 1936 Olympics. There were one or two boys' adventure books, and more adult reading, from which I benefited eventually.

When Dennis was apprenticed at the Institute of Automobile Engineers, on the Great West Road next to Coty's, and had to 'do his bit' fire-watching with the other lads, he brought home things that he bought second-hand as various fads took hold. There was a fencing foil and mask, a baseball glove and face mask, a snare drum and cymbal kit with a stand, Victor Silvester's ballroom dancing instruction book, a selection of astronomical books and charts, and a pair of Indian clubs. More enduringly, a portable HMV gramophone appeared, which was supplemented by a growing pile of 78 rpm records and sheet music that were to eventually arouse my interest enough to make me want to play the piano.

On the south-west corner of the house, the smallest bedroom had a clear view of the setting sun between two houses in Wood Lane that backed onto our garden. In the summertime, especially during British double summertime, it was pleasant to lie in that bed with the last rays of the evening sun bathing the room in a golden light, to be serenaded by blackbird and thrush, and to listen to the swifts shrieking in their mad race as they passed between our house and the Hills's next door, or hurtled up the outer wall to feed their young in the nest under the eaves. The proliferation of sparrows in the loft, and the invasion of the bedroom by strange tropical bugs carried in by the swifts finally caused Father to board up the eaves, which was judged necessary, but sadly took away a little of our house's tradition and character.

The landing was known for three things. Firstly it had a large stained glass window at the top of the stairs, and one night Dennis was stopped just in time as he was climbing up onto that first floor window sill to go into the garden - in his sleep! The second feature was a long brown framed photograph of Father as a member of a large troupe of minstrels, from before the Great War - a precious family souvenir which somehow got relegated to the shed, along with his tap-dancing shoes, and then became lost forever.

The third thing was that it was the site of one of Father's Slight Misunderstandings, whereby he had thought that he might wash down the (brown) lincruster paper with Tide, a washing powder that contained bleach to make our whites even whiter. He soon realised his mistake, but the resulting whitish patch remained on the wall for some time as a discomfiting reminder and 'insider' joke, until a lick or two of brown paint restored both colour and dignity.

The bathroom, which faced east, was a pretty cold place, and not popular. We never missed our morning ablutions, but in winter they were often reduced to a 'cat's lick' or 'saloosh', as Father termed a quick splash round with the flannel. Father wisely had his early morning shave in the warmer kitchen, 'to keep Mother company'. He used a Gillette Valet razor with a single-edged blade which he sharpened each day on the strop that hung on the back door.

Of course, the bathroom could be made warm and cosy enough for baths by pre-heating with the portable Valor paraffin stove, although it meant carrying it up and down stairs. It burnt with what I thought was the pleasing smell of paraffin, a reminder of our Tankerton beach hut days, and if the electric light was put out, the stove's gently revolving fan threw a moving pattern on the ceiling, which was one of my 'treats' . Another was to have a little time to play with my boats, the best one of which was a 'torpedo', made from the bomb-shaped wooden handle of some forgotten implement.

The Valor stove resided in the kitchen, and when I was nine I thought I was quite capable of carrying it downstairs on my own after a bath. I was proved wrong, as the stove and I tumbled head over heels down the full flight, but we landed unscathed and with the paraffin still in the tank. I was left in no doubt as to my foolhardiness, but at least credited with having had the sense to turn it off before attempting the descent.

The bathroom windows were of frosted glass, and on one of those interminable days when the imagination failed to provide a constructive outlet, Mike and I passed some time calling out of the bathroom transom window at passers-by, fondly believing we were projecting mystery voices and could neither be seen nor identified. Mrs Hills from next door was neither mystified nor happy to be so taunted. Curiously, she did not come to my house but called upon Mrs Curwen to make her protest Fortunately for us, Mike's mother was an exceptional lady with a complete understanding of young children, and after discussing the affair with us and getting our agreement that it was a stupid thing to do, the matter was ended. It never reached the ears of my family!

Next to the bathroom was the lavatory - still separate in those days. I naturally spent my share of hours there, dreaming, hiding, performing, although we never took to the habit of reading there, except for the nursery rhymes which were to be found on Izal toilet paper.

I did not notice anybody else's habits except Father's. I was always a little astonished at his totally uninhibited, thunderous torrent, straight into the water (not skirting the porcelain sides quietly, as I would), and his muttered 'Aah, that's better', interspersed with snatches of song: 'Be-au-ti-ful dreamer, lah-dowah-di-dowah, lah-dah-dee, dee-dee-dah, awake unto me.' No doubt it was just a reflection of his acknowledged honesty and directness.

Grandad Fred Betts and Great
Uncle Alfred Baker - 1925.

Grandad Fred and Grandma Ellen Betts
1882.

Grandad Fred Betts (extreme left) with gang from Whiteley's
c1910.

Grandad Fred Betts and a growing
Family - Father extreme right - 1903.

Father with a Harlesden bicycle - and
some of the family - 1907.

Uncle Fred Betts
- tough infantryman.

Uncle Pash Baker
- dashing hussar.

Uncle Bob Cook and Aunty Win.

- and Family! with Packard - 1912.

The delectable Maud Allan
- always asked for Uncle Bob!

Father - hire car driver- Hastings, 1914.

Father - in the Great War.

"We got the bird!"
- Father, right and partner.

Mother, at seventeen.

Aunt Alice Savage, at Enfield.

Three generations of Savages, Enfield in 1912, with Great Granny Beecroft and Grandma Savage at the gate and Mother far right.

Harewood Road 1935 - Pauline outside our house.

A more recent view from our house.

Our house - just completed and occupied - 1929.

Our house - dominated by the bay tree - a local landmark - 1946.

Our House in the 1950's, with recently added garage and brick wall.

- and more recently, further refined with enclosed porch,
double glazing, and side rendering.

Our garden - "a thick blanket of pristine snow".

Our garden - the path to my secret place and the swing.

Next door, Dennis and Pauline in the Scales' pond.

The Cowboy Suit - Pauline and Dennis. 'Big Teddy' - with cousin Peter Morgan.

The back garden - Uncle Harry and Aunty Margaret visiting.

The bedroom plum tree.

Next door again - Pauline,
Dennis and me.

Mother and Father - beneath the kitchen window.

I hold 'Hoppity' while Sylvia rides the rocking horse.

Father, Mother and Sylvia.   Pauline and Sylvia.

Dennis in full flight - Twickenham Tech. - 1939.

Chapter Four

. . . And Garden

'Better than a holiday in the country!' declared Father, whenever he sat in a deckchair under the verandah with his afternoon cup of 'Rosie Lee'. And in many ways it was.

We had both a back and a front garden of a size that was then typical for semi-detached suburbia. At the front of the property, there was a low brick wall surmounted by a small, wooden lattice fence, and divided in the middle by a solid wooden gate. A cement path led up to the front door, and from this, another path led to the side entrance, which was seven feet high and consisted of two large wooden doors. We only ever opened the one nearest the house. This was the door with the latch, but both doors had top and bottom bolts, which we fondly but mistakenly thought would deter any intruder.

There was a lawn each side of the main path in the front garden, and along the front wall there was a flower border. In one corner was a lilac bush (which Father pronounced 'lilock'), and near the gate was an evergreen shrub with leaves which grew in 'buds'. When I needed a little therapy, I spent a lot of time peeling back the ever smaller outer leaves to reach the infinitesimal centre leaves. By the front door, in between the main and side paths, there was a lavender bush, large and untidy but sweet smelling, and often visited by butterflies. The lilac attracted them too, and it was on those branches that I once found a bright green, strikingly-marked puss moth caterpillar.

The dominant feature of the front garden was the bay tree, which became quite a local landmark. It had started life in a pot by the front door, but had grown large enough to be planted in the centre of the lawn, appropriately enough in front of the 'bay' window. That was a coincidence, but it was also one of Father's Slight Misunderstandings, because it eventually rose to bedroom window height, and its pyramid-shaped foliage, which was dense enough to hide the perennial blackbird's nest, blotted out much of the light in the drawing room. When Father faced the inevitable, we were all involved in the huge task of cutting it down and digging up the root, and we were surprised to find that the foliage was laden with soot. Later that night, sitting on the fender box close to the dining room fire, the largest, blackest spider I had seen to date came running down my arm from my shoulder. Father's voice released me from my paralysis: 'Not afraid of them, are you? They're only air and water!' and as it hit the floor he flattened it with the fireside shovel. But, steeped as I was in Edgar Allen Poe and the like, I thought on quietly, as its remains sizzled on the fire, wondering if it had been watching our labours from the sooty depths of the tree and had followed us, homeless and vengeful, to make a desperate do-or-die attack on our very hearth. For a long time afterwards, I took care to check the vicinity for intruders before sitting on the fender box.

Passing through the side entrance, a flat, concreted area ran down beside the house where the back door and door step were situated. The house wall was blank except for the larder window and a couple of drainpipes to which the decorating ladders were tied, so it was ideal for tennis ball games against the wall, such as 'clap and catch', or straddling the bounce, as in 'donkey'.

Opposite the house wall was the coal bunker. The original wooden one with its unique smell of damp coal dust eventually collapsed, and was replaced by one of Father's expedient but unsophisticated solutions, an open-topped brick and cement 'surround', with a few bits of stout wood across the gap at the front ('That'll do, pro-tem!').

The mangle and the zinc bath stood against the fence, hidden by a waterproof cover, together with other odds and ends, but then Father bought a wooden self-assembly shed, which he and Dennis erected and creosoted, and this tidied up the garden by transferring the untidiness to the shed.

The shed was close to the fence, and this left a narrow passage beside the house. Down this gap from the lawn end we were still able to practise our fast tennis-ball bowling at the stumps chalked on the inside of the side entrance, for an equally swift return from the batsman, making hasty and thoughtless emergence from the back door a somewhat hazardous move. We did witness one such inconsiderate forehead resoundingly divert the ball over into next door's garden, turning our demonic glee to chagrin, and the stinging shock of the victim to triumph, but the shout of 'Six!' soon reduced everyone to laughter.

The back of the house boasted a verandah, built by Father and his brother, Uncle Harry, and this overlooked a lawn flanked by path and flowerbeds. Father imported a man-sized wooden beer barrel and set it up to catch the rainwater that cascaded down the sloping glass roof of the verandah. The barrel, which always seemed to be full, was smartly painted in green with black hoops, and one of my interests was to stand on my tricycle and watch the antics of the mosquito larvae cavorting near the surface. We used the water for the garden, but also collected it by the panful to boil and then use to wash our hair, with the bar of special 'green soft soap' that pre-dated shampoo. The softness of the water seemed to leave the hair in particularly fine condition, but I preferred to think that perhaps the magical ingredient of boiled larvae had some beneficial effect.

At the end of the lawn was a 'rustic' (that is, made by Father) trellis, throughout which grew a 'rambling rose', and at one side of which, straddling the path, was a rose-covered arch of similar but more slender construction. Beyond the lawn was a vegetable patch, and at the bottom of the garden, where the path straightened before starting its return journey, was my 'secret place'. Here the path was straddled by another 'rustic arch', and by the homemade swing, the seat of which had to be slung round one of its posts to allow for through traffic.

The back garden was surrounded by a five-foot paling fence, an integral part of which were what Father correctly referred to as arris rails; but owing to his occasional lapses, I always thought they were 'Arris rails, and therefore were vaguely associated with our near neighbours, the Harris family.

This uncertainty, caused by the unreliability of the Londoner's aspirate, gave rise to another of Father's Slight Misunderstandings. My sister was christened Sylvia Helen, because as late as 1942 Father still believed his mother was named Helen, when in fact she was Ellen. It also illustrates the kind of legacy that resulted from the long-standing Victorian custom of maintaining a discreet and formal distance between the generations by not tolerating many 'personal' questions.

The estate had been built upon an orchard, and so in the back garden we had an abundance of the residual fruit trees, although some of the neighbours had evidently removed theirs, or were less fortunate. There were several Czar plum trees on the lawn, which in August were loaded with luscious, syrup-sweet, purply-black-skinned fruit, giving off a heady perfume which summoned wasps from miles around. The ripe plums almost fell out of their skins, and eating them was like eating peaches. No plum since has offered the same delicious combination of fragrance, texture and taste.

After reading the likes of *Robinson Crusoe* and *Coral Island*, I made an unsuccessful attempt to sling a hammock, constructed from a deckchair cover and bits of washing line, between the branches of one of our plum trees. An idyllic notion, but neither safe nor comfortable and, for a landlubber, not as simple as those seafaring stories suggested.

Further down the garden, there were William pears, Bramley cooking apples, and Cox's eating apples, which we learnt had originated with the Mr Cox who had lived a hundred years before in the cottage by the level crossing in nearby Colnbrook, and which we considered were the finest of English apples. Father always laid some out in the shed, or in the air raid shelter, to be brought in and added to our treats at Christmas.

On the vegetable plot, Father grew a selection of salad stuff and vegetables, including runner beans, and there were raspberries and

46

loganberries growing by the fence, and strawberries in the darker area under the apple trees. In fact, although he was a 'townie', Father was quite successful at turning his hand to growing things, motivated by the desire to save money. Pauline took the cue, and was eventually to take over and become an expert on growing produce - enough to feed half the neighbourhood, we used to say, and certainly she gave much of it away, just as Father had distributed basketfuls of our plums among friends and relatives.

The washing line ran at various times between two plum trees, then from the verandah post to a dead tree, and finally from the house wall to a line post, but in direction always from the house down the lawn towards the trellis. The washing was kept flying high by a long prop, and for some reason I always liked to see the washing blowing high, especially on a sunny day, even though the prop was an obstacle to my games on the lawn. On washing days, I was allowed to help with the mangling, and I enjoyed seeing the cogs mesh together and the water pouring out noisily into the zinc bath below. Much fuss was made about keeping little fingers away from the rollers, and not without cause, because they did get lightly but painfully pinched once or twice, but that was during illicit but vital experiments to determine the effect of mechanised squashing upon assorted substances. I always felt such knowledge would come in useful when I eventually discovered the right application.

There was a period when I had my own garden. This was a patch of flower border close to the shed, in which the steadfast lily of the valley and London pride flourished, while the mustard and cress, solitary lettuce and other seedlings nourished the insect population or failed to materialise at all. Pauline and I attributed this failure to my planting the seeds upside down, because we had often giggled at that same mistake, which little Johnny was told he had made, in one of our storybooks.

I made miniature gardens on my patch, with tiny rockeries, mirror ponds, shell borders and twig trees, only to have them wiped out by mock earthquakes, bombing raids, or a real nocturnal feline prowler. I made mobile versions too, in an old baking tray, which could also become a 'sunken garden' and therefore be subject to an exciting and disastrous flood.

My most enduring occupations in the garden were with the tricycle, the rocking horse and the swing. Being 'on' something was always more appealing than just using the legs, and besides, it stimulated the imagination. The red tricycle had a flat metal seat and backrest, with solid wheels and pedals attached to the front wheel. Left to my own devices, I would cycle round the garden path and sideway for hours. The pleasure was further extended when Father made me a 'box barrow' from two pram wheels and a wooden fruit box, with shafts made from architraves, and I would laboriously tie it to the back of the tricycle and tow it round, loaded with a variety of 'goods', which of course had to be delivered to 'customers' at different 'depots'.

Under the verandah was a favourite spot for baby Sylvia to sleep or sit up in her pram. I used to amuse myself by amusing her, and was here advised by Father not to tickle her toes, as it would make her speak with a stutter. He also told how parents in his day would keep a baby quiet by putting a little treacle on its hands and then giving it a couple of feathers to play with. I could well imagine the silent concentration while painstakingly picking a feather from one sticky set of fingers to the other, but I was not allowed to try it out on Sylvia. One could never be quite sure when Father's tales were to be taken seriously.

Also under the verandah stood the rocking horse, and since the family had a hand-me-down cowboy suit and a small arsenal of pistols, riding the horse while playing cowboys and Indians was a favourite pastime, sometimes with a warbled 'Post Horn Gallop' or a snatch of the 'William Tell Overture'. But just sitting in the saddle and gently rocking was a means of losing all notion of time and place, and drifting across the threshold into the world of make-believe.

For sheer simplicity and therapeutic power, however, nothing could compare with the garden swing. It was blissful to be able to slip down the garden, past the rustic fence and the vegetable patch, to my 'secret place', where I could not be seen from the house. There I would sit on the sturdy, smooth, wooden seat, and 'work up' to a self-sustaining rhythm which would elevate me into the world of trees and birds, sunshine and sky. I would be able to see over the fences, enjoy the rush of air and the exhilaration from the tummy as the downward momentum began, gradually freeing the mind and losing all care.

The shed was really Father's kingdom, but as he was only likely to be there on Saturday or Sunday mornings, I soon acquired the right to play 'sensibly' inside. The accessible outsides were kept quite smart by being re-creosoted from time to time, but the front panel by the door was Father's 'wiping off board', and was irreversibly daubed with every conceivable hue of matt and gloss paint that had come his way over the years. 'That will all help to keep the weather out,' he said, and no doubt that panel would have survived long after the rest of the shed disintegrated.

Just about everything that was 'outdoor' was kept in the shed. There was a homemade bench, with boxes of tools, paint brushes, spare parts and innumerable bits of 'just-in-case' underneath, and there were shelves loaded with oil cans, bottles of thinners, balls of string, oddments of wallpaper, and half-used pots of every colour of paint, stain and varnish. Onions hung from the roof, apples were laid out in boxes, and the rest was a jumble of deckchairs, garden tools, bats, racquets, balls, stilts, buckets, spades, shrimp nets, old picture frames, the iron shoe last (Father did quite a bit of 'snobbing' or shoe repair, when money was tight, from stick-on soles and heels to blakeys all round), the sledge, the whooping cough kettle with its long spout, packets of seeds, the watering can, tricycle and bicycle - and still there was room to stand in front of the bench, but to turn round safely you had to spin on the spot. 'It's handy to have everything within reach' said Father. There were times when the rocking horse and the mangle were squeezed in too, but that put paid to any activity within. The annual 'clear out' was an interesting but lengthy ritual in which, on a fine day, the entire contents were spread over the lawn and paths, and some attempt made to throw away the excess junk, but they were difficult decisions as, according to Father, 'You never know what will come in handy tomorrow'.

- Despite a lethal array of chisels, knives, razor blades, hammers, nails, screws, scissors, spirits and poisonous chemicals, no accident ever befell us children, as we were well versed in what was and was not a safe thing to touch or do. But there were occasions when

Father's aim suffered, perhaps as a result of some childish distraction, and hammer would strike thumb. At such moments it was prudent to melt away into deep cover, beyond the rustic trellis, to my secret place, until Mother summoned Father indoors to get ready, a little before 'opening time', whereafter he would proceed, at a leisurely walk, 'down the road' or 'up the top', to learn the latest news from his pals, or take in the life story of a casual customer.

The whole of the back garden acted as a release valve - a happy playground in which it was easy to forget troubles and get lost in the games and imaginary situations of childhood. The seasons also made their special contribution.

On a winter morning, it was exciting to recognise the unusual greyish light, and look out of the windows at a thick blanket of pristine snow, just begging for attention. It was fun to venture out the back, in the cold muffled silence, and make the first ever human footprints to the bottom of the garden, trying to identify the different bird tracks that revealed the urgent search for food and water that had taken place before I was up.

In April and May there was tremendous activity from the large bird population, starting with a powerful dawn chorus, and continuing all day long with the whistling, calling and chattering of every common species in the host trees that populated the gardens.

After a summer storm, it was good to stand under the verandah, listening to the dripping leaves and breathing in the fresh smell of wet earth and grass.

Then there were those special, everlasting, golden days of summer, when grasshopper and bee made a soothing background noise while I looked about for the iridescent greeny-blue dragonflies straying from the Scales's pond next door, and for the painted lady, red admiral, peacock, tortoiseshell and blue butterflies that abounded. The cabbage white, labelled a pest, was everywhere, and therefore easy to observe and catch, but we just watched its colourful cousins until they fluttered out of sight. For a butterfly net, I used the small fishing net I'd brought back from our last seaside holiday at Tankerton. One cabbage white took umbrage at being captured, and when released it flew into my face, hitting me several times before rising and fluttering away over the fence, leaving me swiping the air and feeling foolish. I imagined what it would have seen, looking down on my flailing arms and upturned face full of surprise, and I was always reminded of this whenever I heard the great heavyweight Mohammed Ali deliver his taunting lines: 'Dance like a butterfly, sting like a bee'.

It was summertime when *Wind In The Willows* was serialised for Children's Hour on the radio. When the programme was finished, I would go down the path to my secret place at the bottom of the garden, my head filled with life on the river bank and in the wild wood, and I would lose myself in the natural world of earth, stones, insects, plants, trees and birds, the haunting signature tune filling my head,

'Wind in the willows is whispering low,
Hid in the meadow which dreams in the sun.'

British double summer time, which advanced the clocks by two hours, kept the sun hanging in the sky until nine o'clock at night and then, for me, the world took on a dream-like atmosphere.

We got the full benefit of the late sun at the back of the house, and whether we were still loitering outside or reading in the back bedroom, those long, warm, golden evenings gave great pleasure, with a background accompaniment provided by the rushing of swifts, the evensong of a thrush, the 'pinking' of blackbirds, and the occasional noise or voices of neighbours reluctant to leave their gardens and go indoors.

And was that really a German parachute we saw, descending slowly in the rays of the setting sun, over towards Hounslow West?

Chapter Five

Christmastime

Games and music, laughter and smiles, log fires, fine food, leisurely hours: Christmas was a happy family time, when for two days at least, everybody seemed more than usually glad to be at home.

In the weeks before Christmas, many things contributed to the build-up of excitement and anticipation. Mother would make the pudding, and I would help with the stirring - and tasting - because I loved the spicy, raw mixture, and I would keep watch as it was boiled in the copper. As an employee of J Lyons, Father received a Christmas food parcel, and we usually also received one from Uncle Ben Greenwood and Aunt Eva in South Africa. This contained a very acceptable mixture of fruits and sweet things, and often some of the distinctively perfumed dried muscatel grapes that we all liked. At intervals throughout the year, Uncle Ben also sent us copies of The Cape Times and The Outspan magazine, which showed how different their world was, but it did not implant in me any desire to emigrate.

Once, in 1939, Father took Pauline and me to a children's Christmas party at Chelsea Barracks. This was organised through Father's old army comrades, and although bewildered by the assembled throng of strange children, I was happy enough to enjoy the party food. Children were invited to go up on stage and perform, and Pauline went up and sang. At four years old, I was content to watch and then take my turn to walk down to the front, like everybody else, and collect a present from Father Christmas. My present was Patch, a furry toy dog which became my long-term bedtime companion, although I was soon ordered to keep it out of bed, because it invariably got underneath me, and I would awaken shouting with nightmares as its paws were sticking in me.

Christmas cards would start arriving in the couple of weeks before the big day, and they added a festive appearance to the piano, sideboard and mantelpiece. Those that I gave had to be homemade rather than bought, so there was quite a lot of effort put into finding appropriate pieces of card, and then drawing and crayoning or painting a design with a typical Christmas theme.

The house seemed much busier and less open than usual, with unexplained comings and goings, mysterious noises of rustling paper behind closed doors which were customarily left open, and inaudible whispered conversations that defeated even the most determined eavesdropper.

Outside, in the streets, there was little evidence of Christmas during the war. This was largely due to the blackout, which prevented people from opening their curtains to display decorated trees and lights, and even the shops were subdued, especially as shortages of food and other materials made it difficult, if not treasonable, to promote excessive indulgence. The spirit of Christmas remained strong, however. United by the common bond of resisting the enemy's worst efforts, people endeavoured to cheer each other up, and seemed especially to want children to enjoy themselves.

Indoors it was a different story, and most homes would try to appear as festive as in pre-war days. Our decorations usually went up about two weeks before Christmas, and that meant we had to make paper chains from coloured strips pasted together, and perhaps some painted newspaper Chinese lanterns, to supplement the long held family stock of good quality paper bells, balls, Chinese lanterns and concertina chains. In addition, we had fairy lights in the shape of snowmen and Father Christmases, which were strung up round the dining room and in due course plugged in. At intervals thereafter, they got Father muttering darkly and reluctantly getting out of his armchair, as owing to an ever increasing number of improvised connections, their magic illuminated the room delightfully but spasmodically, and a clamour of good-humoured derision went up from the other occupants every time they went off.

A favourite feature of our decoration was the Christmas lampshade, with a repeated Father Christmas and sleigh motif all round in its coloured leaded glass. It was too small to go anywhere except in the hall, but it gave out a most welcoming and cosy light, and proclaimed Christmas to whoever entered through the front door.

We never did have a Christmas tree. There was no room for it, and it was not at that time judged to be essential.

Christmas Eve was a bustling, upside-down sort of day, with the kitchen permanently occupied and all of us lending a helping hand, whether wanted or not. The radio was on all the time, providing carols and comedy to accompany our efforts, and we kept a look-out through the front window for the appearance of the Salvation Army brass band which, with its smartly uniformed players, gleaming instruments and acclaimed performance of favourite carols, issued a heartening challenge to the pervasive murky gloom of a typical winter's afternoon.

Sleep that night came with difficulty, and expectations would be running high, although this was more due to the occasion and ritual than to any hope of a large or expensive present. We were brought up with the notion that we should not expect anything at all, and so any present was a nice surprise, and that element of surprise, of not letting the recipient have an inkling of what was to come, was a large and essential part of the pleasure. More than once I awoke to hear a stealthy rustling at the bottom of the bed, where my empty pillowcase had been placed with such optimism, but I never wanted to look or get up and interrupt the process. I just wanted everything to be right on Christmas morning.

Like all children, I was always awake too early, and reached out in the dark to feel the lumps and corners through the now partly filled pillow case. Then I would lie back, content to wait until Mother said it was all right for us all to go into their bedroom with our 'sacks'. In the cosy warmth of the gas fire we would take turns to open our presents, while Mum and Dad enjoyed a cup of 'special'

- Father always put 'a drop of Scotch' in their first cup of tea on Christmas morning (a commendable tradition which I have had much pleasure in upholding).

Mother would be the first to go downstairs and start getting breakfast, and Father would follow to get the fires going in both the dining room and drawing room, and that was the signal for us to go down too.

After a hurried breakfast, it was back to the presents. In those early years, the kind of presents I received included various clockwork, friction and free-wheeling toys, paper cutout sets, lead soldiers, tanks, guns, farm animals, paints, crayons and drawing pads, books, jigsaws, board games, torches, model kits - but on any one occasion, there would only be half a dozen items altogether. There was little enough available or affordable in the toy shops, so perhaps some things came from one of the WVS 'toy bazaars' which put unwanted second-hand toys on sale before Christmas. As a final treat, at the bottom of the 'sack' there was usually an apple and an orange, a few nuts, and a bar of chocolate or some sweets.

The largest Christmas presents I ever received were a fort to house my lead soldiers, an aerodrome which Father made, and a red metal, mobile swivel-crane with ratchet brake. I did eventually go one better than all those with a chemistry set, which was all the rage when I was eleven. If there were any more expensive presents, they tended to be the nicer essentials, like slippers or a dressing gown.

The presents we children gave or exchanged were modest, either a small book or plaything, or diaries, socks, ties, handkerchiefs, inexpensive scent, pipe tobacco, cigarettes, and sometimes a cigar. Father was always pleased to have some St Bruno Flake tobacco (what an exotic and intoxicating smell it had while still in the packet!), and Mother's great luxury was a packet of Turkish cigarettes, usually Abdullah, which she smoked using an elegant black and silver holder, and which lasted her until the following Christmas.

At school, we not only made Christmas cards, but also calendars as family gifts, using a piece of card covered with a wallpaper oddment, to which we stuck a penny calendar showing the dates, and a ribbon with which to hang it up. It was usually only Mother's calendar in the kitchen that survived the year, however.

I always got the maximum enjoyment out of what I was given, and the presents were in any event just a part of the whole occasion - two days in which the family was able to devote time to pleasure at home. However, although I was not envious of other children who did better, I did secretly wish that the fascinating toys that were advertised pre-war could have been available in my time.

By half-past ten, there would be a good fire going in both rooms, and the radio on in the dining room, but the real attraction was the front room, where the open grate would have a log or two blazing on top of the coals, transforming the place from its usually fresh and formal atmosphere into a really warm and cheery spot to play in.

This was about the time that Father would have his first drink, which he termed a 'livener': always a bottled beer to 'line the stomach', and we would be offered orange, or orange wine, or one of Father's 'specials', which were 'cocktails' based on a mix of orange and ginger wine.

Sometimes Phil Harris would call in for a short while to see Dennis, placing Father in his preferred role of host and entertainer; then at about eleven, our only regular Christmas day visitors, the Thurlows, would arrive for an hour of good-humoured banter and tale-telling, and, of course, a drink or two. Mrs Thurlow and Mother would embrace the sherry, while Mr Thurlow would join Father in a beer, and then a scotch.

Dinner would be at one o'clock in the dining room. The wartime shortages diminished what Christmas fare we might have had, but although we did not always have everything, as a result of months of saving, making do and doing without, Mother did manage to ensure that we always had enough. The main course was usually a goose, supplied by a contact of old Tommy Downs, the Wood Lane coffin maker, and a joint of ham. To go with it, there would be roast potatoes, brussels sprouts, carrots and thick gravy. None of us were very interested in sauces, and not until later years was wine much in evidence, but when possible, Father did like to produce a bottle of Sauterne for the table. The homemade Christmas pudding was served with cream if we had it, or evaporated milk, or custard, and there were usually homemade mince pies too. We did not go in for igniting the pudding, which was considered dangerous and unnecessary, and for similar reasons, we did not put silver threepenny bits in the mixture, although at that time and until 1944 they were still currency.

If we had them, then nuts, dates and figs and crystalised fruits from South Africa would be on the table, and my favourite crystalised orange slices. Then, of course, there was the chocolate tin, with its precious reserve bars kept back for the occasion. Some years, there were crackers (which Father always referred to as 'bon bons' - this may have been some long-forgotten term, or a 'Slight French Misunderstanding'), although after the war the novelties inside were always judged to have 'gone downhill'. I did make my own crackers once or twice but sad, silent substitutes they proved to be, alas. In any event, there were always paper hats to put on, because we had a number of good quality ones collected from better days, including various colourful caps and coronets, pointed hats, mandarin hats, a fine legionnaire's hat with a sun flap at the back, and the extraordinary 'black cat' hat, which invariably sat on Father's head like a well-fed and contented pet.

Mother and Father would have a glass of port while we went through the ritual of getting our fingers pinched in the nutcrackers - the nuts were usually almond, cob, brazil and walnut. Every effort was made to keep the walnut shells in two intact halves, so that they could later be turned into tortoises. This was done by gluing over the hole a piece of card cut to represent the underpart, legs and head, with a long piece of thread stuck in between shell and card by which to pull the diminutive creature along.

Father always tackled the washing up, and there was plenty of help available to get all clearing up done and fires stoked before settling in chairs in the dining room with a cup of tea to listen to the King's speech, which was broadcast on the wireless at three o'clock. The 'grown ups' would then doze off, leaving the young to play with their toys and look at their books in the front room.

Tea was an informal affair, the dining table being set with ham sandwiches, bread and paste or jam, jelly, blancmange and the Christmas cake, which was a rich fruit cake covered in marzipan and icing, decorated with one or two of the carefully preserved miniature Christmas decorations, such as Father Christmas, the sleigh, the Christmas tree or the little house. Everybody helped themselves, but appetites were soon satisfied after the unaccustomed excesses of dinner time.

After tea, but sometimes beforehand as well, the whole family joined in with whatever amusement was decided upon with common consent. We had a 'Compendium of Games', which was a box that included snakes and ladders, ludo, draughts and a pack of cards. There was also a 'Foulsham's Fun Book', which was a thick and well-thumbed volume only brought out at Christmas time, and containing games, puzzles, riddles, conundrums, jokes, tongue-twisters, tricks and songs, all of which became part of our seasonal family tradition.

We played card games round the dining table, and the most popular would be 'rummy', 'sevens' (which Father termed 'runnin's out'), 'snap' with regular cards or the special picture pack, 'Happy Families', and 'Lexicon', which was a word-forming game. Father would always perform a card trick or two, and he could bewilder us by making pennies disappear from the hand, and reappear convincingly from behind young (wet!) ears - a guaranteed success if we had any young visitors.

If we asked insistently enough, Father would bring down the cinematograph from its year-round hiding place. With much effort and fuss a white sheet was found and fixed with drawing pins to hang from the picture rail in the dining room, and with the cinematograph on the table and plugged into the light socket, we would sit back and enjoy the coloured slides depicting the adventures of 'Sabu the Elephant Boy', or the quietly whirring and rather curious flickering film that showed Gandhi arriving somewhat jerkily by rowing boat at a flight of stone steps on an otherwise unrecorded and certainly quite unremarkable occasion in India during the 1930s. Although we did not clap, I at least experienced the same sort of wonderment that must have been evident among audiences years before at the showing of Lumière's 'man sneezing' or 'people getting off a train'.

Apart from the King's Speech, the radio would be on

intermittently for carols, other music, variety or a favourite comedy show, but our own music was always in mind. So it was that at some point in the evening Mother, flushed from the cooking, the sherry, and perhaps a gin and tonic, would coax some of the old songs out of the piano, while Father, flushed from stoking the fires (or so he claimed), sang in his fine tenor voice, which by this time would be sufficiently well lubricated to emulate anybody, from Richard Tauber embracing the 'mystery of life' to GH Elliot sighing for 'the silvery moon', with falsetto yodelling .

Father was an 'advanced' singer - that is, he was always in danger of being ahead of his accompanist. This imbalance on some songs was compounded by Mother, who played by ear and sometimes struggled to find the right chord, but they were very tolerant of each other and never took it too seriously, even when Father had to keep singing the same line while Mother sorted herself out. As this was only an annual event, everybody competed to recall the song titles, which never seemed to get listed, and so that ritual became part of the fun too.

Under some pressure, Father, who was a great fan of Troise, might be persuaded to play a tune on one of his two mandolins. These were impressively labelled as by Umberto Ceccherini of Napoli (imported in the 1890s through Alban Voigt of Edmund Place, London), and while his repertoire was limited, the delicate tremolo made for a charming and very soothing interlude.

The artistes were always exhausted long before the repertoire. In addition to the better known music hall ditties, Stephen Foster classics, and other 'community' songs, they would resurrect obscure Edwardian hits from when they were young, and items from Father's minstrel and soldiering days, especially those favouring ' 'armony'. A selection might include 'Redwing' (by Mills/Chattaway); 'In The Evening by The Moonlight' (by Bland/Jerome); 'Moonlight Bay' (by Wenrich/Madden); 'Sailing Down Chesapeake Bay' (by Botsford/Havez), which Father, with the true Englishman's unselfconscious disregard for foreign names, pronounced 'Chepassey Bay'; 'Lily of Laguna' and 'Little Dolly Daydream' (by Leslie Stuart); 'Roses Of Picardy' (by Wood/Weatherly); 'Good Bye-ee' (by Weston/Lee); 'Love's Old Sweet Song' (by Bingham/Molloy); 'The

Rose Of Tralee' (by Spencer/Glover), and invariably, 'The Miner's Dream Of Home' (by Godwin/Dryden), with its catchy tune, and words both poignant and appropriate:

> 'The log was burning brightly,
> 'Twas a night that should banish all sin,
> For the bells were ringing the old year out
> And the new year in.'

As Mother's playing was largely restricted to the slower paced numbers, Father would intersperse all with unaccompanied snatches of his livelier specialities, like 'Down In Jungle Town' (by Madden/ Morse), and Harry Champion's 'Boiled Beef And Carrots', 'Mother Don't Want No Peas No Rice No Coconut Oil!', and 'Ginger, You're Barmy!'. Another speciality was 'The Old Folks At Home', to which Father sang a parody in counter melody to the tune of 'Roll Along Covered Wagon'. It had very curious words, which I unfortunately failed to record, but the seemingly irreverent opening line was 'Hop along, Sister Mary, hop along'!

The only real exception to our regular enjoyment of Christmas was in 1940. They were dark days for all, and we were no exception. The winter weather, the war, the shortages, the Blitz, having to sleep on the floor downstairs for our own safety - it was a cheerless time, and on top of all that I had German measles, and was miserable with it.

In contrast, I am able to recall with pleasure one of my early Christmases, pre-war, and of a moment in the dining room after dinner, when we were all wearing paper hats, dancing about under the decorations and lights, with Dennis playing 'The Old Grey Mare' on his harmonica, while Father sang another of his parodies: 'I don't want to go with the Bombardiers, I just want to go home!'.

Chapter Six

At The Seaside

'All aboard! Right guard!' The last door slammed, a whistle blew, and the engine began to huff and puff its way clear of the station. That is how I recall the exhilarating start of the train journey that took us to Tankerton.

The most momentous events of my early childhood would have been the declaration of war in September 1939, and starting school in the summer of 1940, but they had already been eclipsed by the glorious upheaval and disruption of routine occasioned by two holidays at the seaside, in 1938 and 1939.

When my brother Dennis was young, the family had holidays at Clacton and Frinton, but the combination of buying the house and the birth of my sister Pauline, followed by my arrival six years later, meant that apart from outings to resorts like Littlehampton, holidays away were out of the question for a while.

However, in 1938 and again the following year the decision was taken, the booking made and our family of five set off. We walked to Isleworth Station carrying our luggage, and caught a steam train to Victoria Station, a vast, noisy place, echoing with shouts from railwaymen, toots from cars, hoots, hisses and shrieks from trains, and with bewildering movement in all directions. Then we had what seemed a long and tiring, but eye-popping steam train journey to Whitstable, the nearest station to Tankerton.

When we arrived there and headed along the open roadway towards the station exit, I became aware of the noise of the many other passengers, especially the footsteps - the thudding, scraping, tapping, clomping, clip-clopping and above all, shuffling feet - a sound which I was to come across again.

We walked to 'the lodgings', but there, on our first visit, disappointment awaited us. Booked by post without personal recommendation, it was owned by the landlady of music hall comedy. She was miserable and mean, and imposed strict rules in a not too clean house. We were even banished to the 'summerhouse' to eat our meals. Father was not impressed, and was not the man to tolerate that for his family, so he went off up the road and came back to announce that he had found a place nearby that was both pleasant and acceptable.

Our new lodgings were at 'Rosedell', number seventy, Queen's Road, the home of Mr and Mrs Fred K Howard Legg, who made us very welcome. They were elderly but active, although Mr Legg, who had retired from the railways, suffered deteriorating sight.

Their house backed onto the railway line at the end of a long back garden, and the opportunity to watch from such close quarters the great steam locomotives and trucks, or carriages full of people, was to me a great novelty. There was a wooden gate in the fence at the end of the garden, and we were able to venture out and across the railway line for a walk into the fields beyond, where rabbits abounded.

Father rented a beach hut, and our routine each day after breakfast was to walk down St Anne's Road, past the rather grandly named Tankerton Circus, a small roundabout, then over Marine Parade to The Slopes, which Father told us was 'the greensward', and so down the wooden dugout steps to 'The Hutments'. There we would open up our hut and release the heady smell of sea water, damp costumes and methylated spirits.

The huts were all named, and ours was called 'Robin Hood' - for me an intriguing reference that was never satisfactorily explained. Access was up a short flight of wooden steps onto a verandah with a handrail, and then through the front door to the single square room.

Inside the room we kept all the paraphernalia of the holiday, with no worries about security as long as the door was locked. There were costumes, towels, deckchairs, rubber rings, quoits, the cricket bat and tennis ball, toy boats, red Hi-Lo bats with their rubber come-back balls attached by strong elastic, buckets, spades, small fishing nets and shrimping nets, as Tankerton then had shrimps aplenty in the shallows.

There was an oil stove, a paraffin heater, which we were all very careful of, as it was used constantly for drying clothes and towels, and keeping warm when changing, and there was a methys burner, used for heating the kettle and cooking shrimps in the saucepan. The sweet, fumey, cloying aroma of burning 'meths' proved to be pleasantly unforgettable, in much the same way as the smell from the car interiors of those days lingers in the senses, with that magical blend of polished wood and leather, and just a hint of petrol.

We spent most of the day on the beach, with occasional walks along the 'prom', which was the asphalt strip between beach and huts, or a game of ball on the greensward. Sometimes we wandered as far as the kiosk at the Beach Road end where, in addition to the wonderful and colourful array of shrimp nets, buckets, spades and postcards, they also sold cornets of soft vanilla ice-cream which had a different flavour that I thought was superior to the regular local variety, so if Father was with us I always put some effort into trying to secure this treat.

I had a red bathing costume and a blue one, both woollen of course, and a pair of rubber slip-on beach shoes as protection against the stones. My territory was the shoreline wherever Dennis and Pauline were, and if the tide was out, I might venture with them along 'The Street', a spit of shingle extending out to sea. When I trod in the wet sand and the shoes filled up with it, I learned the word 'squelchy', which became a Huge Joke. I invented another Huge Joke by throwing wedges of wet sand at my brother Dennis. Far less of a joke was his eventual retaliation with a bucket of seawater, which left me gasping and, for once, speechless.

Mother could not swim, and did not like the water much, but Pauline had learnt. Dennis was an excellent swimmer, and I liked to watch him far out doing his crawl back and forth. Father enjoyed his daily 'dip', which tended to be brief but boisterous. He had learnt to swim as a boy by diving in at one end of a pool and surfacing at the other. At the seaside, he would kick off his shoes and, with a shout, charge down the beach into the water until it was deep enough for him to plunge in head first, then he would pop up, splashing, gasping and blowing like a walrus, calling to all and sundry to 'Come in, the water's lovely - not a bit cold if you keep moving!' Then after showing his paces with breast stroke, crawl and back stroke, in no time he was out, charging up the beach again and towelling off vigorously amid exclamations of cold, whoops of pleasure, and vocal encouragement to others round about who were contemplating going in, or were weighing up the effort and the temperature and looking a little uncertain.

Of course, there was the occasion when things did not go quite to plan. Mother had knitted him a pair of bathing trunks - quite usual in those days, but as she afterwards admitted, she 'used the wrong wool'. For once the hapless victim, Father had to struggle out of the water and up the beach to the safety of his bathing robe, this time with yelps and tuts of dismay, clutching the severely stretched and quite inadequate remnant of the garment round his middle - to the hysterical delight of family (except Mother) and bystanders. It is on occasions like this that you become aware of that hitherto unnoticed yet surprisingly large body of people who are evidently not intent on going anywhere in particular, but who all manage to materialise in your vicinity at precisely the wrong moment.

As a result of Father's cheerful and extrovert manner, there was always somebody talking to us, and that was how we met and enjoyed the company of a pleasant family from Gillingham, and the Tobin family from Enfield, with their daughter Mary, who became Pauline's companion. It was by arrangement, however, that we met one of Father's pals there, 'old Tommy Jones', a fellow driver and Great War comrade, with his wife and daughters, Eileen and Pamela. Once we were visited by Mr and Mrs Scales from next door, and on another occasion, we spent a cheery few hours with the Cooks from Hayes, Uncle Bob, Auntie Win and other family members who came for a quiet interlude away from their rather more hectic holiday at Herne Bay, just round the corner.

At lunchtime, Father liked to take a stroll - his 'constitutional', which would take him, and perhaps Mother, along Marine Parade as far as the Marine Hotel. He was also wont to refer to his pint there as a 'constitutional', thereby blurring the definition and giving the habit of a lifetime a beneficial but at the same time covert air. The word thus came to mean anything that was good for the 'inner man'. On one such lunchtime visit, Father was able to point out Max Miller, the famous comedian, standing outside the Marine Hotel sporting his fashionable brown and white shoes, with the Rolls parked at the kerb. Father did not wholly approve of Max's 'blue' image, but he was quite happy with a hostelry that was good enough for the stars of variety.

After dinner at the Leggs', in the quiet and balmy August evening air, we would take a stroll towards Marine Parade to savour the sea once more before bedtime. On the way, we would make the detour via Tower Parade to Beach Road, and wander through Jacques ('Jakes') Arcade, where I could stand and gaze at each of its brightly lit and fascinating amusements. From time to time, I was allowed a penny go at the 'crane', and would vainly try to 'grab' one of the tantalising prizes that lay jumbled in the bottom of the glass case. More successfully, I would use the penny in one of the little slot machines that delivered the unique tasting, red-wrapped, flat bar of Nestlé's (always pronounced 'Nessels') plain chocolate - a flavour well-remembered, but no longer to be found. It was a popular and fairly regular treat, as these same machines were then to be found on most railway stations.

On reaching Marine Parade, we would pause on the 'greensward', with the setting sun away to our left - and this stretch of Kent coast is famous for its sunsets - watching the oyster smacks sailing out with the tide from Whitstable harbour. Their sails, treated with fish oil and ochre, were red, and as they caught the last rays of the sun, Father needed no better cue to softly croon for us 'Red Sails In The Sunset', at that time a fairly recent hit on the radio.

Walking back in the gathering dusk, lights would be coming on here and there, and through the wall in one particular alleyway there was always a strange throbbing noise which I was told was made by a generator. And so I absorbed another new word.

Back at our 'digs', while the rest of the family played cards downstairs with the Leggs, I would be tucked away in bed, my mind wandering over the day's adventures, and wishing the holiday would last forever.

CHAPTER SEVEN

THE TRAPPINGS OF WAR

A long, dark and threatening shadow was spreading across the sunny beaches of Tankerton while we were on holiday at the end of August 1939. The outbreak of war was suddenly felt to be inevitable and imminent, causing many people to cut short their stay and head for home.

It was the start of anxious times for parents, and although Father did not seem to change much, except to listen to all the news and mutter about the 'blessed Germans', Mother obviously felt and at times showed the strain.

The first real evidence of war that I saw was on the return journey from Whitstable to Victoria, when the train seemed crowded with men in uniform, mostly khaki, who were behaving with that alternating mix of jolly camaraderie and solitary reflection that comes from being suddenly uprooted and then thrown together with strangers. There were no lights on the train, even in the tunnels, which created a sense of common adventure, but when we reached Victoria, everyone spilled out onto the platform and departed, bustling and intent, knowing where they were going and needing to get there without delay.

Back at home, nothing much happened at first, except that the decision was taken not to evacuate any of us children, but the worrying went on.

We all eventually acquired gas masks, an identity number and a silver identity disc to hang round the neck. My gas mask was the conventional black rubber type, in a little square brown box, but because I was due to start school, Father made me a sturdy case for it out of a large cocoa tin. This he painted yellow, and then threaded cord through drilled holes so that I could carry it over my shoulder. It looked all right, but it gave me and some of my friends a few bruises, and it was at times a burden for a five-year-old to carry round. I had to make an effort to keep remembering not to accidentally leave it at some play spot in the bushes.

Our Anderson shelter was delivered in its corrugated sections, and Father and Dennis set to, digging out the required hole in the middle of the lawn and erecting our personal monument to the ugliness of war. It had an earth floor and entrance area, and outside the roof and sides were covered with earth and then turf. Eventually the Council provided men to cement the structure, and we had the services of two Spaniards, Antonio Gimenez Roman and Manuel Maja Calvo, who were refugees from the Spanish Civil War that had ended in 1939. My sister Pauline persuaded them to sign her new autograph book.

The shelter, which Father referred to as 'the dugout', was damp and smelly even after it had been cemented. Although we used it quite often during the Blitz, it was neither appetising nor comforting, and we abandoned it as soon as Father considered the raids were no longer such a threat to our safety. It became a cold store and a place to lay out our overflow of garden fruit, until peacetime allowed the removal of all but the foundations, which undoubtedly still lie hidden under the grass.

Some people opted for the other sort of shelter, the Morrison indoor shelter. This was in effect a large steel box with wire mesh sides two foot nine inches high, and it occupied a large area in one of the downstairs rooms, where it often served as a table. One of Father's old Great War comrades, Freddie Gould, had one. Freddie was a 'good sort', who had been the regimental flyweight boxing champion and had the hunch, the broken nose and the deafness to substantiate it. Because of his boxing weight, I always thought of him, without disrespect, as 'Freddie the Fly'. He later fostered my interest in boxing, and would pass on copies of the Boxing News when we met. He lived with his wife at Greenford, but they had no children, so in 1941 they invited Pauline and me to go on the bus and stay with them for a few days. They all slept upstairs, but thought I would be safer in the Morrison.

Contrary to their expectations, I awoke in the middle of the night and panicked when I found I was in total darkness (the Blackout was complete) and inside a cage, which was fastened shut from the outside. Mrs Gould had tucked me up and when I was asleep, closed and secured the mesh door. We arrived back home sooner than expected, and I had very pronounced views on Morrison shelters.

The introduction of the Blackout was a significant change that impacted us all, especially in the winter time, but being so young, my view of it was largely from the inside of the house, supplemented by what I glimpsed through the front door when it was opened, or observed on my way home in the late afternoon. We had a mixture of the black curtain material, and paper blackout sheets nailed onto wooden frames that had to be fitted into the windows each night at dusk.

The Blackout was obviously a great hindrance to some people going about their lawful business, and particularly so to Father. As a professional driver, he had to find his way about the country, sometimes in the dark, with all road signs removed. He said the telegraph poles had their cross bars on the London side, but that may have been his whimsical humour. More realistically, he praised the invention of cats' eyes, and of the war-inspired white line in the centre of the road. He also at times had to negotiate the streets of London in total darkness, not to mention the disruption from air raids, bomb damage and the seasonal thick fogs. He knew London as well as any taxi driver, but no doubt he also drew upon his Great War experience as a driver in France.

The old order of night and day was further disturbed when British double summertime was introduced in 1941 and lasted through 1945, to return for a final year in 1947. It meant that we were permanently one hour ahead, and two ahead in summer. This gave us nice, light evenings in summer, and as I grew to enjoy reading in bed before going to sleep, it made for a very pleasant atmosphere. In contrast, we paid the price for this on cold, wet mornings in winter, when we had to wrap up well from head to toe before venturing out into the darkness at 8.15, which was really 7.15, and hurry along the glistening, windswept pavements to arrive damp, miserable and reluctant at the start of another day's schooling, where we sat in the yellow artificial light of the classroom, while rain pattered in gusts on the windows.

There were other signs of the change in our lives. A gas warning board appeared on the waste ground above the level crossing in Wood Lane. It was supposed to turn yellow if gas was in the air - but who would see it, we wondered? And supposing it was at night?

The premises of Frazer Nash, a car factory and showroom on the London Road, were taken over by the Royal Navy, and sailors were therefore billeted on houses in the neighbourhood. As their canteen was in the grounds of Borough Road College, the lads could often be seen marching up College Road at mealtimes.

The nearest air raid siren was located at the corner of Syon Lane and the Great West Road, along with the sandbagged blue police box and a strategically placed pill-box. The siren was frequently and inescapably heard within the radius of a mile or so. Thankfully in less frequent use were the stirrup pumps and buckets of sand that were suddenly to be found in strategic places around people's homes, usually near doorways or in the porch. They were intended chiefly to put out the fires caused by incendiary bombs, and one night Harewood Road was showered with incendiaries, but our house escaped. They mostly bounced on roofs and fell in gardens and were dealt with by the residents; Mrs Scales next door had to put one out in her garden, and one did set the Harris's front gate alight. More stark evidence of the reality of this danger was provided by the burnt-out shell of Woolworth's and Curry's stores in Hounslow High Street.

All around us there was quite a lot going on while the Blitz lasted, from September 1940 to May 1941, and during the subsequent bombing raids which persisted irregularly until the Germans switched to attacking us with 'doodlebugs' in the summer of 1944.

A sizeable bomb fell in the grounds of Borough Road College during the Blitz, blasting out windows and roof tiles of houses in surrounding roads, including the top of Harewood, and causing Mrs Penman's hens to flap up into the trees and lose their feathers through shock. Other property round about also fell victim to high explosives, incendiaries, oil bombs, land mines and sometimes even our own ack-ack shells, one of which seriously damaged two houses in nearby Albury Avenue. Neighbouring houses were hit in College Road, the Flats, the London Road opposite the fire station, Sidmouth Avenue, Harvard Road, Osterley Road, Thornbury Road, Church Road, Jersey Road, Wood Lane, Ridgeway Road, Amhurst Gardens, The Grove, Hartham Road, and in many other roads too. Damage was also incurred at other sites and buildings, like the Central School, the Green School, the County School, and the Friends' Meeting house in Quaker Lane.

There were unexploded bombs too, that took time for the hard-pressed Royal Engineers to deal with, like the one just west of the footbridge on the Southern Railway line, which temporarily closed the Marlborough Schools. We acknowledged that Harewood Road was relatively lucky.

As part of the various 'salvage drives', a pig swill bin was located outside Miss Shepherd's house, next to the sand bin at the corner by Northumberland Avenue. We dutifully carried to it the peelings and scraps of unused food, although there was little enough of that in our house. Despite the bin being emptied or changed regularly, the pungent smell released by opening the bin was considered to be a real killer.

Food rationing was apparent every day because of the paraphernalia of ration books and coupons which Mother often referred to and which I saw everybody consulting whenever I accompanied her to the shops. I was aware of the scarcity of chocolate and sweets, and of the absence of ice-cream, and I could not remember what a banana was like. At the end of the war, I was a little disappointed that bananas were not as creamy as I had recalled.

'Mr Chad' (or the 'goom', as he was also known), was the barometer of shortages, and appeared on walls and in newspapers with his comical 'Wot, no beer?' and other complaints, and we all learnt to draw him. The more official Squander Bug was also on display everywhere with the message 'Wanted for Sabotage' on hoardings on the London Road, in Father's newspapers, and on a poster inside Isleworth Post Office. I contributed my scarce sixpences to buy National Savings stamps, which I stuck rather untidily in the booklet provided, but I was always ready to cash them if there were a good reason. Father always said 'Income sixpence, expenditure sixpence - happiness; income sixpence, expenditure sevenpence - misery', but he did not have a useful precept for 'income nothing', when I had to make do with what turned up on birthdays and Christmas. There really was no money to spare most of the time. Father was also in the habit of saying, 'You have to cut your cloth according', so revealing another of his Slight Misunderstandings.

He never finished the phrase, and it was years before I realised that in fact I had to cut my coat according to my cloth. Even so, despite the transposition and abbreviation, his meaning was clear and the philosophy unassailable.

As well as slaying the Squander Bug with War Savings, we participated in special efforts like the 'Wings for Victory' weeks, and the ongoing salvage drives, and I knew that we had to 'Keep It Dark', and that 'Careless Talk Costs Lives'. That was why my pals and I were always on the lookout for German spies, an occupation that was stimulated by radio plays and books about schoolboys who had more luck than we did in identifying and capturing these 'quislings'. It was not our destiny to become war heroes, but we did remain suspicious of a man over the road who went to work each day dressed in a light macintosh with upturned collar, wearing a brown trilby hat and carrying a small brown attaché case - we knew these were classic clothes for a Gestapo agent out of uniform. Fortunately he moved away before our ambitions led us to an embarrassing confrontation.

There was plenty of evidence of response to the 'Dig For Victory' slogan, encouraging people to grow their own food. Public allotments appeared on open spaces, like the Spring Grove Allotment Association (SGAA) plot at the Great West Road end of Borough Road College, and other similar plots at the back of Syon Park Gardens, in the Jersey Gardens Field, on the Jersey Road edge of Osterley Park, from Thornbury Road to the 'hole in the wall', and on the railway embankment near Syon Lane Station, and in common with many of our neighbours, our back garden had a vegetable patch beyond the lawn.

The SGAA were our largest local allotment enthusiasts, and Mr Brown from Roxborough Avenue was in charge of their hut on the allotment in the grounds of Borough Road College, where he and daughter Shirley dispensed seed and other essentials on Sunday mornings. The Association held an annual show in the hall of St Francis Church, at which Mrs Rose from up the road, always recognisable by her ankle socks and colourful beret, was one of the highly respected judges. The proceeds were given to the Red Cross so Mrs Hamilton, wife of the Principal of Borough Road College, would be invited to receive the donation in her full Red Cross regalia. I was taken only once, probably because I let the social significance pass me by, as well as failing to show sufficient interest in vegetables.

When I reached school age and was allowed to wander up and down our side of the road, I went further and further afield. If, as was not uncommon then, someone was leaning over their front gate, I would say hello and ask if I could see their back garden. Refusal was rare, and I got to know the neighbours and their vegetable patches, and came away often having had a drink or something tasty. Old Mr Cleveland was a case in point and an opportunity lost, or rather unrealised. He was a gate-leaner in a front garden which had a mass of lavender bushes - a gruff but kind, elderly man with a grizzled appearance, sporting a thick, bristling, white beard. He was a retired farmer from Suffolk, living out his years with his unmarried daughter, Maude. Little did any of us know then that Father's ancestors had been labourers on Suffolk farms. What conversations Mr Cleveland and I might have had!

Public air raid shelters were another visible sign of the conflict. My first experience of these was when I started at the Marlborough Infants School. The underground shelter was in the middle of the playing field, and both these facilities were shared with the Marlborough Senior School. We went into the shelter in rehearsal first, and then in reality whenever there was an air raid, each class being marshalled in by the teacher, often at the double! The shelters were all to a common design, and consisted of cemented passages with slatted wooden benches fitted to the walls on each side, and as well as the entrance doorway, the junctions of corridors had an iron wall-ladder leading up to a heavy steel escape hatch. They smelt of cement, and the air was full of cement dust, although eventually many shelters took in rainwater and became partially flooded. We would try to continue our lessons, but often resorted to singing or spelling bees, or listening to stories being read.

There was a large public shelter in 'the field' by the tennis courts in the eastern part of Jersey Gardens, and another by the allotments on the Great West Road/Wood Lane corner of Borough Road College. Later on, this one was used by tramps, and became the regular home of a lady of the road known as 'Hatsandboots'. She was very like my Aunt Alice at Enfield in that she was six feet tall, of large build, and wore huge boots and long black skirts from another age. The similarity ended there, however, because she also wore various coats, sometimes several at once, including an army greatcoat, and one, two or three hats at a time. Whenever we saw her I became curious about her life, but we did not speak to her. Her muttering and grim countenance led all the children to think she was slightly mad, if not dangerous, and we were apprehensive about what she might do.

Nearly opposite us lived the Webb family, and they were as English and as nice a family as could be found. He was 'something in the City', we understood, and his wife was in manner and appearance a combination of dowager and farmer's wife. She fussed over her two attractive daughters, Jessie and Sylvia, who were then teenagers. From the age of about five I liked Sylvia, and by the time I was ten years old, I thought she was as pretty and glamorous as a Hollywood film star.

The surprising fact was that they had no air raid shelter, and so another wartime routine was created. The Webbs were related to the Spooners, who lived at the back of us in Wood Lane. Father obligingly removed some panels from the dividing fence, and instead of bolting our side entrance at night, it was left undone. Thus, when a night raid occurred, the Webb family would come across the road, through our sideway, down the garden, through the back fence, and into the Spooners' Anderson shelter until the all clear sounded. In my later dreams, I escorted Sylvia down the garden with my torch, rescued her from the bombed shelter, carried her back to our house and earned her undying gratitude and love. In the real world, the raids became sporadic, the shelters were no longer used, and eventually the Webbs retired to Dorking, quite unaware of any broken 'threads'!

After that first winter of sleeping on the ground floor for safety, some confidence returned and we resumed sleeping upstairs, but made for the shelter with dressing gown and blankets when the siren went. Sometimes I walked, but sometimes I could not be roused sufficiently and had to be carried. It was a miserable time, especially for parents, but we knew from what was happening to others that it could be a lot worse.

Perversely, the night raids were fascinating for me, and whenever I could I watched, peeping from the window of the darkened bedroom. There was usually an interval of silence after the siren stopped wailing, then we would hear the ack-ack (anti-aircraft) batteries, a sound that got nearer until our nearest, the Redlees Park battery opened up. This would be followed by the intrusive and unmistakeable drone of the German bomber, with the sinister ebb and flow of its engine noise, as irritating and persistent as a mosquito round the bed. The sound was in complete contrast to the open, honest, consistent note of our own planes. The searchlights could be seen as long or short shafts of powerful light, and circles of fainter light high in the dark sky , illuminating clouds, and switching this way and that in their desperate attempts to find the source of that infuriating noise. Even when they caught it and focused cross beams upon it, I never had the satisfaction of seeing a plane brought down, and despite the comforting sounds, inevitably the guns were seen as having more bark than bite.

In daylight, the raids were viewed more openly, at least in the early days, and we consulted our 'Enemy Aircraft Silhouettes' which were hung up on the wall of Dennis's bedroom, hoping to get the opportunity to identify Dorniers, Junkers, Heinkels, or Fokke-Wolfs. In the sunshine of August 1940 I watched Battle of Britain 'dogfights' from our back garden, probably when Fighter Command at Northolt Aerodrome was under attack, and once when Mother and I were out shopping, I watched from outside Wood Lane Stores, while the battle raged over the Surrey hills and the blue sky was criss-crossed with vapour trails. It was an almost silent struggle and somehow detached from reality, because apart from a rare snatch of gunfire, no sound could be heard from the ground and people felt safe while watching.

Barrage balloons, operated by the 'beer-beer' units, could be seen in the distance over London and the Thames. I had a small inflatable replica of one, with cardboard fins, but it was rather a disappointment because, inflated with air rather than gas, it would not stay aloft.

There was more down-to-earth evidence of war from the metal plate reading 'Air Raid Warden', which was fixed to the front door or gate of those who performed this valuable role. Mr Morrison on the corner was one, and Mr Curwen at number seventy seven was another. They were among the very few households with a telephone, which must have been a great asset.

Our local ARP unit, known as 'F3', was in fact staffed by nine of our neighbours, from Northumberland Avenue and Roxborough Avenue as well as Harewood, although we did not see much of them in their official capacity, since we did not suffer any significant damage. Our house remained fairly intact, except for shrapnel damage to roof tiles and the glass verandah, and the appearance of a few cracks due to blast or shock waves. Shrapnel abounded in the gardens and in the streets, and despite the warning of booby trap devices being dropped in the form of sweet tins, thermos flasks and 'butterfly bombs', we were confident we could recognise those, so all boys collected the rusting, jagged pieces, and bigger was definitely better. In addition to my large haul of the small stuff, I acquired a shell cap, the wing of an oil bomb, a piece of parachute silk, and a piece of a Mosquito aircraft, being a small section of very thick plywood. Both the latter items were patently unused, and no doubt fell from a lorry rather than from the sky. Later in the war, on some mornings on the way to school we would find the streets littered with small aluminium discs which the Germans had dropped to confuse our radar, and these too we assiduously collected.

Father was approaching forty seven when war was declared, and deemed too old to be recruited to fight for his country a second time. His job was now that of driving the Chairman-designate of J Lyons, and it meant he had duties in connection with the Ministry of Food, which was based at Colwyn Bay. For some years I kept the shilling piece given to him as a tip by Lord Woolton, the Minister from 1940 to 1943, until one day my desperation for cash forced me to make the agonising decision to spend the shilling, thus consigning the coin back to anonymity.

The local Home Guard proved to be an appealing alternative part-time contribution and Father joined, to be followed by my brother Dennis, who was by that time an apprentice at IAE (the Institute of Automobile Engineers) on the Great West Road next to Coty's. Their Home Guard unit was based at Redlees Park, and it was there and at Osterley Park that they did their training, learning about tactics, communications, sabotage and unarmed combat, and drilling with imitation rifles.

Early on in the war, our friend and neighbour Phil Harris was a senior member of the local scout troop at St Francis church. He and others were selected to undertake small tasks in support of the Home Guard and Air Raid Wardens, and Phil found himself with a pal on regular fire-watching patrols round a large ornamental pond in the grounds of Campion House, the seminary in Thornbury Road, under the supervision of a warden named Miss Bee. Nothing much happened, except that they got caught trying to cross the pond on a makeshift raft, so it all proved rather monotonous, and Phil jumped at the offer of a change of duty, helping the Home Guard in Osterley Park.

They were in the charge of Tom Winteringham, who at that time was directing training with homemade land mines. The mines were being made in the garage of a house in Ridgeway Road, probably without the knowledge of the neighbours. They consisted of a section of drain pipe, with a screw-on top and bottom, coarse gunpowder being placed in the bottom section, and fine gunpowder on top. The detonator consisted of a torch bulb with the glass filed down to expose the elements, and this was inserted into the top of the mine and attached to a very long wire.

Phil's first job was to file down the glass bulb without damaging the elements. He was later taken to the trials in Osterley Park. Here they had a car which towed a homemade trailer by a very long tow bar. The mines were laid in the ground (of Osterley Lane), with each long wire attached to a switch, which was under the control of the Home Guards who were lying in the ditch alongside the road. When the car drove by, and the trailer was over a mine, the switch was turned and sometimes nothing happened; but if it worked, the trailer got blown up and they had to reconstruct it.

John Mundell, a fellow IAE apprentice and friend of Dennis' who lived at Sudbury, spoke of his typical experiences in another local 'Dad's Army' as follows:

'Like Dennis, I was also in the Home Guard, but with the unit based at work (IAE). We had manoeuvres in Osterley Park, and one weekend we even "captured" Northolt Aerodrome. We were supposed to be a mobile group using bren gun carriers which were always in at Packards factory for servicing. There never seemed to be any available when we wanted them, so instead we became a Smith gun battery. These were "Heath-Robinson" weapons made from three-inch gas pipe, firing ten pound shells made from a smaller sized gas pipe. They were towed on their side by cars. To prepare for firing, they were tipped over onto one wheel, which provided a firing platform, with the other wheel providing a bullet-proof shield above.'

'We were also equipped with old long (barrelled) Lee Enfield rifles. At one time, when invasion looked imminent, we were issued with one clip - five rounds - of ammunition, and told to fight our way through to our unit, or if this was not possible, to join up with a local unit. I have often wondered how I would have managed the seven mile bike ride to work, fighting off the cream of German paratroops with my five bullets.'

Dennis and John were also part of the widespread 'fire-watching' network - people whose duty involved keeping a lookout from the roof of their office or factory at night and reporting enemy action and bomb damage to the local civil authorities, to assist the emergency services. It was not all fear, flak and freezing fog, however. For Dennis, it proved to be a spawning ground for exploring many new if short-lived hobbies and interests picked up from his colleagues.

John had this to say: 'I was also involved with fire watching, at home and at work. IAE and Coty combined for works purposes. We were based in Coty, and it was their roof we watched from. My group included a pianist of sorts, and a ukelele player, and I was recruited to join them on drums. We occasionally had a violinist as well. If there were no air raids, we would spend the evening playing in the Coty canteen. One evening some of the Coty girls invited the officers from a local army unit in for a party, and we played for them to dance to. On another occasion when there were no air raids, we had a good night's sleep, only to be told next morning that the "Better 'Ole Cafe" had caught fire during the night. Coty's roof had a wonderful view across the City, and one night we were watching the 'doodlebugs' going across the sky. These could be seen by the flames from their jet motors. We noticed one which did not appear to be moving, then someone realised why. It was coming straight for us. With fingers crossed we watched it eventually pass very low overhead. Later we heard that a fire watcher on the Gillette clock tower over the road saw it pass below him!'

Following the surrender of thousands of Italians in North Africa, a number were housed in a camp in Osterley Park, to be joined later by a few Germans, and on our local walks we saw them from time to time, with a large diamond sewn into the back of the tunic of their dungarees. There were Land Army girls working in the park too, and there was much interest (but little action, despite the credibility given to their motto 'Backs to the Land') from the older lads in the local gang, when one girl remained there for some time after the war was won, still in uniform.

It was a tremendous if not very frequent thrill to see our Lancaster, Wellington and Stirling bombers flying overhead, on their way to give Hitler and the Germans some of their own medicine. However, although we had hit Berlin in 1940 and were later impressed by what were called 'thousand bomber raids' on other German cities, there was added interest when the first full strength combined British and American 8th Air Force raids began happening in 1942. Even so, we were quite unprepared for the astonishing display of allied might that filled the skies when they came our way. Everyone was jubilant and so excited that we ran out into the street to stand and watch while wave after wave of Flying Fortresses passed over our houses in broad daylight, heading east to stamp on the enemy.

In June 1944, with the Allied Invasion of France, the news on the radio suddenly became much more exciting, with the real hope of victory ahead. It was the war that had turned radio from pure entertainment into an essential part of our lives. Possibly it would have happened anyway, but war made it 'the link', the most immediate way in which we learnt what was happening, what people were thinking and doing, how they were managing, what we should and should not do, how to make the best of things. It mattered not that some of the information might be distorted, or over optimistic, or that we were not given all the bad news. BBC radio gave us the best information available, and the best entertainment when we were confined to our homes or other locations. Moreover, we knew everyone else was listening too, and it helped to form and maintain the common bond. Above all, it gave us hope.

We listened to the BBC News throughout the war, whenever it was possible. It was broadcast hourly, and we became familiar with the announcers, who had to give their names - Bruce Belfrage, Stuart Hibberd, Alvar Liddell. We listened to old Mr Middleton telling us how to grow our vegetables and look after our fruit trees, and to Charles Hill, the radio doctor, making earthy references to bodily functions and telling us how to look after ourselves. Mother listened to the Kitchen Front for comfort from Gert and Daisy, and for those economy recipes, given out by Freddie Grisewood, using dehydrated meat, powdered milk, dried eggs and no sugar. But she tried to give us as nearly as possible the more appetising pre-war dishes, and whale meat and horse meat were certainly non-starters.

Mealtimes may have been a headache for Mother due to rationing, but for the younger generation they were always an opportunity to provoke each other into fits of laughter over nothing at all. A friend of Dennis's came to Sunday tea, and his surname was Parsons, which set Pauline and me off in a chain of giggling throughout, because in Father's paper a day or two before, a classic early Giles cartoon showing the newly arrived Americans fraternising with British housewives was captioned 'Moonlight with Mrs Parsons. Gee, baby!'

Backing up the radio, the newspapers were as popular as ever, but unable to furnish too much detail except on matters that were not strategically important. They were indispensable to Father, who did a lot of waiting about in his job. One of the attractions was the football pools, or 'Unity Pool' as it was called, because for economy reasons the coupon appeared in the newspaper, but alas, although Mother often said things would be much better 'when our ship came in', Father's luck was no better in war than in peacetime.

In fact, although he did the pools and knew all about pitch and toss and the three-card trick, he was no gambler and often said the dogs and horses were 'a mug's game' with the bookie the only winner. A race meeting was all right as a social occasion, however, and a flutter on the Derby or a sweepstake ticket for the Irish was quite acceptable, even if the outcome was a foregone conclusion. On a couple of occasions when we were in the West End, he pointed out to me the tipster Prince ('I've got a horse') Monolulu, and obviously appreciated the contribution made by such colourful characters.

As the air raids upon us became fewer and seemed less and less threatening, we were lulled into feeling safe. Then along came the V1s, unpleasant and much-labelled devices which the Germans apparently named Vergeltungs Waffen (Revenge Weapon), while we referred to them as 'flying bombs', 'doodlebugs' or 'buzz bombs', and some comedian called them 'Bob Hopes' (bob down and hope for the best). For the first time I experienced serious apprehension, if not actual fear, when one night a doodlebug approached so noisily that it seemed to fly slowly up our road. It took us by surprise, since we had not heard the siren, and as I awoke to the noise of the infernal machine, I heard Mother and Father moving to the windows to look out. The harsh, crackling roar of the motor was suddenly cut, and we waited the eleven seconds in contrasting eerie silence while the thing crashed to earth and then exploded. It had evidently been further east than I thought, and landed on rough ground near Wyke Green golf links, where it did little damage. Perhaps it was the one that passed 'below' the Gillette fire-watcher.

We were again fortunate in that of the five thousand that fell on London and the south-east, not many reached us, and the dozen or so that did landed far enough away not to cause us any damage.

The V2 rocket added quite another dimension. At four thousand miles an hour, compared to the four hundred reached by the V1, when the first one struck at Staveley Road, Chiswick in September 1944, we learnt that now there was to be no warning, no indication of danger, and no moment of apprehension. The V2 that fell on Packard's factory on the Great West Road in March 1945 was our only taste locally, but we realised it was a fearsome weapon against which England had no defence.

Once the invasion of Europe got underway, we put up on the dining room wall the 'Daily Express Map of the War', and soon had the French coastline covered with the little flags they supplied. Then it was exciting to listen to the news and move the flags to show the progress of the Allied armies across France and heading for Germany.

Mr Scales next door, although a man of few words, was something of a heroic figure to me. He had been with the 3rd Battalion Rifles in India in the 1920s, and was called back into active service at the beginning of the war, so now, more legendary than real as he had not been seen for so long, he was a member of a tank crew in the 11th Armoured Division, REME. He had the distinction of being in the crew of the first tank into Brussels when that city was liberated, but unluckily, after having been on active service since the beginning of the war, in March 1945 he suffered an injury to the jaw, and was for a while to be seen in his garden, dressed in the blue uniform of the wounded.

Bob Thurlow, the eldest son of my godparents, was killed while serving with the Royal Air Force in Burma, and a memorial service was held in St Francis church. For reasons which were not explained, my Mother and Father did not attend, but instead they dressed me in my best and sent me round to the church with instructions to be sure and give their apologies to Mr and Mrs Thurlow. It was a daunting task for a nine-year-old.

I was unable to catch them on their way into the church, so I managed to get an aisle seat halfway back, and sat through the hour-long service, which was delivered to a full congregation. At the end, Mr Thurlow proudly lead the assembly out, with head held high, a ramrod straight back and Mrs Thurlow on his arm. I summoned up all my resolve and stepped out as they went past, gabbling, 'Mum and Dad said they were sorry they couldn't come, but they sent me instead.' To my relief and his credit, without averting his gaze Mr Thurlow said, 'It's all right, son.' I was able to go home and report mission accomplished, but I just knew it was all wrong. Again to his credit, Mr Thurlow did not let this incident alter his close relationship with my Father or the family.

The Old Wall, Northumberland Avenue.

St Mary's Sports Club - looking towards the railway and the oak tree.

The Osterley Hotel ("up the top") and Wood Lane entrance.

The Great West Road - looking west from Wood Lane
- the site of Wood Lane Farm is in the foreground.

Baxter's Corner, Wood Lane - the shop is on the right.

The Rising Sun ("down the bottom") and Amhurst Gardens.

Wood Lane Stores - and 'Health and Efficiency' alley.

The Southern Railway - looking east from the level crossing
towards where the unexploded bomb lay.

Isleworth Post Office - guardians of my capital.

The Odeon Cinema - from 'Hoppity' to 'Henry The Fifth'.

The black cat hat that Father wore.

Tankerton - Marine Parade and "the greensward" nowadays.

Tankerton - Marine Parade many years ago.

Tankerton - 'The Street', a stretch of shingle exposed at low tide.

21. TANKERTON AT LOW TIDE.

Tankerton - a view from 'The Street'.

Tankerton 1938 - outside 70 Queen's Road, with the Legg's
- I am clutching 'Jock'. (upside down!)

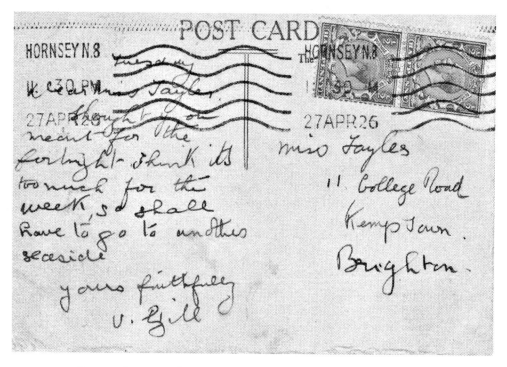

Postcards were often used to sort out holiday arrangements
- in this instance to register a protest.

'Robin Hood' - the hut at Tankerton.

Aunty Win and family visit us at Tankerton - Father with 'the old gun'.

At Tankerton with Mr Tobin (left) and Mary (second from right).

Freddie Gould - champion boxer.

HESTON & ISLEWORTH A.R.P.
WARDENS POST F.3
3RD SEPT., 1939 TO 8TH MAY, 1945

WAKEFIELDS LTD.,

G. Tobitt,   C. Thorp,   H. Shrubshall,   C. E. Galley,   A. S. Bird,   R. E. Morrison.

G. D. Curwen,   R. G. Barrett,   F. W. Reynolds.

Our Air Raid Wardens.

3RD SEPT., 1939 TO 8TH MAY, 1945

WAKEFIELDS LTD., CHISWICK

P. Chesworth, R. E. Morrison, G. Tobitt, H. Shrubshall, C. E. Galley, H. Bissell, F. Nott, W. Stannell.
A. Mulvey, Miss Capper, Miss Smith, Mrs. Emmett, Mrs. Hills, Mrs. Walford, Miss Brown, Mrs. Smith, D. R. Sampson.
C. Thorp, C. Beer, A. S. Bird, F. W. Reynolds, R. G. Barrett, G. D. Curwen, F. Saltsbury, W. H. Soffe, G. Vinten.

The F3 Wardens among local colleagues.

Quaker Lane.

Marlborough Infants' School - Quaker Lane.

Marlborough Infants' - front gate in Quaker Lane.

Marlborough Infants' - the top classrooms and the grassy bank.

The Footbridge - Quaker Lane.

Looking east to Syon Lane, from the footbridge.

Mrs (Saunders) Jackson in class - Marlborough Infants'.

Mrs Jackson in the playground - Marlborough Infants'.

CHAPTER EIGHT

THE INFANTS' SCHOOL

It was one of those moments that remain indelibly inscribed on the memory. The covered passageway we walked along was shaded, but the quadrangle which it skirted was filled with warm sunlight, and from the hall at one end came the sound of children singing 'All Things Bright and Beautiful'.

That sound lingers on, with its associations of sunshine, innocence and a sense of great anticipation. Never quite out of mind, and always revitalised every time the song is sung by children, it is as if, even when I first heard it, it was already a distant memory, recalling forgotten friends, games, hopes, dreams - every lost childhood.

The occasion was my first visit to the Marlborough Infants School on a bright, sunny day in May 1940, when Mother took me for my introductory interview with the headmistress. It was a momentous occasion for me, but I was quite happy about the idea of starting school.

We walked there of course, and it was along a route that was to become very familiar, in many moods and many kinds of weather, over the next three years. From Harewood Road, we went round the corner to cross Northumberland Avenue just before Campion Road, then walked past the pillar box and along until we turned down Roxborough Avenue. At the bottom of the hill, it was left into Quaker Lane, then over the railway footbridge, past the 'rec'

85

(recreation ground), and up to the school gates, which were in the Lane.

The interview with Miss Culham was brief. She was grey-haired and tweed-suited, but smiling and encouraging as I read a little, and counted the buttons on my jersey for her. Then we were on our way home and I gathered all was well, and I was to start school in a few days' time.

Mother accompanied me on my first day, but although I was only five, it was not long before I was making my own way there and back, after being seen across Northumberland Avenue. Traffic was very light in the war years, although there seemed to be hundreds of bicycles passing through at rush hour, with people cycling to work in the factories on the Great West Road. It was a lively and interesting procession, with all shapes, sizes and ages, and all going in the same direction. There was a certain amount of calling out, banter and flirting, and every now and then a skirmish as somebody tried to overtake a rival.

For a couple of months, until the summer holidays, I was in the 'baby' class in the charge of Miss Carter, who was young and pleasant and evidently strong enough to rise above the chaos in the classroom. I did the obvious thing and watched the other children, then either copied their actions or joined in with my own contribution.

In addition to our desks, chairs and tidy bins, there was a piano, a life-sized doll's house which you could enter, a big model boat and various dolls, trains, lorries, bricks and other toys. Outside was a sandpit, and we were allowed to play in that for an occasional treat, two at a time. The damp soft sand was reminiscent of Tankerton, but the confined space and wooden surround caused it to have a strong, dank smell.

Miss Carter's job appeared to be mainly one of keeping the noise down, organising 'turns', quelling arguments and reading stories. The children all seemed younger than I was, and the next term I was moved up into Miss Wylde's class next door. Here we were introduced to discipline by being made to sit at desks in rows, and grapple with the serious business of reading, drawing, writing and counting.

It was in this class that I first noticed poverty. A number of children had torn trousers, coats and dresses, and no socks or handkerchiefs. Miss Wylde had to cope with it all, but she did not show any 'side'. It did not affect my actions either, although I did not like the runny noses or the smell that surrounded some children. However, like tended to attract and play with like, and associations between particular children started to emerge.

This was the time of the Blitz, and every so often Hitler interfered with our lives and my education, whether it was through being kept at home because of an air raid, or being taken across the school field into the shelters when the siren went. We also had to spend time on gas mask drill, putting them on and keeping them on, giving our hair painful tugs as it caught on the rubber, and trying to breathe normally while the screen misted up as we got ever hotter inside. Carrying the gas mask to and from school was a nuisance, but discipline and constant reminders as to the mask's purpose were such that, on the occasions when I took it off to climb a tree or stop for a play in the 'rec', I did not forget to pick it up again. In due course, the danger of gas attack was judged to have diminished, and we stopped carrying the masks after a year or so.

Since my birthday was in May and on Empire Day, when this fell on a schoolday it was always memorable as well as pleasant. At that time of year there were usually warm sunny days with the promise of summer to follow, and on my big day the schools always had a half day's holiday to celebrate the existence of the British Empire, so we were sent home at lunchtime. In Miss Wylde's class, she led up to this by introducing us to the Union Jack, and getting us to make paper flags of the crosses of St Andrew, St Patrick, St George and finally the Union Jack itself.

I progressed in due course to the class of Miss Sayers, who was strict but very nice, although she appeared rather severe because she dressed in long black clothes that hearkened back to the Edwardian era. I was made milk monitor, which meant ensuring the availability of the correct number of free third-of-a-pint bottles, one for each class member during morning break, together with the paper straws which were inserted through the hole in the centre of the cardboard milk top. The milk was delivered in wooden crates, which had to be placed outside the classroom door, and I had to supervise the collection and return of the bottles from the crate. During the bottling process, something that bore an unfortunate resemblance to the contents of one's nose used to be left behind as a deposit on some bottle tops, so there was some competition to be first in the queue and get the bogey-free bottles. The milk monitor was well placed for this, and also for appropriating or handing out any excess bottles!

Long before the invention of Blue Peter, teachers and children found ways to use the cleaned and dried milk tops. They were good for throwing or 'skimming', and for making wheels; but a more ingenious use was to weave them together with wool or raffia and create table mats or pot stands, which we used to take home and give as presents.

My next move was across the quadrangle into Miss Spencer's class, which was sometimes looked after by our 'supply' teacher, Mrs Tilbury. She lived quite near us, in Albury Avenue, and so never seemed to me like a real teacher.

Fortunately it was Miss Spencer, not my neighbour Mrs Tilbury, who was in charge when my behaviour showed some unacceptably anti-social tendencies. Once, in the playground, a boy deliberately tripped up another unsuspecting boy and, no great harm being done, it was a Huge Joke shared by all. My first opportunity to become the star of a similar performance occurred when Malcolm walked past my desk, looking at some papers and heading for Miss Spencer. I stuck out my leg and sure enough, down went Malcolm, scattering the papers. Instead of the expected raucous laughter, the act was followed by a sudden silence, during which Malcolm picked himself up and said, 'He tripped me up!' The bemused 'star' got the offending legs soundly slapped, and was left to reflect upon his 'nasty and dangerous action' while the rest of the class instantly resumed normal activities.

Unfortunately, the lesson was only half learned. There was a subsequent occasion when I observed a boy playfully pinching the bottoms of several girls in the playground. I remembered this when we were lining up in the hall and, in copying mode, without even thinking that I might be doing anything wrong, I tried it on the girl in front of me. 'Look, he's pinching her! Did you see that!' I heard the shout and realised I was in trouble, but it was not the offending hand that was punished, it was once more the long-suffering legs.

It was thus demonstrated that my general approach to education had been inadequate. It was not enough to copy or join in, one also had to use judgement. For me, this was perhaps the beginning of the loss of innocence.

When, in the autumn of 1941, I moved up into Class One with Miss Saunders - Mrs Jackson, as she became shortly afterwards - I suddenly made great strides forward in knowledge and understanding. This was partly due to my age, no doubt, but it was also due to the exceptional quality of the teacher. Miss Dorothy Saunders was an outstanding athlete and local celebrity, having represented Britain in the 1938 British Empire Games in Sydney, but she was also a great teacher. I was lucky enough to later encounter another such teacher, Miss Esther Groves, in the top class of the junior school, and what they seemed to have in common was the ability to be authoritative (overruling the unruly), to give direction that enabled all to follow, and to carry everything and everybody through to the required conclusion with an impetus that left no room for boredom or distraction. They also possessed an underlying sympathy that made these exceptional teachers approachable and helpful when difficulties arose.

At seven, I was coping with arithmetic, just. We were multiplying hundreds, tens and units, adding and multiplying shillings and pence, and starting to learn pounds, shillings and pence. An old exercise book shows I was getting about half of it right, but as for the rest, I had not fully grasped the idea of 'carrying over' from one column to another, and every so often I was evidently distracted by something else and gave a nonsensical answer.

Handiwork was another subject I had limited success with, although I produced the required items in raffia or paper, and a passable flowerpot and saucer in papier maché, duly painted and varnished. Our efforts were not dignified with the word 'art', but we did draw a lot and coloured our pictures with chalks, crayons or poster paints.

We were taken out into the playground or onto the field for exercises and team games, and we all enjoyed playing our part. We wore coloured sashes to distinguish the teams, and there were games and races with hoops, balls and skipping ropes, all controlled by Mrs Jackson and her silver whistle. There were also ring games like 'The farmer's in his den,' (and who could forget 'Ee-aye-addy-o the farmer wants a wife'!), all of which games and words the girls seemed to be more familiar with, no doubt because they had become part of street lore and were played out of school as well.

I had no problem with reading, and I really began to enjoy the printed word. We learnt originally from *Janet and John* books, and the *Beacon Readers* with stories such as 'The Cobbler and the Elves', 'The Cock, the Mouse and the Little Red Hen', and 'The Sky is Falling Down', but by now I was borrowing books from Miss Culham's library, which was housed in the medical/ quiet room, and also making progress at home, away from the nursery rhymes and towards such story books as *Rupert Bear* and *The Water Babies*.

Sometimes Mrs Jackson read to us. There was a good story of Victorian times about an old gentleman called Mr Periwinkle, Joel Harris's *Tales of Uncle Remus* about Brer Rabbit and Brer Fox, *Aesop's Fables*, and the unforgettable *Epaminondas Stories*, about the little boy of that name who could not get anything right, especially when he was sent on errands and applied the carrying instructions for the previous errand to the current one, so that the cake got crushed in his fist, the butter melted under his hat, the dog got drowned in the cool stream and the loaf of bread got dragged home on a piece of string. His mother would say, 'Epaminondas, you ain't got the sense you was born with!', and we found it hilarious. Most successful of all was Hugh Lofting's incredible story of Doctor Dolittle, well illustrated and challenging our imagination with creatures bearing extraordinary names like Chee-chee, Gub-gub, Dab-dab and the pushmi-pullyu.

One story concerned a curiosity shop, and there was a picture of it showing the old fashioned bow-fronted window crowded with relics from old ships and trophies from foreign parts, and an old banded sea-chest, and suspended above all, a stuffed alligator. I used to dream of finding such a shop and being allowed to play in it and choose something to take away, and discovering the chest had a secret compartment full of treasures. I also dreamed of exploring the forgotten part of an old house and finding an old chest, and of the pleasure of discovering what might be in it, although this became complicated when I was taken to one of the London museums and shown what was allegedly the original 'Mistletoe Bough' chest, wherein according to Thomas Bayly's version, young Lovell's bride had hidden herself with such tragic consequences. The antique shops that I saw were rather dull by comparison, and distinctly lacking in treasure chests and alligators, but that picture did kindle an interest in things from the past

Reading increasingly opened my eyes to the boundless world of print, where anything was possible, and I eagerly drank it in. Poetry became a part of that too, the rhyme and rhythm appealing as much as the descriptive content. They were, of course, just children's poems, or at least children's verse:

> 'If I were a bee, I know what I'd do,
> I'd gather some honey and give it to you'

> 'Wagtail, I would like to know,
> Why your tail keeps wagging so,
> Up and down it goes all day,
> I'm sure you'll wag it all away.'

> 'Good morning, Mother Mousie,
> Have you need of any corn?
> I'm Goblin Green the Pedlar,
> And I pass this way each morn.'

> 'Under a toadstool crept a wee elf,
> Out of the rain to shelter himself.'

And there were many more. These were plainly not the inspiration for most of my 'stories', which we each had to write regularly in our exercise books. My fictional tales often contained a dash of brutal realism that showed I was probably more in tune with the war than with the world of the 'wee elf' in the poem:

> '3rd March 1942. One day Billy climbed a mountain, when he suddenly tripped over a stone and fell to the bottom of the mountain and broke his neck. When his mummy heard of it she began to weep, she told her father [sic] when he came home from work what had happened.'

> '27th April 1942. When I grow up I am going to be a tank driver. I am very intrested [sic] in tanks. And sometimes I might drive my tank through the woods. And I expect I will like driving a tank.'

> '15th May 1942. Once upon a time there lived a little elf. He was an artist who could draw good pictures. All the little elfs [sic] came to him to buy pictures because he draws such pretty ones. One day a man trod on the toadstool and crushed it to little bits. And that is the end of the story.'

Some of our 'stories' were just first hand accounts of actual events:

> '1st June 1942. Last Sunday evening I went to the Hare & Hounds and I had a glass of ginger beer. And I saw a drum and fife band in Wood Lane. And I went to my anties [sic] on Saturday.'

> '21st August 1942. The week before last I went to Hide [sic] Park. And the sparrows are very tame up there. I swam in the Serpentime [sic]. We had dinner there and we went home at half past four.'

> '26th August 1942. I went on a trolleybus to Epsom Downs. And I went in the woody part of it.

There wer [sic] lots of wild birds and a few wild animals there. And there were men shooting rabbits to cook and eat.'

The visit to the Hare & Hounds was the culmination of a walk up Wood Lane on a fine summer's evening. Father was in his element as we sat at the tables outside the pub, and he kept disappearing into the bar to 'top up' and pass the time of day with the locals. The old original building was still there at that time, at right angles to the road, and Father showed me in to see how it was used as a skittle alley. On the way home, the drum and fife band was a big surprise, and a fitting end to a very pleasant outing.

The visit to 'anties' was one of our fairly frequent two-bus trips to Angel Lane, Hayes, where Father's sister Win held sway over the Cook family. It was always a full house, with much banter and some music, and everybody came away feeling the better for it.

On the Hyde Park trip, we saw anti-aircraft guns, barrage balloons and soldiers, contrasting rather incongruously with the sheep grazing in the park, but these symbols of war and tranquillity were evidently too commonplace to be considered worthy of a mention in my 'story'.

At Epsom, we came to a field where the corn was being cut in ever decreasing circles by a horse-drawn reaper and binder, and the remaining area of uncut corn in the centre was surrounded by men with shotguns, killing rabbits as they fled into the open. A truly rural scene, which I watched until I was dragged away.

Another interesting part of the curriculum was the time spent looking at the environment. Our nature study lessons started with Miss Wylde, and each year, in season, we collected specimens of chestnuts, spinning sycamore seeds, beech nuts, acorns and sticky buds, to take into the classroom to exhibit or draw and to write notes. We even went on short rambles round the grounds and into the Lane, where oak, elm, beech and chestnut stood along the Green School boundary.

In Class One, we noted in our exercise books each day the kind of weather outside. We went out to the quadrangle to look at the golden weathercock on the vestibule roof to see the wind direction (did the arrow show where it came from, or where it went?), and inspected the white box which measured temperature and rainfall, and if it was sunny, we might look at the time on the sundial. When in the quadrangle, our eyes would be drawn to the two white stone statues of Peter Pan and Wendy, located at opposite ends, and we would also take the opportunity to talk to the other resident, Snowy, a white rabbit in a hutch, because children were not allowed to set foot on the grass of the quadrangle at other times.

Some of the poems we heard increased our interest in nature, the seasons, and the weather. Those about the wind particularly captured my imagination:

> 'I'll sing you a rollicking, frolicking song,
> As gay as the wind when it jostles along.'

I loved EH Henderson's

> 'The merry March wind is a boisterous fellow,
> He tosses the trees; and the daffodils yellow
> Dance and sway, as he blows by
> To hurry the clouds across the sky.
>
> He plays such pranks with the weather vane,
> Turning it round, then back again.
> But the game he enjoys the best of all,
> Is blowing my bonnet right over a wall.'

I never wore a bonnet, well not after the age of two anyway, but on blustery days when the wind would whistle and roar through the huge trees in the Lane, accompanying me on my way to and from school like a big, noisy, playful dog, it was as familiar through the poems as a family friend, and I felt quite at home with it.

I mixed well enough with other children, or at least with my classmates. It was then mostly a matter of casual encounter rather than the formation of lasting friendships or arranged meetings, but there was soon a notable exception outside of school.

By playing outside my gate, I met Brenda Morrison, who was my first friend. There is an entry in my exercise book which reads: '4th February 1942. My freind [sic] name is Brenda'.

Brenda went to Ashton House, one of several local private schools, like Wyndhams and Pelham House, which other children said were for 'posh' people. This made no difference and was not even cause for comment between us, though I was aware that her family was comparatively 'well off'. They were Scottish and came down from Edinburgh, and her father was chief chemist at Garvin's 'Bear Honey' factory. He was further distinguished because he was a local Air Raid Warden with a metal plaque on the front gate declaring the fact, and because he had a large Austin car and a telephone in the house. This was uncommon enough but, uniquely in our area, the family also had a housemaid. Annette Bassi was a professional maid in cap and apron, who had been with a titled family and now saw to the needs of the Morrisons, walking daily to and from her home in Worton Gardens.

I liked Mr Morrison because he had a sense of humour, and he accorded me the rhythmic name of 'T for Tony Anthony Betts'. When Brenda had a party on her eighth birthday, Mr Morrison organised the games, and he played the piano, making us stand round and loudly sing 'The Grand Old Duke of York' - and enjoy it.

As Brenda lived just a few doors away, on the corner, we often played in each other's house and garden. Sometimes her older brother Robin would take charge of the game, and we would get to play with his train set or his wonderful collection of lead soldiers, which included many on horseback, as well as horse-drawn carriages. He was also fond of involving us in setting up his dinky toy vehicle collection on the floor, with the carpet pattern forming traffic routes. We would each be assigned an area, and on his given signal of 'Rush Hour!' we had to change the direction and route of all our vehicles - and got told off if we got it wrong. Robin was a very fine pianist, one of Mrs Freeman's best, specialising in Bach.

Brenda and I played other games too. When the rest of the family was not around, we would become doctor or nurse and

95

patient, and examine forbidden talcum-covered trouble spots behind the armchair or in the cupboard under the stairs. We knew enough not to want to get caught in our most secret games, and failed only once when, at the height of our familiarity, Brenda decided to 'do a wee wee' behind her shed. I was posted as lookout, and my head nearly clashed with Annette's as we both peered simultaneously round the corner of the shed. I was sent home and heard no more, but Brenda was marched off to await summary treatment from her father when he came home from work. I concluded at that moment that 'old maids' who appeared to look kindly upon me were not necessarily on my side, and were not to be trusted.

It was at the Marlborough School that I became acquainted with Mike Curwen, whom I recognised because he lived up the road from us. I approached him in the playground during my first year, while he was in the top class, Class One.

'Hello, Michael, what are you doing?'

'I'm a car. It's good being a car. You can start and stop and go to places. Well, I'm going to drive off now.'

With a noise of gear changes and engine-revving, he was off round the playground, hands on the steering wheel, hand signals clearly given, and then with a squeal of brakes he arrived at his next destination.

He was two years older, but when I reached eight years of age and went to the junior school we became fast friends, although once again he was ahead of me and in his final year there.

While we all seemed to spend most of our infant playtime wandering about and watching, and occasionally getting a drink at one of the fountains against the wall, we also played 'follow the leader' or did 'bussing up' to gallop round like horses with various partners, and I sometimes played at being a car, like Michael, or an aeroplane, with arms extended and a whining 'Nyee-ouw' as I weaved, banked and turned to dive bomb targets and narrowly miss more preoccupied pedestrians.

In the classrooms, our desk positions seemed to change quite often. It was not until I was nearly seven in Class One that things settled down and relationships began to develop with those in the surrounding desks.

Peter Cooper and I communicated easily, and we were to form a lasting friendship. He already had a following from his locality in Hartham Road, and so I also became acquainted with his pals, Tony Carter, Bernard Francis, David Potter, Valerie Hockliffe, and Brian Bidgood. Unfortunately, they all went home down the Lane to the London Road in the opposite direction from me, so our early contact was confined to school hours.

From Syon Lane and Busch Corner came Dorothy Attewell, Joan Smith, Pat Kidd, Bessie Osmond, Carol Atkins, Sylvia Richards and Joan Holford. Joan was at the next desk to mine, and as we became friendly I looked upon her as somebody special, with her golden hair and red dress with white polka dots. One day she said, 'On Fridays, I 'as me bath and washes me feet, then I pricks all me blisters and scrapes all me corns.' I did not realise she was only repeating what she had heard, and this timely domestic revelation stopped me forever from asking her to marry me.

There were only two children at school who were not entirely English. One was Raschid Ali, who appeared briefly and then disappeared again, and was understood to be a refugee from North Africa. The other was Jacqueline, whose father was English, but whose mother was very French. Jacqueline sat at one of the front desks in Class One. She was a spirited girl with a fascinating French accent, and an even more interesting predilection for waiting until Mrs Jackson left the room, and then standing on her desk to hoist her skirt and dance round showing off her blue knickers. What seemed odd, even at the time, was that nobody ever said anything about it.

I had brief, exploratory close contact and visits with children who lived in my homeward direction: Jill Fenn in Roxborough Avenue, one of the nicer girls, whose garden we played in; Brian Tancock in Parkwood Road, an enterprising lad who made some boats by nailing together scraps of wood, and sold me one for a penny; Guy Nichols in Downs View, who had a doting mother and lots of toys. My Father, some years later, had a chance encounter and conversation with Guy on a bus (Father talked to anyone within range), when Guy told him he had 'duffed Tony up in a fight'. Father relayed this to me with some amusement, and I was quite irritated by the fact that he was so impressed by it, especially as I had no knowledge of the alleged event. Then there were the brothers Peter and Jimmy Howes in Wood Lane, who had cardboard boxes of chicks in the kitchen as part of their war effort, and Alan Gibson in Redesdale Gardens (one of the roads known to us as 'the Flats'), who invited me to his eighth birthday party. This placed me in an awkward situation as I dearly wanted to go but had no money for a present, and none was forthcoming from Mother or Father. I made do by wrapping up some comics that had been given to me, and I knocked on Alan's door with considerable apprehension; but he was delighted, and the party was a great success. We even had sparklers after tea.

On several occasions I went to play with another boy called Alan, in Roxborough Avenue. Once, when I was admitted through the front door by his mother, a tall, dark-haired, attractive lady, she closed the door and said to him, 'Now go and fetch the cane.' She turned to me and said, 'I'm afraid that Alan has been a very naughty boy.' Alan re-appeared holding a shiny, dark brown rod. 'Now go into the kitchen and take your trousers down.'

'Oh, no, Mum!' Alan sobbed. I was ushered into the front room. 'We won't be long, Tony,' she said. Doors were closed, and shortly afterwards a tearful Alan appeared, and we got down to playing with his toys, a favourite being his lead set of a window cleaner, complete with miniature ladders, leather and bucket, into which we put real water.

Among the hundreds of incendiaries and high explosive bombs that were dropped on our district, several bombs that fell on the Southern Railway line did not explode. They had to be defused and removed, but the Royal Engineers were very busy at times, and as a result of one such bomb which fell just west of the footbridge during the Blitz in November 1940, the authorities had to ban for a while the use of the footbridge in Quaker Lane, and close both the Marlborough Schools. We went temporarily to other venues for our lessons. Mrs Jackson took some pupils in the Hall at Isleworth Town School, and others like me gathered at various houses. I went to Alan Walford's house, in Roxborough Avenue, where Miss Wylde came and taught a small group of us.

A number of children went home in my direction up Quaker Lane, but none lived in my road. They were heading for the Flats, Parkwood Road, Roxborough Avenue, Downs View, the Great West Road, Syon Park Gardens and even Oaklands Avenue. In addition to Brian Tancock and Jill Fenn, others who ran, played, talked and shouted along that route included Malcolm Champion, Gillian Wright, Marian Humphries, Colin Bowles, Kenneth and Peter Harbron, Ann Yateman, Daphne Wise, Derek Martin, Diana Good, Michael Dunkeley, Evelyn Milton, Nicholas Trickey, Brian Ritter, Bran Mcgrath, 'Jasper' Freeman (Brian Ritter convinced us that 'Jasper' was short for John), and Rex Ingram.

With Rex, I had two Slight Misunderstandings. The first occurred in Quaker Lane. I usually turned off into Parkwood Road on the way home, but because Rex lived across the Great West Road, I sometimes went with him up the Lane as far as Northumberland Avenue. On this occasion, just before we reached the parting point, we discovered a large sack on the path, which was of course irresistible, and upon opening it, we saw a number of small black and white creatures which Rex immediately declared he recognised as dead badgers. He assured me my parents would be very pleased if I took one home, as they had valuable fur. We hid the sack in the bushes and went our separate ways, carrying one priceless limp corpse apiece. Mother and Father were both home, and I went as usual through the side entrance and straight into the kitchen where I proudly presented my prize. Mother was aghast, her horrified expression stopping me in my tracks. Dreams of a fortune in fur faded as the words 'Dead cat!' rang in my ears, and this began indeed to seem more akin to the bedraggled thing I was clutching. Then we all headed for the dustbin.

I fell into the second Slight Misunderstanding, probably because I had forgotten the first. A couple of years had passed, and I was walking down Amhurst Gardens to the Town School in the company of 'old Rex' when suddenly we both saw a large, dark bird fly off a housetop and disappear over the back towards the school field. I was interested in birds, and able to recognise the common varieties, but this had been a very brief glimpse of what seemed an unusually large bird, and in my moment of hesitation Rex said, 'That was an eagle!'

I wrestled with the statement, matched it against my knowledge and experience - I had seen eagles at close quarters in the zoo and in books - but while I was still struggling, Rex reaffirmed 'It was definitely an eagle! Let's run to school and see if we can see it again.' I once more gave way to his confidently superior knowledge of British wildlife, and together we raced for school and into the playground. At this point, Rex unwisely called to one or two acquaintances, 'We've just seen an eagle, it's out on the field!' We ran to the back of the school, followed by a straggle of our peers, already jeering in cynical disbelief. The field was almost empty, except for a lazily flapping crow in the distance. The jeering broke out into predictable howls of derision and mirth as we filed back to the playground - 'These blokes reckon they saw a' eagle!' - and our gullibility and lack of expertise were exposed to one and all. I joined the sceptics.

Olive, who lived in Wood Lane, was a very energetic girl who attended dancing classes, and also had a talent for storytelling. When requested by the teacher to fill a gap, she was quite at ease standing in front of the class inventing and telling a long story, often about a little girl and the fairies. We exchanged garden visits, and she confided in me: 'My brother's got ever such a funny name - his first name is Archie, and his second name is Bold!' One day, as we walked to the Infants School together along Northumberland Avenue, she said, 'I need to do a wee-wee.' I watched with astonishment and interest as she moved to the kerb, pulled down her knickers, lifted her skirt and peed into the road. She adjusted her clothes and said, 'Come on, we mustn't be late', and was off, while I hurried along behind, still trying to absorb the sight, sound and smell and this unselfconscious shattering of the rules.

The 'copy or join in' philosophy led me to try something similar. At the beginning of Northumberland Avenue, near Wood Lane, there was a green electricity box set on the pavement, but recessed into Mr Murray's high brick garden wall, and with a cement path all round. The area out of view behind the box was a territorial wetting place for the many stray dogs that roamed the streets then, and a haunt of small boys wishing to hide. While Mike and I were returning home from a jaunt, we decided we would use this safely screened passage to relieve ourselves. As we then walked off round the corner into Harewood Road, two things happened. The 'evidence' trickled down across the pavement into the road, and in one of those typical but incomprehensible and irritating strokes of bad luck that dog the miscreant child, Mike's mother walked round the corner behind us on her return from a shopping trip, and had to pass the junction box.

Once again, this exceptional lady proved that she knew how to deal with the situation, and we got off with an admonition, in her soft Derbyshire accents, that it was 'unhygienic, unnecessary and not very nice'. We did not get caught again.

I did not witness any fights at the Marlborough Infants School, although I did have a push and shove altercation with Neil Spokes over who owned some worthless item we found. The two 'big fellows' at the school were Joe Hollis from Brentford, and Brian Ritter from Oaklands Avenue. They were much bigger than the rest of us, and their size seemed to lend them a maturity which was almost adult. We did however speculate upon the outcome if they fought each other. I was in the school lavatory, standing at the wall alongside Joe, when Brian came in and I wondered what would happen, as if just being in the same place might be a challenge for them. But the anxiety was all mine. 'Hiya Joe,' said Brian, and 'Hiya Brian,' said Joe.

At the end of the summer term in 1942, because of the overcrowding at the Marlborough, the older pupils, comprising half of our year and including Peter Cooper, were transferred to the top classes of the Town School Infants, leaving me and the younger half of the class to stay at the Marlborough for another year as 'Class One Juniors'.

At home, our social life, like most people's, was very limited by the war, as well as by our financial status. We did manage to visit some of the family, however. As well as visiting the Cook family at Hayes, Mother took us a couple of times on the tube to Enfield to visit her mother, Grandma Savage, who was very small, ailing and housebound, and being looked after by Mother's sister Alice. Alice had outgrown her strength at about twelve years of age. She spoke softly, but was six feet tall and wore large black boots and long black dresses.

The little old house was dark inside, but quite cosy and full of recollections for Mother. The music boxes that played old songs and marches were still there, and the harmonium that Mother had learnt to play as a girl. The little stone-flagged scullery smelt of boiled greens, and I was pleased to be outside in the sunny garden, with its old world atmosphere. At the far end of the garden was Bush Hill Park, with its now deserted bandstand from which Mother recalled marches and popular songs being played in concerts before the Great War. In the quiet of the afternoon, we were able to slip through the garden railings for a walk in the park, empty of people but crowded with memories. On other occasions, we visited Mother's brother Charlie, who managed Howard's Cycle Shop in Enfield Town, and we visited Tom, another brother who had a drapery and men's outfitting business.

Father took us by bus to visit his sister Rose, who had remarried after Uncle Albert died, and sold the Marylebone guest house in order to buy a semi-detached in Chatsworth Avenue, Wembley. There she had a walled garden, a cat and a beautifully furnished home, but what took my eye particularly was the huge ostrich egg in a stand on the mantelpiece. It was undoubtedly yet another souvenir from one of her widely-travelled gentleman lodgers. Fervently but in vain I hoped it would find its way to our house one day.

One very hot day in summer, the family had an outing to Chessington Zoo. Although I enjoyed it, when I got home and into the garden I felt unwell and was put to bed. This was my first experience of the headaches that were to plague me for the rest of my life.

I played with Tommy Tippell, who lived at the top of the lower end of Harewood Road. Neither Tommy nor his brothers went to my school, but his father and mine were acquainted through being friendly supporters of Vic Samuels, mine host at The Rising Sun, 'down the bottom'. On a fine summer's day, the boys and I were all playing soldiers in their back garden when my legs began to hurt. They gathered round and we discovered I was sitting on an ants nest. They delayed destroying the nest in order to take me home as a genuinely 'wounded soldier'.

One night in December 1942, there was a lot of coming and going in our house, with Mrs Scales from next door and Mrs Webb from over the road popping in and out. It all seemed to centre on the front bedroom, while I lay half awake and wondering in the back bedroom.

The next day I found I had a baby sister, Sylvia, which was a pleasant surprise and a novelty for all. Unfortunately it doubled Mother's workload and worries, and I was packed off to stay with Aunty Win and Uncle Bob Cook at Hayes for a couple of weeks. It proved to be such a thoroughly enjoyable visit that I gave no thought for home or the school I was missing.

At Hayes, the house was one in a row of typical turn-of-the-century, brick built, terraced 'villas', with a hallway and stairs on the left, the two main rooms on the right and, at the back, the scullery and outside toilet. Upstairs there were three bedrooms and a bathroom. I shared the front bedroom with my cousin Derek, who was some eight years my senior. He went off to school each morning while it was still dark, while I lay in bed listening to the scores of shuffling feet, reminiscent of the crowd at Whitstable station, only this time they belonged to people walking up Angel Lane to the Uxbridge Road to work, or to catch a bus. There were occasional shouted greetings, but mainly the footsteps - continual, purposeful, tireless and quite anonymous.

On some evenings, from the drawing room window, I saw them returning, but then, although interesting enough, they were simply people, and unlike the morning procession, there was no mystery surrounding the sounds they were making, no cause to conjure up an imaginary sighting of the shuffling throng.

Derek introduced me to the 'William' books of Richmal Crompton, but they were too advanced for my seven years, although the pictures of the scruffy schoolboy and his pals aroused my curiosity and interest

During the day, I kept Aunty Win company, sometimes going to the shops over the main road, or on the trolley bus to Ealing.

Another son, cousin Bobby, lived and worked at Wicks the butcher's, and my developing word sense was quite tickled by the frequent call that somebody was 'over Wicksies'.

Another son, cousin Charles, was a local decorator, and he would be in and out of the shed in the back garden, picking up materials and equipment. Cousin Cecil was an engineer, and cousins Joan and Winifred worked for HMV (His Master's Voice Gramophone Company), Joan at Hayes and Winifred in Oxford Street.

Uncle Bob was a chauffeur/mechanic at Hayes Hospital. Like Father, he had started as a hire car driver before the Great War, but had been additionally trained as a Rolls Royce chauffeur, and was therefore at that time in the top flight of the London business. He was always immaculately turned out, and it had long been a family joke that he was a bit of a ladies' man because in his Rolls Royce days, glamorous Maud Allan, the Salome dancer, always asked for him to drive her.

Bob and Win enjoyed a lot of banter, especially when guests arrived, and there always seemed to be visitors in that very full house. Aunty Win's large dinners were legendary, but Bob, in his 'dry' fashion, would greet my parents with 'Hello Nell, hello Charles. Thank goodness you've come, I might get a decent dinner today. It's the only time we get any food here, when we've got visitors!' Father could hold his own in similar vein. When Win and Bob had been to visit us, and we were seeing them off on the trolleybus at the bottom of Wood Lane, they would clamber onto the rear platform helped by the conductor, and as the bus drew away, Father would call to the conductor, 'See that they pay their fares!'

During the Great War, Uncle Bob had served in the Royal Flying Corps as a sergeant mechanic, based at the aerodrome on Hounslow Heath. He possessed a real sword, which he kept in the cupboard by his armchair in the living room. I was allowed to inspect it, which I frequently asked to do, and got quite a thrill out of holding it, although it was far too heavy for me to manipulate.

Their dog, Rex, was too old to be bothered with a restless seven-year-old, although he was company on the odd occasions when Aunty Win slipped out to visit a neighbour, like Old Granny

Beagley, the blind lady a few doors up. I explored the back garden, and got to know Sonny Bourne, the boy who lived next door. He was my age and we played together, sometimes rambling over the field at the back, right up to the rear of the baker's shop on the main road. It was in this part of the field that Billy Smart had stored all his circus and fairground wagons and rides under wraps while the war was on. In peacetime, Billy's show was to be found at places like the Southall showground, and he later became famous as head of one of the greatest families of showpeople, as well as for his quaint catchphrase 'Automatically speaking ... ' when he was beginning a statement. Needless to say, we had a good look under the covers, but the fascinating vehicles, the fantastic shapes and designs, the gilt and the gay colours, all seemed very sad and lifeless, hidden away in the wintry gloom and damp of that deserted field.

Because the girls worked for HMV, they had a fine electric radiogram with automatic feed, which was housed in a smart, wooden cabinet. Quite an advance on our wind-up gramophone. They also had many of the latest hit song and swing records, among which my favourite became Roger Edens' 'Minnie From Trinidad', sung by Judy Garland and Tony Martin in the film Ziegfield Girl. My liking for it was probably as much to do with the novel title and lyrics, introducing 'Minnie Breeze' and 'Calypso Joe', as with the music.

There were times when I was alone there during the afternoon, that I would listen to the radio, and I got my first real taste for listening to plays as a result of the BBC's matinee performances, especially enjoying those with a touch of mystery.

When I eventually returned to school, just before the term ended, Christmas preparations were in full swing, and we made decorations and cards, and learned carols. Only the traditional carols were sung, and the two I most associate with that time are 'Away In A Manger' and 'Once In Royal David's City'. My class were about to perform a Christmas play for the school and parents, but my absence meant I had not got a part. Mrs Jackson, not wanting anyone to be left out, kindly dreamed up the notion that I should deliver a short prologue instead. She drilled me with the little speech until we thought I was ready.

On the great day, when the parents and pupils were all assembled in the hall, I was given my cue and amidst an expectant hush, dutifully carried my chair into the centre of the floor in front of the stage area, arranged it 'square', and climbed up onto it to face the audience. The silence was total - and so it continued. I had no idea what I was supposed to say. Mrs Jackson came to the rescue, walking over to my side and defusing the situation by saying somewhat superfluously to the amused audience: 'He's forgotten his lines.' She quietly reminded me, so that I was able to stand and deliver - to immense applause.

Between the school and the railway was the recreation ground, or 'rec'. Sometimes I would play here for a while on the way home from school, or come back on Saturdays or during holidays and play.

There was a seat on each of three sides of the 'rec', used mostly for off-the-ground tussles, but probably meant for doting parents. The official apparatus included single bars, connected in line at three different heights, parallel bars, baby swings with seat bars to keep little ones in place, ordinary swings like the one in my back garden, 'boat' swings which accommodated two people facing each other and had a two-handed central lever for working up impetus, and a brown-painted, multi-seated rocking horse with a carved head that had a handle projecting from each side. On this latter beast, the person at the front had the handles and most control, those in the middle, each holding to the saddle in front, felt the least movement, and the one on the back end usually finished up shouting 'Too high! Too high! Let me off!'

When the 'rec' was closed, the swings were chained and padlocked to their frames, and the horse immobilised, but that did not discourage us from climbing over the gate to go in and play, and the bars were always available for climbing and swinging on. There was a concrete base around each apparatus, and during official opening hours a coconut mat was laid out to break the inevitable falls.

The mats were kept in a little hut to the right of the gateway, and in that hut during official hours resided the 'keeper', who was recognisable by the regulation dark-coloured uniform and peaked cap. He was an elderly man, specially selected by the Council for his taciturn, humourless manner, and his potential ability to frighten off the more adventurous sparks, whose uninhibited and overenthusiastic use of the equipment wrapped swings round poles, stood horses on end and caused cautious would-be gymnasts to wobble and fall protesting to the ground. He would sit just inside his doorway, an eye to the crack, and offer up the occasional shout of warning, but in cases of extreme provocation, he seemed to shoot out of the shed and perform a sort of double-take-and-rage dance while simultaneously brandishing his walking stick, before bearing down upon the rapidly scattering demons, easily distinguishable from the reeling righteous or stationary stricken, who leant where they could or lay where they had fallen.

The Lane itself consisted of an asphalt path, and the surviving part of the original lane from the London Road to Northumberland Avenue was bordered by bushes and small trees on the eastern side, probably the remains of an old hedgerow. Immediately behind these trees was a scarcely discernible dirt track, alongside the boundary fences, and here we would loiter on our way home, chatting, chasing, hiding, and climbing the trees to look over the Green School field, or to view the back gardens belonging to the flats or to the houses in Roxborough Avenue.

It was from near the top of one of the trees just north of the footbridge that Brian Ritter called out to me: 'Who do you love?'

I hesitated, because I had given up Joan Holford, but it was evidently important to have somebody as a replacement, and they would not know who I meant if I said Sylvia Webb, so I said the most glamorous name that came into my head: 'Betty Grable.'

It was a mistake, albeit a minor one. Brian slithered down the tree, and went to the others, saying: ''Ere, this bloke loves Betty Grable!'

Beyond the name, I knew nothing about Miss Grable, so for a day or two I had to bluff my way through the jeering questions, and I learned that it was wiser to know what you are talking about when you give an answer.

Towards the end of my time at the Infants' School, some incidents occurred which cast shadows over my otherwise pleasant life. The war imposed its own grimness and interference, but these things were more personal.

The first was a seemingly minor incident, but it affected my self-confidence. Standing in the Lane outside the 'rec' with a group of boys, Gerald Gage got pushed by somebody. An older boy decreed that nobody else was to touch Gerald. I thought I would gain recognition and make a Huge Joke by giving Gerald another push. This proved to be an error of judgement, as the others all turned on me and I was chased away over the footbridge. It might have been forgotten as quickly as it happened, but to my dismay, another older boy trailed me all the way home, calling out that he was going to tell my parents what I had done. When we reached my house, I was quite perturbed that he came right into my garden and waited with me in the porch, telling Mother the tale when she opened the door. He went away and Mother dismissed the matter, but I was shaken because an ill-conceived joke had been made to seem like a serious misdemeanour, and because the sanctuary of my home had been invaded. Despite this, my judgement in such matters continued to let me down, and I plainly did not heed the lesson.

That was an isolated event. The second was repetitive and more difficult to understand. The small group of lads I walked home with every day were sometimes incited by our leader, Brian, to turn on me. I was chased off a number of times, and they would throw stones after me until I rounded the corner into Roxborough Avenue. It was worrying and perplexing for me, as I could not relate it to anything I had done. It just seemed to suddenly develop, yet immediately afterwards, perhaps on the way back to school and at other times, everything was fine. Brian even came to my house to play.

The third and more lasting problem came with the appearance of the 'Air Force Twins'. These two lads moved from 'somewhere up north' into a house in Northumberland Avenue near the corner of Harewood Road. They were of similar age to me, but at that time did not go to my school, and they were often dressed in imitation Air Force uniforms, because their father was seemingly in the Royal Air Force. Basil and Colin (I never knew which was

which) would hide and wait for me to come along the road, or deliberately show themselves to be waiting for me, but they only accosted me when I was alone. One would advance up to me and start to make fatuous conversation, then snatch anything from me that I could not hold on to. Meanwhile the brother would skulk behind to cut off my escape attempts, and to receive the stolen items, which they would pass from one to another, easily defeating my attempts to recover them, then eventually throwing them somewhere out of reach, over a wall or up a tree, for me to retrieve - if they allowed it.

This got to be a regular thing on my journeys to and from school, and I did not know how to deal with it. I lacked the three Gs - gumption, guts and aggression - and although I tried to explain to Mother, it did not lead to any solution.

The lowest ebb was on an occasion when I spotted them from as far off as Roxborough Avenue, and in despair I walked all round Roxborough, coming down Harewood Road from the top end. I could then see my brother Dennis standing in the road, hands on hips, waiting for me. However, he was only there because Mother had asked him to look out for me as I was late. Right behind him stood the twins, grinning as always. I pointed them out to him and tried to explain, but Dennis merely dismissed the matter and ushered me in.

I felt badly let down. Dennis was seventeen and my hero, but did not pay any heed. The problem persisted, but I made no further attempts to get help. Intermittently over the next four years, apart from a spell of a few months when they were evacuated, I was frequently ambushed, with two onto one. Every time I left the house or returned alone, I had to take precautions to avoid them, but they had the necessary cunning to ensure that I got caught time and again.

It was not until I had left the junior school that I eventually resolved the problem myself, and it happened this way. Returning from a second year football game with my boots round my neck and wearing my County School uniform, I had acquired more confidence, especially as I was taking boxing more seriously and had entered the school competition. The twins appeared ahead of me, one loitering on the opposite side of the road while his brother approached me. 'What's them?' he said ungrammatically, pointing to my boots and obviously weighing up the possibilities of snatching them. I walked up to him and shot out a straight left, catching him full on the mouth in a most satisfactory manner. He reeled back, covering his face with his hands. His brother yelled 'What did you do that for?' but stayed where he was. I strode on towards home. I knew that was the end of their reign.

CHAPTER NINE

ENDLESS FUN

We dressed him up, sat on him, laid him in the pram, pummelled him, cuddled him, rolled around the floor with him and loved him dearly - that was 'Big Teddy', three feet of battered, golden-fur-encased sawdust, with a skew-whiff face and faulty squeaker: one of my earliest toys, handed down from cousin Peter Morgan to Pauline, then to me.

Considering there was little money to spare in our household, I was fortunate to have such a quantity and variety of toys to play with. A few were bought especially for me at Christmas or birthday times, and some were home made, but most were handed down from within the family or from thoughtful relatives or neighbours.

Most of the indoor toys were kept in the cupboard under the stairs. Here were also to be found the Ewbank carpet sweeper, brush and dustpan, and electric and gas meters, but in the further depths was a wooden box and a couple of cardboard boxes, which were hauled out into the daylight when the room cleaning was finished and I got the 'all clear'.

Besides 'Big Teddy', the toys that kept me quiet at a very young age were 'Bonzo', an equally battered black and white, rubber cartoon-character squeaking dog in a sitting position; 'Jock', a Scottish doll in traditional tartan and kilt, that I took on holiday to Tankerton when I was three; 'Patch', the furry standing dog I got from Father Christmas at Chelsea Barracks; a floppy, furry black

111

and white dog; Walter, a large papier maché man with a rounded bottom containing a weight, so that if you knocked him over he would stand up again; a papier maché policeman which had once contained sweets, so he was in two slide-on halves and hollow inside; a man made of polished wooden pieces and joined by elastic threaded through all his moving parts so that he could be made to adopt any pose; and a dancing man made of cardboard joined up by thread, with a larger controlling thread which could be pulled to make the limbs move.

There were also some mechanical toys - a lifesize, clockwork, walking, furry chaffinch, given to me by the Willises over the road; a blue tin, clockwork whale that rolled along spouting sparks; a furry, clockwork penguin that wobbled from side to side as it moved along on its webbed feet; and a Japanese, tinplate clockwork motorbike with sparking exhaust, and with a rider that had a sinister Japanese face with goggles over sightless eyes.

I also used to pester Pauline to be allowed to play with some of her toys - particularly an early Mickey Mouse made of padded velvet over a wire skeleton, wearing velvet trousers and leather shoes, and a grey, papier maché standing elephant that had a removable nodding head.

The first ball I played with was a coconut-sized woollen one that was considered safe for indoors. We were not allowed to throw it, but I had endless fun chasing it across the linoleum in and out of the furniture and round people's legs, especially in competition with Dennis or Pauline.

When the world was a much larger place and I could safely hide under the sideboard, I developed a strange trait. On the rare occasions when I felt frustrated or could not attract the required attention, I would walk up to a selected, seated adult, grasp their legs and bang my forehead repeatedly on their knees. The reaction was usually one of surprise, and so had the desired effect. Fortunately I gave up being a knee-banger before it aroused greater curiosity and more probing analysis.

Of course, as in most families, there were bricks to play with, kept in the wooden box. Some had letters or words and pictures on, and if built up in the right sequence they formed a nursery

rhyme. Others were coloured red, yellow, blue and green. All were used for building house-like structures or bridges, and they were supplemented by a coloured set of wooden columns and arches, and a set of wooden imitation house fronts, windows and doors.

There was quite a selection of musical toys, the centrepiece of which was a tin drum with sticks, but because of its ear-splitting potential, nobody banged on it, not even me. There were various mouth organs that Dennis had discarded (he kept his best German Hohne in its box in the bedroom); a wooden xylophone and a chromium dulcimer, each with the notes marked on the keys; a little concertina with silver keys and an air leak; a Jews harp that nobody liked playing because it went rusty (our talented friend Phil Harris could actually get a tune out of his); a green wooden imitation ukelele; and a couple of 'der-ders', the party blowers that squeaked and shot out with a feather on the end.

Gradually I acquired some lead farm animals, a tree or two, a wooden stable with a 'thatched' roof and half-door, and these were supplemented by zoo animals. I then had to think hard to create acceptable scenarios for the co-existence of ostrich, zebra and gorilla in the midst of sheep, cows and pigs. I also had a cutout farm, the contents of which I could stand around on the floor as a background to the more manoeuvrable lead animals.

A small number of dinky toy cars came into my possession, the pride of the collection being racing cars, especially the Auto Union, Alfa Romeo and Mercedes Benz. I was also fond of the silver three-carriage model of the 'Mallard' express train, although we always erroneously called it the 'Coronation Scot'.

I eventually got a Hornby Dublo green and black clockwork engine, which pulled three rather battered pullman coaches round an oval track. The carriages stabilised it and if I left them off, the engine went round at breakneck speed, and usually took to the air on one of the bends. Part of the fun was to try and convert my perspective to that of the train, and to achieve this, I would set it in motion and put my head on the ground and close one eye. I discovered there was an element of risk in this, particularly while enjoying the best view, which was watching the train approach. The track was old and had been trodden on in a number of places, so the joins on the curved sections were liable at any time to suddenly launch the locomotive on an unscheduled route across the carpet towards the watching eye, requiring a rapid restoration to the upright position and an unerring grab at the angrily buzzing engine.

The train kit was enhanced at times. I got a set of points, and some straight track with buffers at the end. There was already a tinplate station, a hand-operated signal and a small tunnel with a rough green surface. To these was added a tinplate level crossing with gates that swung open and closed and could be bolted in position. Many a horrendous but carefully staged accident befell cars or 'leaden footed' members of my 'public' who loitered on the crossing when the six o'clock express came through. I was given a petrol wagon, a coal wagon, and a freight wagon into which farm animals or soldiers could be loaded. Largest item of all was a green turntable. This was good in principle, because you could turn the train to move off in any of four directions, but there was only room for the engine and one wagon. This meant you had to disconnect them, turn the table round by hand, and either abandon the rest of the wagons or go back in the opposite direction with the engine pushing the wagons. This much labour was only rarely invested.

As time went by, the fascination of the train set diminished, and it became more an occasional 'good idea' to get everything out and set it up, but less absorbing to actually play with it. Because it occupied most of the living room floor, nobody was too upset when its popularity waned.

There was a brief revival when Aunt Rose passed on to me cousin Peter's steam engine. This was a little bigger than the Hornby, and it had a real copper boiler and brass pipes. After you put water in you heated the boiler with a methylated spirit burner - well, Father did. It got up a head of steam and puffed along the floor well enough, but each time we got that far, one of the pipe joints would melt and Father had to re-solder it. We all got tired of that.

A less complicated toy that gave me some fun was the large, red mobile crane, with a weighted hook and a ratchet brake on the winder. Several toys had a convenient place for hooking, or could be 'roped' round, and I spent a lot of otherwise valuable time moving things laboriously from location 'A' to location 'B'. That too became boring, although it had the merit that there was hardly any set-up time, and relocation of the crane was instant, on demand.

When my territory consisted of the living room floor, or sometimes the drawing room floor, only the train set required a reserved area; and while this was not always convenient, it was at least plainly visible to all. However, the war, and natural tendencies, led to my burgeoning interest in military matters, which meant lead soldiers. The setting up of a base and battlefield required a more flexible layout, with as much variety in the terrain as the imagination could conceive. Furniture feet became rock formations, a cushion was a range of hills, patterns on the lino or carpet were roads and rivers, and all sorts of objects could be used as mountains with passes and valleys.

This made it more difficult for non-combatant adults to go about their lawful business. Another dawning restriction was that new baby Sylvia took up an increasing amount of room, with the pram to be accommodated in the hall and the playpen set up in the dining room. Gradually the little-used drawing room became more acceptable as a regular play area.

I started off with one or two 'old soldiers', and I was given, over a period, a shilling box of Grenadier Guards with rifles, bought from Woolworths by Pauline, a brass band of Grenadier Guards, knights in armour both on foot and on horseback, nurses and stretcher-bearers, and various soldiers in khaki, some with machine guns, and also a radar spotting device.

The war zone vehicles comprised the civilian racing and other cars, a couple of tanks with caterpillar tracks, a grey battleship and a submarine, and several bomber and fighter aircraft. 'Live' armaments included an anti-tank Howitzer, with the disastrous combination of a weak spring and heavy metal shells that were in consequence reluctant travellers. The real attacking strength lay with several cannons, which were metal guns on two wheels, with a very efficient firing mechanism that would shoot 'dead' matchsticks or small nails with devastating accuracy and power.

What pulled the whole thing together was the fort I was given one Christmas. It was of wood, about eighteen inches square, with a moat and drawbridge leading into a raised courtyard or 'square' which was surrounded by walls and turrets, all of which were detachable and could be packed away into the hollow base, At the back of the 'square' was the barracks or living quarters, which could be lit up inside by a bulb and battery.

This staggering present from Mother and Father kept me amused on and off for two or three years. The enemy (inevitably German) 'army' could be set out in and around the fort, with a parade band, sentries and off-duty men, such as cowboys and knights in armour, supplemented by sundry animals. The attacking force, of which I had the honour to be Commander-in-Chief, would sneak up over rough terrain, take up its positions and attack at dawn with the benefit of total surprise and superior fire power.

Facing us would be a combined force of snipers' rifles, withering machine gun fire, tanks, planes (grounded), and even knights on horseback with lances, but they were no match for the cannon. Fired matchsticks would knock over a 'balanced' foe, but fired nails were certain death. Lead-casualties did occur, the commonest being decapitation, but this was not considered fatal, and in fact lead-surgery was sufficiently advanced to remedy this 'in the field' by inserting a matchstick to reunite head and body, and enable the victim to rejoin the fray. Fatal wounds were broken legs or crushed body, usually suffered as a result of unwisely taking up a forward position beneath the advancing army's foot.

The Victory Parade, or sometimes the warm-up parade, took place with a 'borrowed' line up of the Grenadier Guards band blowing to the strains of Purcell's 'Trumpet Voluntary', my favourite (twelve-inch 78 RPM) record of that time, which I was eventually allowed to play on the large, wooden wind-up gramophone whenever I wanted. It was always a stirring moment, and I would go off into a bit of a trance while the music lasted.

Sometimes, when going to a friend's house, I would take a few soldiers and cannon with me, and it was through such a visit that I found another dimension was added by playing with them in the garden. The natural terrain was infinitely superior to carpets and cushions. There was the 'jungle' of real grass, real hills of earth or sand, rocky cliffs of stone, and it was possible to make lakes of real water. Of course, casualties were higher, and in the next parade at the home base, gaps were discovered and verdicts of 'lost, presumed killed' would be proclaimed. It was also heavy on ammunition, which was hard to find after it had been fired, but for a while the garden campaigns breathed new life into the old 'war horse'.

One Christmas, my present was a fine aerodrome which Father had made. It had a painted plywood base, two camouflaged hangars, and a windsock that was permanently extended as if in a stiff breeze. It gave a boost to the aerial activity over the battlegrounds - and took up yet more floorspace, of course.

I also had sets of cutout card soldiers which stood up, and their varied uniforms added a very colourful backgound, since all manner of British and Colonial troops were represented.

Playing at being a soldier was another natural pursuit in the midst of the War, when we lived and breathed conflict. A central item in this game at home was the rocking horse. It had been bought for Dennis at Pontings, around 1930, and passed down. It was of traditional design, with a large woodblock horse, painted white with black markings, rocking on a stand with two pillars. Also handed down was a cowboy suit with hat, shirt, trousers, scarf and spurs, and a holster with a selection of hand guns. An inherited but discredited weapon was the wooden pop-gun, which comprised a wooden barrel and wooden handle with rod attached, but it had lost its cork and string and, lacking compression, could no longer be fired in anger. My favourite was the silver cap-firing Colt with revolving chamber. There were no caps available in the war, of course, so more effective, and sometimes lethal, was the black potato gun, which fired pieces of that (unrationed) vegetable, and which got re-armed whenever a specially trained raiding party found the kitchen unattended.

Homemade swords, consisting of pieces of flat wood, shaped and nailed together, were often being fashioned to replace breakages and bows and arrows were frequently made with whatever branches and canes could be found. Shields were desirable but rare, as they required a large piece of plywood and the fixing of a sturdy handle. Peter Barratt in Northumberland Avenue was the envy of all, as his father had made him a fine shield with the cross of St George painted in red.

Dennis's Home Guard unit progressed to real rifles, so he was able to give up his wooden rifle used in drill, and this was a valuable addition to my armoury. The wooden rifle was kept in the shed, along with a tin hat, but the hat proved too cumbersome for a nine-year old gnat-weight to wear, and in any event I did not like being compared to a toadstool.

After the war, Dennis bought a Webley air rifle and made a good wooden case for it. Dennis was mature and sensible enough to ensure no live targets were put in the sights, but we had some real fun and satisfaction firing down the garden at the bullseye target cards

We made some attempt to introduce 'baddies' into our war games. Chicken feathers were stuck into strips of cardboard to make Indian headdresses, and bandits wore scarves or handerkerchiefs over their lower face. Germans, when anybody could be persuaded to take the part, wore improvised black moustaches, goose-stepped and shouted 'Achtung - Heil Hitler!' but it was not a popular role, although the lampooning of Germans and of Hitler was common enough.

When I wanted to be a pirate, I made a triangular hat out of folded newspaper, and a sword out of rolled and folded newspaper, both of which accomplishments were learnt from Father. We also made masks out of paper, with cut-out eyes, nose and mouth, but the 'borrowed' knicker elastic soon tore through the sides, unless you could get hold of the rarer strong brown paper.

The only other dressing up I did was as a bus conductor. I had a conductor's outfit, which consisted of an oval lapel badge, a coin bag, and a silver ticket-punch which rang each time a ticket was punched. The bus was a couple of dining room chairs, or the underneath of the table, or the cupboard under the stairs, which had an actual door you could pass through before paying your fare and sitting on a wooden box for the 'ride', although it was perhaps more akin to being on the 'tube'. Tickets were readily available,

because everybody trav̱elled ̱by bus and often saved their tickets.
Trolleybus tickets were ̱ ̱ ̱ as ̱ ̱ the single card bus tickets,
they were printed off a ̱ ̱ roll of flimsy paper by the conductor's
machine, and were no̱ ̱ robust enough for my punch. However, for
a long time one of m̱y p̱ri̱ze possessions was an unused roll of
trolleybus ticket paper with a mauve line printed through it - given
to me by a friendly conductor on the 657 route to Hounslow. It
was a highly 'desirable' object, and yet I never did find a good use
for it.

We had a jack-in-a-box, the box being of painted wood and jack
having the head of a clown, but it was rather sad because nine
times out of ten, when you undid the catch on the lid, jack would
just sit there, bent over, head in lap, with no hint of spring or
surprise. There were glove puppets too, from the Plasticine doll
with woollen hair, whose features could be altered at will, to the
more realistic clown and monkey. The script for my puppet shows
left everything to the imagination, as there was a certain impatience
to reach the climax, a no-holds-barred 'puppet fight', which
boisterous and enthusiastic finale signalled the end of the
performance.

Drawing was a continual sideline occupation of mine from
the age of five until about ten. Paper was in short supply, but in
the way of presents from various people I used to receive very
small pads of greyish or cream coloured 'utility' paper. On these
I drew minute aeroplanes, tanks, warships and soldiers, which
would be bombarding houses, trees and each other against a
background of mountains, woodlands and oceans, while
overhead the sun or moon shone and seagulls flew unconcernedly
by. As a direct result of my education at school, I was able to
introduce further detail including union jacks, toadstools,
weathervanes and flying insects.

I used wax and pencil crayons, and the three tin boxes of water
colour paints that we shared, so most drawings had the benefit of
colour - as did my fingers, shirtsleeves and sometimes the tablecloth.
Tracing was a good wet day time-filler, although it was only possible
when greaseproof paper could be found, and I also had a set of
stencils in the shape of animals and trees that made drawings which

were irritatingly superior to even my most painstaking copies.

I had a slateboard and pencil given to me, and these were well used, as the results were easily erased. Similarly, we enjoyed using chalks on blackboard and easel, of which we had two - the smaller board naturally being allocated to the smaller (or weaker) participant.

Plasticine, in its various colours, was fun to model with in idle moments at home, leaving on hand its strong if familiar smell, and it was also available at school. In modelling vein, I inherited a tin of coloured wax sticks with a collection of hinged metal moulds in the shape of ships, lighthouses, and cars, intended for the shaping of the hot wax, but that interesting prospect was officially denied me as being too dangerous. There were no instructions, but I guessed that there was a piece of equipment missing, and so the technique for melting the wax and getting it into the mould whilst hot was something I spent a lot of time wrestling with. Mother would have been relieved to know that, despite deciding that her milk saucepan with the pourer was suitable, I never got round to trying it, although I afterwards considered that there would have been a certain appeal in offering a nightcap of cocoa with elements of boiled wax as a 'moustache stiffener and late night embalmer'.

Pauline had other prize pre-war toys that appealed to me at an early age. One was the doll's house - which had belonged to Sylvia Webb - a moderately large 'suburban villa' style dwelling with a hinged front, and each room furnished with fascinating miniature pieces. The other toy was a cardboard, foldaway shop. When this was opened out and stood up, it was divided off into a butcher's, a grocer's and a confectioner's, each with its proprietor, its counter, and produce. There was a set of scales, a scoop and little paper bags, and one could serve from jars containing a variety of groceries like rice, and lentils, or sweets like miniature dolly mixtures and 'hundreds and thousands', and hanging on hooks in the butcher's there were realistic joints of meat, some just imitation, and some made of very edible sweet stuff, very hard to resist

I was given a discarded (metal) Meccano set, and it undoubtedly helped my manipulative skills, once I was old enough to control the spanner and screwdriver. It was also frustrating, because it was a very basic set, and although it had some wheels, a crank handle and some red string, I could only make very simple models, like a cart, or a bridge for the Hornby train to pass under. With it came an instruction book, but this covered the whole range of Meccano kits, and I spent more time gazing longingly at the working models of cranes, windmills, and electrically driven motor vehicles than I did in becoming more ingenious at making what I could. We were asked into Phil Harris's house to see in his bedroom the massive, mobile and highly manoeuvrable crane that he had designed and built. It was very impressive, and my limited kit dropped still further down the ratings, but we did come away with Phil's catchphrase 'Swing 'er round on the jib!' which stayed forever in the family lore.

There were things that we made ourselves - for instance, with cotton reels. By threading an elastic band through the middle and securing it with a matchstick at each end, then cutting grooves across the two outer rims, we made a 'tank', and when you wound up the elastic band with the two matchsticks and set it on the floor, it would move cumbersomely along.

At the junior school, we gave 'George Formby concerts' to audiences of one at a time. This required the cotton reel to have a double thread of cotton through the middle, secured by a matchstick at one end, and with the other end fixed through the centre of a matchbox tray. The audience put the tray to his ear, to act as a megaphone/'receiver', while the performer kept the thread tension adjusted and made the story into a running commentary punctuated with noises from the reel and thread, so we would talk of George giving a concert and playing his ukelele (to plucked cotton), leading up to George falling off the stage and breaking his leg (to matchstick 'snapped' smartly against the side of the reel). The climax came when George emerged from hospital and gave a celebration performance to immense applause, for which the tense thread was grated round the ragged edge of the centre hole, producing an ear-splitting crackling through the matchbox tray that invariably caused the 'audience' to flee the auditorium, nursing the afflicted orifice.

In the absence of fireworks and caps, which were not available during wartime, we made bangers by getting two hefty bolts screwed into opposite sides of a nut, and loading the gap in the middle with red Swan Vesta match heads. When this was hurled at the pavement, the match heads ignited with a cracking report. At the Town School, Brian Ritter produced one of these 'bombs' from his pocket with some matches, which were strictly forbidden on the premises, so he wanted to set it off outside. I agreed to accompany him, and we slipped out of the playground and round the corner to Mandeville Road, under the illusion that it was miles away and perfectly safe from all vestiges of authority, although why we assumed any adults within earshot would also be stone deaf is not clear. He duly loaded it and hurled it to get a very satisfying 'crack' and then, retrieving the bomb, we fled back to the playground. For once our luck was in, and nobody confronted us with the 'crime'.

Dennis had a joke rose that I used to borrow. It was a lifelike celluloid red bloom with green leaves that fitted into a lapel buttonhole, and you invited the selected victim to smell the perfume, and then squeezed the hidden rubber valve full of water that squirted into his unsuspecting face. Of course it only worked on anybody once, and one soon ran out of victims, especially the few who could be relied upon to take it in good part and not retaliate.

At the end of the war, shops like Baxter's suddenly had a supply of slim, elegant, silver metal pea shooters, and Dennis and I had some fun with a couple of those - and so did a number of school pals. Mother's stock of pearl barley was continually depleted, and got put on strict rationing.

From time to time we made catapults, but it was always impressed upon us how dangerous they could be to people, and how damaging to windows, so we were inhibited in their use in the garden and road. Usually ours were of wood with just ordinary rubber band or knicker elastic tied on, but there were boys with more lethal weapons, where the wood was heavier or the frame was metal, and from somewhere they got a double strand of quarter-inch elastic tied to a proper rubber sling for the missile. I did not take a serious interest in the possibilities of this improved specification, because we were aware of people whose sight had been damaged by stones, like Mother's sister Emily, and I knew it would only lead to trouble.

A less aggressive pursuit was collecting cigarette cards. Although they were not produced during the war, they were plentiful from pre-war days, and everybody seemed to have some. We kept them in cigarette packets, except for those few special sets for which we had the ready-made album, with the text printed alongside the space to stick the picture in. Dennis had the main collection, which by degrees I borrowed from and then took over. We used to try and get complete sets, usually around fifty cards, by swapping or trading but not by buying.

The sets covered a huge range of subjects, and among the common ones we had were Aeroplanes (Civil), Aircraft of the Royal Air Force, Motor Cars, Cycling, Hints on Association Football, Household Hints, Film Stars, Cricketers, Association Footballers, Kings of Speed, Railway Equipment, British Railways, RAF Badges, Radio Celebrities, Straight Line Caricatures, Uniforms of the Territorial Army, National Flags and Arms, Coronation Series (dress etc), Butterflies, Garden Flowers, Animals of the Countryside. My favourite sets were Churchman's 'Howlers' ('a myth is a female moth', 'Julius Caesar entered Rome wearing a coral reef ', and worse), Senior Service's 'Our Countryside', which were real photographs of England at its best, the colourful De Reszke silk 'Flags' given to me in their paper album by Aunt Rose, and 'Boxing Personalities', with their blunt, impassive faces like that of the curiously named Moss Deyong, and the rugged heroes in fighting stance, like Jack Johnson, Jim Driscoll, Jimmy 'Ghost With A Hammer' Wilde and Joe Louis - and I also valued as rarities two cards I called 'Chinese', because they had oriental script on the back, but this may equally have been Japanese, and they were likely as not issued in England.

Just about everybody collected stamps, mostly pasted or hinged into little pre-war 'Excelsior' albums, although gradually these were replaced by loose-leaf albums, and more care was taken to preserve the condition of the stamps. At school, the real enthusiasts seemed to have emerged by the age of ten, mostly owing their ever-growing acquisitions to the sponsorship of a philatelic father, or in extreme cases like Geoffrey Over, to a father who owned a shop which happened to sell stamps. I acquired some very attractive stamps, especially one from Ecuador featuring a golden eagle, and the two New Zealand triangular 'health' stamps which I bought from Geoffrey as an investment - never, alas, to give the hoped for return. Gwen Dalton's brother returned from his army duties in Germany, and I was consequently able to buy from her a set of unused 'Hitler' stamps - as did most of the class, I discovered afterwards. I was disillusioned by my inability to find a penny black among old envelopes, or a rare misprint when buying stamps from the Post Office, and when my prized 'Victory' stamps fell on the mat, stuck onto my own handwritten envelope, and I saw the smudgy ink and crooked stamps, and noted the Post Office's failure to mark it as a 'first day cover', my collecting days were more or less over. However, I was left with an unsatisfied hankering to own a really smartly bound, old-fashioned album, with a fine collection of Victorian and Edwardian English stamps already neatly stuck in.

Badges somehow came into my possession, given by grown-ups, or found on pavements, or in fields and through swapping. Military hat badges were quite common, and there were small lapel badges about, like the 'Spitfire Fund' or 'Spitfire Library' badge, or pre-war ones like the RNLI. My best was the Royal Artillery hat badge, but I also valued a large Victorian round brooch that I found in a field - it was marcasite, and probably worthless, but I sensed it had history.

We accumulated Easter egg cups. They were popular pre-war, mostly of glazed pottery chicks, ducks, rabbits and other animals. My best was a smartly attired elephant, standing on two legs and holding a top hat. They were used for ever afterwards to hold the breakfast boiled egg, kept warm under its knitted cap, with bread and butter 'soldiers' lined up on the side plate, although this was only a once-a-week treat during the war. Easter eggs could be quite large, and their presentation packaging even larger. Thus we had baskets that had held one or even a clutch of such eggs, and even a small yellow cricket bat that had had several eggs fastened to one side. At Easter time during the war, we usually got an ordinary egg, and we would decorate it with paint for the Sunday breakfast - and I would gaze at it and imagine what it would be like to once more have a real dark chocolate egg, with its unforgettable flavour, as unique as the Nestlé's penny bar, or a Walls lemon or strawberry water ice.

Indoors, on wet or wintry days, as well as playing dot-to-dot, noughts and crosses, building a house of cards, drawing silhouettes or playing 'I Spy', there were always jigsaws, and ours were all surprisingly complete. Among many, we had Buckfast Abbey with surrounding fields, Bentalls of Kingston and surrounding streets, 'Bubbles' (Millais' famous Pears' Soap picture), a fox-hunting scene at 'the meet', a wooden rusticity depicting 'cows in a field', a World War II 'battle at sea', Pauline's large 'Snow White' with scenes from the Disney film, and her huge thousand-piece foreign scene of girls picking flowers in a terraced garden.

Mrs Harris gave me a polished wooden solitaire board, made by Mr Harris, who was a ship's carpenter. To play, I used my collection of marbles, which fitted the holes perfectly, but eventually discovered a routine for 'getting out', which took the edge off the solo game, but it enabled me to demonstrate how clever I had become.

We had a nice green bagatelle board with ball bearings that pinged their way down into the wire nail scoring enclosures, and on the reverse was shoveha'penny, with its shiny coin-sized brass discs with a hole in the middle. The score was chalked up in five bar gate form on either side of the concourse, and there was something hypnotically addictive about trying to nudge the discs between the lines.

Christmastime triggered the appearance of the 'Compendium of Games', and although we always ended up playing cards, the board games of ludo and snakes and ladders were always popular, largely because four could play. Cribbage was reserved for teenagers and above, and so too was chess, but draughts, and 'ducks and drakes' were played by all, as were dominoes.

In addition to playing real card games like rummy, sevens and whist, we played noisily at snap, happy families and lexicon, in which the competition was always strong.

I had a miniature set of playing cards, but they were too difficult to manipulate. That difficulty was one of two problems I had with the second hand conjuring set I received when I was seven. It was a fascinating thing to possess, in a fine red box with a picture of Louis Golding on the front. Inside were various compartments with ready-made tricks and illusions, an instruction book and a gold-topped magic wand. Unfortunately the instruction book did not enable you to manipulate, and it did not cover the other problem - patter - so essential in distracting the audience from the manipulation. Father had seen the great illusionists Horace Goldin and Maskelyne and Devant, and Cinquevalli the juggler, and Chung Ling Soo who caught bullets in his teeth (until he was accidentally shot), and he tried to encourage me from time to time. In addition to his prestidigitating skills in making coins disappear and reappear, he would occasionally demonstrate for me a trick or two from the box, using the magic word 'Abracadabra!' or his own 'Kiskawoski - tombolo!' I practised and had a measure of success with some card tricks, and with the coloured spot that mysteriously changed hue when you slid it in and out of its case, the cricket bat with its three holes and the matchsticks that changed location unaided, and the three cup trick with its vanishing ball. But unlike Father, I was never at ease being the centre of attention and talking my way through the action.

We had a roll-a-ball game in which the balls had to be rolled purposefully along the table to climb up a sloping card that had scoring holes, so the balls either scored or rolled back. I was playing this in the dining room on one occasion when the air raid siren went, and there was a knock at the door. Mother answered and brought in a neighbour from Roxborough Avenue who wished to shelter until the raid was over. We did not know Mrs Hutchings until then, but she was very pleasant and took to me. She always spoke to us thereafter until she and her husband moved to Cornwall at the end of the war. 'You must come and visit us,' she said, but at that time Cornwall might as well have been at the other end of the world.

There was another table game in which coloured cardboard rings were fired from a sprung metal 'catapult' in the attempt to score by landing them on hooks attached to a standing board. In similar vein, we had a game called 'quoits', with scoring hooks on a wooden board that hung from the picture rail, and we pitched rubber rings at it to catch on the hooks.

My godparents, the Thurlows, gave me two excellent games at different times. One was 'Over the Alps', which consisted of a hinged board that stood up like a mountain, on which the Alps were depicted, together with a trail and hazards like avalanche and crevasse. By throwing the dice you moved your lead climber along the trail, hooking him into holes by his pick, over the mountain via rest hut and base camp, but getting knocked back by landing on a hazard. The other game was the tantalising 'Magnetic Fishing', with magnets at the end of a rod and line which were used to blindly catch metal-tagged cardboard fish that were heaped inside a painted cardboard 'aquarium'. The larger the fish, the bigger the score, but bites were nearly as rare as prizes on the arcade crane, until I got some 'real' magnets, which caught two or three fish at a time.

I received a second-hand John Bull printing outfit, which required the setting up of tiny rubber-based letters into wooden frames, after which they had to be banged on an inked pad and banged again onto paper, to achieve the printed result. The lengthy painstaking set-up time, followed by the discovery of the inevitable errors of missed or reversed letters, eroded the initial enthusiasm, and ideas of newspaper and book publishing receded into oblivion.

The biggest, best and most grown-up game I had was Monopoly, which never palled, and all the family enjoyed it. The other best one I never owned but had access to was Father's horse racing game.

Dennis had 'Blow Football', which was more fun when we got the larger, square dining table. The player at each end had a cardboard tube through which to blow a ping-pong ball into his opponent's goal, in which hung a swinging, revolving tin goalkeeper which had to be blown into the required defending position. The cardboard tubes soon got soggy and had to be constantly changed, until we substituted tin pea shooters, but there was still the problem that the ball would shoot off the table and in the frantic excitement would get crushed underfoot (and it was not unknown for it to go straight into the open fire), which temporarily dampened what was otherwise always a lively and humorous contest

Table tennis was also feasible on the new draw-leaf dining table, although the ball left scores of tiny indentation marks in the polish, and the net clamps had to be packed with newspaper to avoid damage. This was quite a civilised game, but for mindless fun we would punt a balloon about, while stocks lasted, going to extraordinary lengths to try and keep it off the floor.

I had a red wooden yo-yo, at which I became quite adept. I also inherited from Dennis a small, brass disc with a boxer in relief on each side, and when you blew the disc to make it spin in its wishbone-shaped holder, it appeared as if the boxers were fighting each other.

Dennis was ten years older, but he knew how to 'rough and tumble' with me without causing injury, although there were occasional accidents and subsequent bruises. We had two pairs of boxing gloves, and sparring became a favourite occupation, after ball games. It was merely feinting and tapping, speed being of the essence, but there were also bouts of shoulder-to-shoulder 'in-fighting', until one or other was exhausted.

Apart from the connection with 'Freddie the Fly', we had a long- standing interest in boxing, and with Father we later listened avidly to the radio commentaries given by Stewart Macpherson and Barrington Daulby. During the war, Joe Louis remained everybody's favourite, but Father knew about the many other champions, and had much admired Jimmy Wilde, and he had watched the great black fighter Sam Langford, against whom Jack Johnson had refused a rematch, running, skipping and shadow boxing in the lanes around Harlesden in preparation for his 1909 victory over Ian Hague

Outside in the garden, we boxed on the lawn or threw the rubber quoit which we had brought back from Tankerton, or played cricket with a tennis ball. The outdoor toys were kept in the shed, and my earliest was the red tricycle with flat wooden seat and pedals fixed to the front wheel. I spent a lot of time going round the path which went right round the garden, either pretending to be a car or a bus, or just taking in the trees, plants, birds, sunshine and clouds. The 'box barrow' was often tied to the back end of my tricycle, and loaded up with toys or 'passenger' dolls, and sometimes I used my conductor outfit to collect fares and drop the 'passengers' off around the garden.

On washing day, which was invariably Monday, if I was home I would help with the mangling, although it was a lethal trap for little fingers. I also liked playing with the wood and glass scrubbing board, and then perhaps I would get a bowl of soapy water and blow bubbles with the small white clay pipe that was shaped like a tobacco pipe, but with a face on the bowl.

On the pavement, there was more scope for certain things, and here I ran with one of the two wooden hoops, one large and one small, or whipped one of our wooden 'peg' tops to keep it spinning, until it went off at a tangent. I also had a large, painted metal humming top, which had a central, vertical handle that had to be pumped to get it going and produce the rich, chorded note that went up the scale as the speed increased, but because the paint might chip, this top was reserved for the smooth, polished lino indoors.

We marked the pavement out in chalk squares and used a smooth pebble for hopscotch. With childish logic and humour we thought that in Scotland they must have called it 'hop-english' (although I have since heard it is actually called 'peevers', perhaps a reference to the paving stones on which it is played). Skipping ropes were always to hand, although not always with handles. We would skip while running or jumping on the spot, or while running along. The girls always seemed more skilled at skipping, whether solo with arm crossing and 'bumps' (a double turn of the rope), or doing singles and 'bumps' with two others swinging the rope, and they knew the traditional rhymes to skip to:

> 'Deanna Durbin
> Wore a turban
> Till she was 2,
> 4, 6, 8'

'Early in the morning at eight o'clock,
Sure to hear the postman knock,
How many letters has he brought,
1, 2, 3, 4, 5, 6' (and so on)

'My Mother said that
I never should,
Play with the gypsies
In the wood'

'Italy was Hungary,
Had a bit of Turkey,
On a piece of China,
Dipped in Greece.'

The significance of the words of that particular chant escaped me completely, as did those of the contemporary hit song 'Oh, what a surprise for the Duce, they do say, he can't put it over the Greeks!' A sure sign I was not destined for politics.

Rhymes were also used for bouncing balls or throwing two to the wall and catching, and for 'dipping' or 'counting out' to decide who was going to be 'it' for a game of 'he' or 'hide and seek':

The dipping rhyme everybody knew was:

'Dip,dip,dip,
My little ship,
Sailing on the water,
Like a cup and saucer,
You are IT!'

But individuals had their favourites. Mike used:

'Inky pinky ponky
Father bought a donkey
Donkey died, father cried,
Inky pinky ponky.'

Brian Ritter used:

'One potato, two potato, three potato, four,
Five potato, six potato, seven potato, raw.'

Inevitably, vulgarity was to be heard from those who wished to appear racy:

'Each, peach, pear, plum,
Stick your finger up your bum,
Tell the teacher what you done,
Each, peach, pear, plum.'

Sometimes we would tie the end of the rope to one of the cherry trees in the road and hold the other end to allow the others to jump over it, gradually raising the level until a winner was found. It was called 'Higher and higher', and to avoid unpleasant accidents you had to hold the rope loosely, but it was hard to resist the Huge Joke of raising it just as somebody jumped.

When a neighbour over the back cut down some poplar trees, Father made me a pair of stilts from the trunks. They still had the bark on, and the blocks were crudely fashioned by splitting the trunk, but they worked, and it was great fun to walk up the road high above everything and everyone. Mike Curwen got his father to make him a pair, and as I feared, his were superbly fashioned, painted green with a sheen, and slightly higher than mine, but there was no real envy on my part - it was just more fun, because we could both roam around and share this new perspective on the neighbourhood.

A pair of second-hand roller skates came my way when I was about ten years old. I learnt to use them in our sideway, which was concreted, but to make real progress I went up and down the pavement and 'round the block'. I quickly grew out of them, even though they were adjustable, but by the end I could travel backwards or forwards, standing or stooping. I never really mastered the emergency stop though, and tended to use anything that was handy - lamp-posts, trees, fences, or friends.

I had long outgrown my tricycle when one day, at seven years of age, I was given a bicycle. It had come from Pauline's friends, Jacqueline and Lorraine Thomas who lived with their grandmother in Wood Lane. They had outgrown it, and soon afterwards they left the district, but for me it was a great and unforgettable gift that transformed the scope of my play.

One size up from a 'fairy cycle', it still had a curved cross bar, but it was a proper bike, with inflatable tyres, a bell and a stand and carrier on the back. Learning to ride came easily, with a little help from the family, although there were no stabilisers then. Once I had learnt to keep my balance, I rode endlessly, and had more pleasure from two or three years on the little red bike than from anything else previously . Mike Curwen, being older, had a slightly larger blue bike, and we cycled around the local roads together, adopting as our theme song the 1942 hit 'Jingle, Jangle, Jingle', which had the pertinent lines:

> 'I've got bells that jingle, jangle, jingle,
> As we go riding merrily along.'

There was almost no motor traffic then, except on the main roads, owing to petrol conservation and the restriction on private motoring, so we had the luxury of being able to use the road with comparitive safety, although we had already learnt and were conscious of the rules and correct procedure. Mike was already a car enthusiast, and because his father owned a car, driving and road usage were things he knew about at an early age. I assimilated his knowledge, adding to it what I learnt from Father.

Once again we became 'buses' and 'cars', only now our journeys were on a grander scale, and our stops for pickups, refuelling and meetings were more ambitiously scheduled at various landmarks around the estate.

With carriers on the back we were able to carry (small) passengers or a bit of 'freight', but apart from all those added extras, there was the sheer joy of just being able to cycle around freely - the streets were very quiet on weekdays - and we could get to distant places like the Flats and back in no time at all.

When I grew too big for that bike, I had to endure a long and very frustrating wait, running alongside Mike and other luckier free-wheeling friends, before I was able to have a replacement.

Around 1945 there was a craze for fretwork, and I was pleasantly surprised to receive a fretsaw and patterns as a birthday present. This interest was short-lived, because we did not have a vice in the shed, nor very much suitable, spare plywood, and the blades kept getting stuck and breaking, and I never solved the problem of getting to the centre of the wood if the other end of the fretsaw prevented it. For a while though, the shed was further littered with sawdust and offcuts, and there were those who appreciated the fact that I was 'out of the way'.

Another fad, when I was eleven, was for chemistry sets. Once more my family surprised me, and I got a set that was about number two up from the bottom of the range. So began a brief exploration of a whole new world. Just to own the mauve box with its yellow label, and the contents, was exciting, and the possibilities for experiment seemed endless. It soon came to light, however, that without the application of heat, chemicals do not do very much that is amusing or even watchable. Heat required a Bunsen burner, which was an extra that I did not have, but Mike had one, so we used to get together in his kitchen for our more advanced work.

My set did include packets and phials of chemicals and other materials, all labelled, and their properties and reactions were described in the leaflet. The list included soda, sulphur, graphite, charcoal and the seemingly indispensable 'logwood chips'. There were test tubes, glass rods and tubes, a metal heating pan and, of course, litmus paper.

We tried heating everything in turn, discretely or mixed, and we watered it and tested it with litmus. For the most part, the results were unspectacular, and we kept resorting to heating sulphur for the production of 'rotten egg perfume'.

More promising was the development of invisible ink, using a solution of copper sulphate, although even with that you had to heat the paper in order to read the message, and since there was a tendency for it to catch fire, we developed speed reading. The other problem was that many a vital message on a seemingly blank sheet got lost or overwritten, because we forgot to put on the visible secret mark that identified it as containing an invisible message.

Surprisingly, we never managed to blow up anything, nor to poison anyone, perhaps because we never lost sight of the warning held in the ditty Pauline brought home from school:

> 'Poor little Johnny's dead and gone,
> His face you'll see no more,
> For what he thought was H20
> Was CUS04.'

CHAPTER TEN

THE JUNIOR SCHOOL: INITIATION

It was difficult to believe that it was late August and still the height of summer, when I started at Isleworth Town Junior School. It seemed instead a cold, gloomy, joyless time, as if winter, sensing a weakness in the end of season sunshine, had sent advanced warning of its intentions. This was not merely a matter of the weather, however.

After the airy brightness of the Marlborough Infants School, with its light and well-ventilated classrooms, fresh and green surroundings, pleasant teachers and the now familiar route, the contrastingly dark decor and the oppressive atmosphere at the new school came as an unpleasant, unwanted shock, and I spent my first two years there trying to come to terms with that.

The Town School was only just over thirty years old, having been opened in 1910, but it seemed to hark back to the 'Board School' age, when school buildings still had that rather overpowering, 'institutional' air, outside and in - and here there were no sunny floor-to-ceiling windows, no decorative sundials, weathercocks, rabbits, statues in the quadrangle - not even a quadrangle.

I tried to understand everything about the place and what was expected of me as I was carried back and forth on the ebb and flow of the daily routine, with home as the welcoming beach and school

135

as the unknown and sometimes frightening depths of the ocean. It was perhaps partly due to the war, and partly to the business of getting to grips with life, but although I did manage to have some fun, I felt as though I was always under threat, always in unsought-after competition, and always just about to be betrayed or exposed or defeated.

Many of those from my class at the Marlborough Infants were placed with me in Class Nine, along with some old friends and familiar faces who had earlier left the Marlborough and spent a year in the Town Infants, and as many again who were unfamiliar. The latter had been infants at the Town School, the Woodlands or elsewhere. There were always over forty of us in the class throughout our time here, each with a desk and chair, in seven or eight rows facing the teacher. In Class Nine, this was Mrs Nicolson, a small, stoutish, elderly, grey-haired lady with a loud, rough voice that brooked no argument.

Outside, the asphalt playground was always quite tidy, and the school building looked neat enough, but although the inside was also clean, the colour scheme was dismal, with its dark brown stained and varnished woodwork, green painted brickwork up from the floor to the dividing black stripe, and cream painted brickwork above. The classroom seemed crowded and confined, and the windows, above distraction level, offered little relief.

Our classroom had a blackboard, some cupboards, a high shelf holding books round two walls, and massive radiators heated by water from the coke-fed stove in the boiler room, which was stoked and fed by the caretaker. The permanent caretaker was Mr Taylor, who lived in the house on the Twickenham Road, between the school's two front gates, but he was called up into the army and during that time we had a temporary caretaker. The caretaker was always intent on his job, quite detached from us children, and rarely if ever spoken to, let alone annoyed, because we all understood that he was protected by the stern authority of the school.

Early in September, the Italians surrendered, and we got a half day's holiday to celebrate, but this glimmer of joy and hope was shortlived as we were soon back reluctantly but nevertheless rigorously applying ourselves to the task of learning the basics of maths and English. The three Rs were the priority. Sums were put up on the blackboard and copied into our books, to be calculated and marked. Maths proved to be a bit of a struggle for me, partly as a result of a lack of understanding, and partly through carelessness, but to my surprise I kept pace with the middle ranks. Tables were learnt by repeating them out loud in concert, and reinforced by individual questions, and the drone of recitation contrasted with the silence while we struggled with sums in our exercise books. We graduated from pencil to pen and inkwell. We learned how to form letters correctly, and how to join them together. We read aloud in turn, and received 'speech training', or we read silently. We took dictation or copied phrases, sentences and vocabulary off the blackboard. We were put through spelling tests, and we were taught the basics of grammar: verbs, nouns, adjectives, plurals and punctuation.

Luckier than some in one respect, I had at least a little aptitude for English. I could read and spell, and string words together grammatically. When Mrs Nicolson introduced us to the word 'prodigious' from a storybook, I incorporated it into my next story, just as she had recommended we should try to use all new words we encountered. As a result, I was singled out and made to read my story out to the class. It was an uncomfortable feeling, being used as an example of how to do it right, especially for such an apparently easy thing. I tried to keep a lower profile after that.

There were reading books on the shelves above our heads round the classroom, and every so often we had a period in which we could choose a book and read to ourselves. In this way, and also partly through listening to stories being read to us at school or on the wireless, I absorbed more of the classic children's stories that we did not have at home - *Treasure Island, Rip Van Winkle, William Tell, King Arthur and his Knights of the Round Table, Ali Baba and the Forty Thieves, The Just So Stories* and *The Jungle Book*.

A book off the shelf I returned to time and again was an ancient volume that gave an account of the daily life of a native boy in the Belgian Congo. The narrative describing the constant search for food, the boy's serious demeanour and the very starkness of his existence, together with the coloured illustrations that showed him nearly naked in the jungle and in a canoe paddling up a dark, tree-lined river, created a picture of life so foreign to my existence that it seemed quite unbelievable.

Our routine was interrupted two or three times a week when we were marched outside to the playground or field for 'drill', but if the weather was too bad, we used the hall. 'Drill' involved forming up into lines to do regimented exercises, and then perhaps (but only if we had been good) playing a team game or two.

Singing was another regular lesson, which unfortunately was to leave me at odds with the majority. The song book was comprised of traditional airs which at the time I found very uninspiring. 'The Two Crows' was quite incomprehensible and one of the worst, but whether the songs were more lively, like 'Soldier, Soldier, Won't You Marry Me', 'Fire Down Below' or 'What Shall We Do With The Drunken Sailor', or more melodic, like 'Early One Morning', 'Sweet Lass Of Richmond Hill', or 'The Rio Grande', I nevertheless felt the apparently spirited and joyful sounds were forced and false, perhaps akin to the desperate enthusiasm with which hymns were sung prior to a Victorian workhouse dinner. My favourite, or the song I found least depressing, was 'Pretty Little Polly Perkins', and I would perhaps have paid even more attention had I realised that my forebears had lived in Paddington in Victorian times. Popular music of the day never got a mention within the school walls, although I have no doubt we would have put heart and soul into singing 'Deep in the Heart of Texas' or 'Beat me Daddy, Eight to the Bar'.

However, the seemingly dull material and dismal circumstances were not the only reason I became disenchanted with singing. One day early on in that first class, we were marched into the hall (we were marched everywhere), lined up with other classes, and told to 'sing up' on the selected piece, then, while Mrs Nicolson pounded her accompaniment on the old upright, other teachers moved up and down the lines listening to each individual. 'This one can't sing a note,' one said, her ear at my mouth. 'You - go over there.' I walked to the side of the hall, and saw a few others pushed out in my direction. The rest of the class were to sing in a concert with other schools, but we were not. Consequently, on their rehearsal lessons, and on the Big Day of the concert, the unmusical relegates were taken into one of the wooden hut classrooms at the back of the school, each so remote as to have its own coke stove, and we had to participate in acting out *Alice In Wonderland*. Although music became an important part of my life, I never again had the confidence to sing in public, and I never liked *Alice In Wonderland*.

The school hours were nine o'clock until twelve, then half-past one until four, although we had to be in the playground by ten to nine and twenty past one. Whenever we were in the playground, either before school started or during the mid morning and afternoon breaks, we were controlled by the whistle. There was a duty teacher, sometimes visible, sometimes not, but when it was time to go in, the first blast of the whistle meant 'stand stock still', and anyone who moved had their name taken for punishment. On the second whistle, we ran across and 'lined up' in our classes facing the school, with the duty teacher out front and others prowling the lines. All being well, each class was told to march off into school in turn. If Mr Hunn was on duty, he would call out, in his thick accent, 'Heyft, heyft, heyft right heyft.' It was always a sobering, almost sombre preparation for being swallowed up by the dreary darkness of the building, and we were never in any doubt as to who was in control, and what was our proper place.

We always entered school through the side door, the front door by the hall being reserved for visitors. Beyond the side door, and round the back of the school, was the playing field, the furthest half of which had been excavated to provide an air raid shelter, in the standard form of a network of concrete tunnels, with a main entrance facing the school and the whole being covered by turf.

The register was called in the classroom, and we answered 'Here' or 'Present'. We filed into the hall for assembly on most mornings, where Mrs Nicolson would thump out the hymns 'And Did Those Feet', 'The Lord Is My Shepherd', 'Jerusalem', and Mr Brown, the headmaster, would lead us in prayers. He was regarded with some curiosity, owing to the persistent legend that he had a removable glass eye, and this appeared to be confirmed because he sometimes wore a black eye patch. He usually spoke to us about life in general, and I especially recall his account of the time he spent as a student in Berlin in the 1920s. When he told the story, the war against Germany was at its height, and if he was trying to make a point about Germany in peacetime, I must have missed it, because the only thing I retained was his interesting description of the storks that built their huge nests at the top of the factory chimneys there.

One morning the playground was buzzing with the story that someone had been murdered in the school hall the previous night, and that there was blood everywhere. Nobody was sure, but some said it was a sea-scout, and that it had been a shooting, and others that a knife had been used. A very brief official statement was made, but it told us little except that a boy had died, and one knew better than to question teachers. Our parents knew no more, but years later I learnt that the hall was hired out to the sea-scouts each week, and on this occasion one lad had secretly brought in his father's pistol to show the others. He did not know it was loaded, so when he pulled the trigger a bullet ricocheted off wall and floor, fatally wounding another boy.

At around the same time, we heard that two boys had burnt down Holy Trinity Church in Hounslow, and All Saints Church in Isleworth. We did not know who the boys were, but were baffled by the motive for such a terrible thing, especially in the midst of all the destruction of the war. The enormity of the act was difficult to comprehend.

At the Marlborough Infants, children said and did 'rude' things, which we all took in but kept hidden from adult awareness. It was there I learnt that in addition to discovering Australia,

'Captain Cook done a poop,
Behind the kitchen door,
The cat came in and licked it up,
And said he wanted more'

and puzzled over the seemingly patriotic but irreverently antipodean verse:

'Red, white and blue,
Ya dirty kangaroo,
Sitting on the dustbin
Doing a number two.'

Swearing was, however, rare enough then among the infants to be virtually unknown. In contrast, I was immediately made aware of swear words at the Town School, because despite being forbidden, it was common among the juniors, although more habitual in certain individuals and only occasionally indulged in by most. It was nevertheless still largely successfully hidden from the teachers.

Falling once more into a trap which I seemed unable to recognise, I lifted my desk lid to get the appointed reading book out, and as a Huge Joke said to my nearest classmate: 'Bloody Black Beauty!' At the end of the lesson on Anna Sewell's masterpiece, I saw little Rose, my classmate, talking to Mrs Nicolson and pointing at me. I was summoned.

'I hear you've been swearing.'

'Yes, Mrs Nicolson. '

'I'm surprised at you. Swearing's not nice - don't do it.'

'Yes, Mrs Nicolson.'

I could not believe my fortunate escape.

For some reason - whether through the stress of air raids, over-confidence or sheer stupidity - within a short time exactly the same thing happened again. Little Rose scuttled out the front and I thought, surely I was for it this time.

'Is that right you've been swearing again?'

'Yes, Mrs Nicolson - sorry.'

'Is it a hobby of yours?'

'No, Mrs Nicolson.'

Pointing to the large silver pin that was fastened across the front of her tartan skirt, she said, 'Any more of that and I'll have to pin your mouth shut with this! Now go and sit down and don't swear!'

I could only surmise that she was not too enamoured of tell-tales, and perhaps my known family, slight frame and politely apologetic manner suggested it was out of character. I heaved a sigh of relief - again - and resolved not to show off any more, and not to trust little girl classmates.

Betty Knight was different. She and I were made class monitors, looking after the milk and the blackboard and doors and windows, and for a while we were quite friendly. She lived in North Street and her house was damaged by bombing, so they were in temporary accommodation. I was impressed by the calm way she talked about it. We had had bombs and incendiaries round about our house, and plenty of shrapnel, but little actual damage. Betty was a real casualty and, I thought, a brave one.

My route to school lacked the attraction of the old route to the Marlborough, but I gradually got used to the new journey, although there was still always the hazard of getting trapped by the Air Force twins, and that was something I dreaded more than dodging along during an air raid.

Of course, air raids continued all the while, if sporadically. Sometimes I would leave home in the morning and be pleasantly surprised to find the streets exceptionally quiet, with no other people about, leaving me to pick up and carefully select the best shrapnel, or the silver discs, but when I got to the playground and found it empty, I knew I was in trouble again. I would then run round to the back of the school, and there, on the far side of the field, in the shelter entrance, would be an irate, arm-waving teacher, shouting 'Hurry, boy, hurry! - get in here! - don't you know there's an air raid warning on?'. With a clipped ear, and listening to remarks about negligent parents, I would join the rest, reading, listening to stories, pretending to sing. Neither Mother nor I ever solved the mystery of how we kept missing those early morning warnings, as the Syon Lane siren was designed successfully to be a noise one could not ignore or fail to hear, even inside the house.

On the journey from home, I went down the road and round the corner, along the short stretch of Northumberland Avenue to Wood Lane. Then down Wood Lane to the Southern Railway level crossing. There was always a chance of picking up a companion along the way - Neil Spokes came down Wood Lane, and I passed the houses of Olive Millar and the Evans twins, Iris and June, who could not be told apart and were really too shy to speak to anyone. Crossing Parkwood Road I might encounter Bobby Minnis, Jack Trigwell, Betty Hervey, Malcolm Champion, Margaret Hensby, Irene Russell, Brian Tancock, Frances Lowe, Harry Sutherland and many others.

The level crossing was frequently closed, by great white mesh-covered gates that were normally at rest across the lines, but were swung round to crash shut and bar the road by the signalman, high up in his box on the west side of the crossing. On the east side, there were other narrow wooden gates through which pedestrians crossed the line, and these too would be locked shut with powerful springs just after the road gates.

There were usually several people waiting for the gates to open, and a number of cyclists as well as an occasional cart or motor vehicle. Watching the steam train go by was always interesting, and one never knew quite what to expect - an ordinary passenger train, with faces at the windows, figures in the doorways, and newspapers held up by invisible readers, or a goods train, with open trucks for coal, enclosed trucks for milk, petrol, animals, and flat trucks with great boxes of freight covered in tarpaulin, or camouflaged military equipment like guns, tanks, or other less easily recognised items.

The engines were all different too and interest grew, turning some boys into trainspotters, and others eventually into railway fanatics. I learnt to distinguish the different types by counting the wheels, the 2-4-2, the 2-4-0 and so on, and to watch for the nameplate and get the 'class', so I started to record the details in a book. Eventually, the keen spotters who also had pocket money began travelling to other crossings and stations, and to main junctions like Clapham and Willesden, where they 'got' the cream of the stock of the various lines - GWR, LMS, LNER as well as our Southern Railway. Mike and I made one journey to Willesden, equipped with sandwich and water bottle, but I never became a dedicated spotter, although I remained interested in whatever passed through our crossing. The boyish delights of steam stayed with me too - the powerful sound of the great engines blowing and pulling away from the platform, a glimpse of the fireman stoking the furnace, the clank of the signal, the rattle over points, the distant whistle, the soothing effect of the puffing rhythm in full flight, and of course, leaning over the footbridge to be enveloped in steam and billowy smoke.

A similar interest developed with buses, as they too were of many different types and individually numbered. Mike and I began recording the red buses, the LTs, STs, STLs, RTs, locally on the Great West Road and around Hounslow's Kingsley Road bus garage. Eventually we each got the London Transport bus number pocket-book, which was a register of all types and individual numbers in service, and we assiduously crossed through each one spotted. Sometimes we went as far afield as Brentford or Chiswick to get a bigger selection, and always carried our book if we were taken anywhere. We 'got' the Green Line buses too, but the Reading 'B' express bus was excluded, not being London Transport. It was nevertheless observed with interest as it stormed down the Great West Road every hour between Reading and Victoria, rather in the manner of a motor age stage coach.

Cars on the road were few, but still too numerous to bother with number plate spotting. Instead, we contented ourselves with recognising the make and model, and there was a huge variety, dating back to the 1920s. The common makes included the Hillman, which Mike's dad owned, Austin, which Mr Morrison and Mr Scales owned, Ford, Singer, Riley, Morris, Wolseley, Standard, Rover and others. Less commonly we saw the Alvis, Lanchester, AC, SS, Talbot, Lancia, Morgan three-wheeler, Lagonda, Aston Martin, Crossley, M.G., Bentley, and Jowett, like the one owned by Ray Plowman's dad in Roxborough Avenue. Mike, already a motoring enthusiast, claimed the distinction that his father was a friend of Mr Goff, who lived up Wood Lane, the man who had designed the superior but ill-fated Atalanta car, built in Staines, but lost to the world through bankruptcy.

Continuing the journey down Wood Lane, once over the level crossing, on the west side were a few light industries. The first, behind a high wooden fence, was the coffin maker's, which belonged to one of Father's friends from the Rising Sun circle, 'old Tommy Downs'. He was a short, rounded man, who wore a suit and waistcoat with fob watch, and sported a small ginger moustache.

In 1943, Father bought me a rabbit, a brown Dutch Buck with a white collar, and I named him 'Hoppity', after the rabbit character in a cartoon film entitled 'Hoppity Goes To Town'. We built a cage out of old boxes, with a wire mesh door, and he lived in that, under the verandah, being let out to roam in the garden each day.

I used to have to go round all the waste ground in the district looking for groundsel and other tasty bits for him to eat, and of course he had to have bedding. This problem was solved through Father arranging for me to collect wood shavings by the sackful from old Tommy Downs. The smell of the freshly cut and shaved elm in his sheds was quite overpowering, but I liked it, and drank it in. As it was wartime, quite a number of older men were employed there, and they were kept very busy sawing and planing the planks which were stacked everywhere, in racks, on trestles, and on the floor, but they always had time for a cheery greeting for me as I filled the old hessian sack.

We once went to visit the Downs' home in Whitton, where he lived with his wife and daughter, and I was a little disappointed that it turned out to be a house and not a farm, because it was 'old Tommy' who supplied us with our goose at Christmastime.

The next unit down Wood Lane was that of the scrap metal dealer who owned my treacherous acquaintance, the bulldog. Behind his high, rusty, corrugated iron fence could be seen the tops of piles of metal, ranging from old cars to the smallest components. Besides giving off lots of noise from metal handling and cutting, there was always spillage on the pavement outside, and we often took home pieces that looked interesting or 'useful'. There were small discs, wheels, rods, blocks, and a variety of turned and bored pieces, the condition of most being an irresistible shining silver. They found their way into our shed, and into oddment boxes, then eventually into the dustbin, and so probably back to the scrap yard. The collecting had to be done with a wary eye on the bulldog, watching the proceedings with fidgety unease from the Hudson Terraplane, and when it suddenly decided enough was enough and set up a barking alarm, we would scamper up the road clutching what we could. It was here, too, that we got the prized ball bearings, which we used as substitute marbles in our obsessive games along the route to and from school.

The last business at the bottom of the hill was a car bodywork and spraying unit, also behind a high metal fence, from which emanated more noise of cutting and welding, and the heady and overpowering fumes of what we were told was amyl acetate.

At the end of Hartham Road, I usually met up with Peter Cooper, and perhaps Tony Carter, Bernard Francis, or David Potter. We walked past Wood Lane Stores, where, on our better-off days, we could buy from Mr Loughram the butcher, a penny slice of Spam, the penny being handed carefully to Mrs West, the cashier. Then we were at Baxter's shop, on Baxter's Corner, where Peter always knew what all the latest lines were, whether it was sweets, stamps, drinks, as when Tizer became available, or some novelty, like the the day they started selling lemonade in green bottles with a glass marble for a stopper.

The London Road had to be crossed, and there was usually a policeman or 'special constable' on duty to see us over. Once, when Peter and I were dawdling home to lunch, a different special constable wearing a flat hat pulled out his truncheon, scowled at us and growled, 'If you come up here late like this again, you'll get this across your backs!' We were startled, and sufficiently impressed with his sincerity to regularly make fast time up Amhurst Gardens, until he disappeared and the memory faded.

Amhurst was to us a rather boring residential road, although but a few years earlier it had been Pound Lane, a narrow country lane flanked by ditches, with a number of resident tramps inhabiting the shrubbery on its borders. My elder sister and her schoolfriends used to often encounter 'Blind Jack' here, and some children would regularly pester him until he gave them pennies - a strange reversal of roles.

One day I met an older girl emerging from Alton Close, and we walked to school together. We got talking about Children's Hour, an important part of our daily lives, and I was surprised to learn that way beyond my limit of simply listening, although only eleven, she had corresponded with Uncle Mac, and supported some of his charitable efforts. She enthused over his efforts and bravery, as she said he had been badly wounded in the Great War, and then suffered again as a result of a serious car accident, but still did all he could for all children. I was not inspired to take up any active role as a result, but I did regard Uncle Mac in a new light. It gave greater significance to the disembodied but familiar and very comforting voice that we all listened to each night, and I felt there was a personal message in his 'Goodnight children - everywhere.'

Towards the bottom of Amhurst Gardens, on the way back from lunch one day, we were playing three-handed catch with the ubiquitous tennis ball (which seemed to defy the wartime shortages), when Miss Goff, a pleasant and attractive infants' teacher, walked by. For reasons which I could only explain as a desire to perpetrate another Huge Joke, I picked that moment to blow a raspberry, although not even remotely towards Miss Goff, of course. Nevertheless, she politely enquired my name and walked on to school. As I got nearer to school, my companions, Peter Cooper and Brian Bidgood, were able to confirm that I was in deep trouble and that, as they had not given their names, they were not, and suddenly I felt very foolish - my action had made no sense at all. I made a quick decision. I went into the playground and across to the Infants School, found Miss Goff's classroom, and luckily she was inside. I apologised, and said I could not explain it, but had not meant to be rude to her. She graciously accepted, and I walked away feeling both humble and relieved, but also wishing she was my teacher instead of Mrs Nicolson.

Small boys are inevitably drawn to explore waste ground, alleys, open gateways, and any other such irregularities off-road. I had become familiar with Quaker Lane and its little pathways, special trees, bushes, and smells, and the views through fences, like that of the bomb-damaged flat with the huge wooden beams holding the walls up. At the top of our road was 'the alleyway', which led to Wood Lane, and in it was the last piece of spare ground retained by Mr Allen the builder. His handyman, old Jim Connor, lived with his daughter at number thirty one Harewood Road, and he used this patch of land to park his handcart. We used to climb over the flimsy fence and have a game with the cart, and pick the apples off the only surviving tree on that patch.

Other local landmarks or registered hiding places included the pigbin and sandbin outside Miss Shepherd's, and the gap behind the electricity junction box in the stretch of Northumberland Avenue leading to Musgrave Road. On my new route to school, I found or was shown other places. There was the spare ground on the east side of Wood Lane, just before the level crossing, and over the road, the open access to Tourell's, the coppersmiths and welders, which had once been Marsden's nursery.

Off Hartham Road, Peter Cooper showed me the back alleys that ran up the side of the houses and round the back of the gardens by the railway. We had many a wild chase round those, as red indians or British soldiers, with other members of his gang. The houses on the north side of the London Road, opposite Pears' factory, also had similar alleyways, and as Brian Bidgood lived there, we got to play in those too.

On the south side of Hartham was an alley that led through a right angle to Wood Lane Stores. It was here that we retreated to inspect Tony Carter's find of a collection of black and white photographic studies culled from the magazine 'Health and Efficiency', and other forbidden sources. The astonishing pictures showed naked grown-ups disporting themselves in every conceivable outdoor activity, and for a first sighting of such variety of adult form and behaviour we had to give Tony top marks.

Further afield, at the top end of Wood Lane, there was the alley leading to Jersey Gardens, and another in Highfield Road, connecting it to Osterley Crescent, although this was considered to be the territory of the College Gang. The gloomy, fir tree-lined alley from The Grove to Harvard Road looked more interesting than it proved to be, because there was too much visibility through from either end. Similarly the alley that ran alongside the County School offered no protection from adult eyes, although it did have a certain charm that I did not recognise until I attended that School and became a fan of the thrush that sang all spring and summer from the branch of a gnarled fruit tree that stood just inside the old nursery wall.

We explored all these alleyways, and others like them. We knew which nearby inhabitants were vigilant, and which were usually absent. We knew the alleyway ruts, potholes, bushes, overhanging trees, the varieties and weaknesses of fence and wall, and the smells, overriding most of which was the 'doggy' smell - at that time, there were lots of local dogs wandering loose but not lost, singly or in pairs, and sometimes in packs of three or four. Often we encountered them, and often we knew whose they were, but many owners allowed them to wander during the day, and so we mostly ignored them and they ignored us.

In these secret places, we would have discussions, make plans, take decisions, and act out more of our fantasies.

In contrast with such pleasant distractions, at school we had a salutory lesson in discipline which probably helped many of us to studiously avoid being caught out in misdemeanours. The cane was reserved for the more flagrant and wilful breaches of the rules, although there were one or two lady teachers who did not like using it, or were not sufficiently adept, and they tended to send the girls to Mrs Redgrove for punishment, and the boys to Mrs Nicolson. Such niceties did not apply to Mr Hunn, who was both happy and adept and not infrequently sent the whole of his class out into the corridor to queue up and await their turn.

On this occasion, the first such in our experience, three older boys filed into our class carrying the cane and punishment book. Their names and punishment were duly recorded in the book, and the ritual commenced. 'Put out your hand.' Thwack! the hand recoiled and disappeared under the opposite armpit. 'Now the other one!' Thwack! the other hand disappeared under the first armpit. Two boys were dealt with, but the third, one of the many Joneses, took the first stroke, then set up a loud howling and danced about from one foot to the other with both arms firmly crossed over his chest. Mrs Nicolson, nothing loathe, swiped repeatedly at the crossed arms, which accelerated the dance and brought forth yelps that we thought would surely bring the whole school in, but it was no doubt a sign of the times that nobody looked in. Then it stopped, and she thrust the cane and book into his arms and bundled him out of the room. Turning to us, in our stunned silence, she said, 'He thought the more he cried the less he'd get!'

At Christmas, we were pleasantly surprised to find that the tradition of a classroom party was to be continued here. Mrs Nicolson's son and daughter, Kenneth and Jean, came to help out, and we were again surprised, this time to see that she had two normal and pleasant children. Her discipline was strict and she had no time for flippancy, but in hindsight we all benefited from her efforts to drum in the three Rs. It was in her character to be hard-working, and other circumstances no doubt resulted in the no-nonsense approach, for we were not to know that she was widowed, and only thus able to work on as a 'married' teacher, and we knew nothing of the determined single-handed struggle with which she got her children to university, from whence they both became doctors.

For the Christmas party, despite the rationing, we brought whatever our mothers could spare in the way of cakes, drinks and sweets, and we had a few decorations round the walls, mostly of our own making. We were told we could bring games, and I asked if I could bring my conjuring set, to which Mrs Nicolson agreed. This turned out to be one of my Slight Misunderstandings. I had no idea she would make me stand in front of the class and give a performance. Some would have jumped at the chance, no doubt, but not being a natural performer, I gabbled and fumbled my way through one or two of the easier tricks until she said, 'No, no, no - not like that. You've got to tell them what you are doing, and show them all, like this: "Now ladies and gentlemen [my magic 'spot' box in one hand, and the wand in the other] you see this ordinary box, I am going to make it disappear!" ' Then she handed it to me and said, 'There you are then, now off you go, like that!' I unfortunately was not going anywhere. I did my best, but I could not do 'the business', and I had been compromised by her suggestion that I could actually make the box disappear, when in fact it was a mere change in the colour of its spot, so I was glad to exit stage left at the first excuse and reclaim my anonymity.

At the end of March, Mrs Nicolson left to become head of the Isleworth Blue School and her place was taken by Miss Richmond. She was pleasant and competent, and in addition to the normal subjects, had a special responsibility for needlework in the school. Consequently there was something of a drive to encourage our practical skills, not only with the raffia making, but also by getting each of us to make a purse, cut out from canvas, lined with material and covered outside with our knitted woollen decoration. It took weeks, but mine was eventually presented to Mother. Another smaller one that we made, I used for keeping my small collection of foreign and special coins, and hid it safely, or so I thought, in the red money-box made like a pillar box, that I kept on the dressing table. A few years later, a daylight intruder climbed over our side entrance, broke in the back door, burgled the house and the treasured contents of the little purse were taken.

There was, in Miss Richmond's time, a vogue at school for 'French knitting', a technique based on winding wool round nails banged into the side of the incredibly useful cotton reel. It was simple enough to occupy an idle child's hands, and we all had a go before leaving it to the girls, who produced many an iron or pot holder, or place mat, and even shopping bags.

I was not afraid of the dark, but every night at this age, fear visited me in the hour between going to bed and falling asleep. I still suffered from the 'shrinking furniture' syndrome, but I believe I was also subconsciously affected by the anxiety which Mother felt each evening in anticipation of the air raids, or perhaps I was just going through a natural phase of self-induced terror. I did not mind going to bed, but I had become convinced that there were hostile and malevolent beings able to enter the room as soon as I was alone. Certainly, as Mother's footsteps grew fainter down stairs, and the landing light went off, foreboding gripped me, and when she went into the dining room and the door shut, leaving total darkness (it was so in the 'blackout'), my mind began working furiously to combat the fear and to think what to do, or of some absorbing distraction. I tried to last out until Pauline came to bed, usually about an hour later, and if an air raid occurred, the activity was as welcome as a real-life rescue. When I had learnt a prayer or two, I regularly added my own, 'Please, God, do not let there be any burglars, murderers or ghosts'. When that did not produce any relief, I might try calling out for a drink of water, and then summon up the courage to ask for the light to be left on, although that was not agreed to very often, as neither Mother nor Father could determine what I was afraid of. That was not surprising - well, 'they' were only there when I was alone.

When I heard the dining room door open, I would watch and hope the landing light would go on next, because then it usually meant Pauline was coming up to bed, and when she did, providing nobody else came up, we would often hold a hushed conversation 'through the wall'.

'Is that you, Paul?'
'No - dees is Funf shpeaking.'
'Have you come up to bed?'
'No, I've come for my dinner.'
'What have you been listening to?'
'The Happidrome.'
'How does that song go?'

(To the tune of the 1941 hit 'We Three')
'We three, in Happidrome,
Working for the BBC,
Ramsbottom, and Enoch, and me.'

'Do the one about the squashed tomato.'

(To the tune of 'The Ash Grove')
'Old Tony's got a bunion,
A face like a pickled onion,
A nose like a squashed tomato,
And legs like matchsticks.'

'Tell me about what happened at school.'
'What about school?'
'You know - Trevor Cullum.'
'Well, he was always acting the fool, and he used to give silly answers to Miss Keene's questions, and she would say, "Don't be a clown, Cullum!" '
'And what does Miss Cook call people?'
'A grubby little scrub.'

'Do the one about going to the pictures.'

(To the tune of 'My Bonnie')
'I went to the pictures next Tuesday,

And took a front seat at the back,
I said to the lady behind me,
I cannot see over your hat.
She gave me some old broken biscuits,
I ate them and gave them her back,
I fell from the pit to the gallery,
And broke a front bone in my back.'

'Say that poem, the Latin one.'

'Tum garitulus merulae,
Dulcia alludit,
Philomena carmine (kar-min-ay),
Dulcia concludit.
- you will have to go to sleep now.'

And, reassured as I was by company, the real and imaginary
worlds would merge into dreams.

Isleworth Town School and playground.

Isleworth Town School - 'the bushes' and 'the hut'.

'Lawn Lodge', with the Town School on the right,
and Mandeville Road on the left.

The Duke's River, St. John's Road, where ducks dabbled.

Isleworth Town School staff and sports teams - 1938. Staff: seated extreme left: Miss Keene; extreme right: Miss Grout; Standing from left: Mrs Nicolson; Mr Constable; Miss Marshall; Mr Bevan; right side: Miss Pegg; Mr Hunn; Mr Brown (Head).

Isleworth Town School - post war pupils, 1953. Sylvia Betts, back row, third from right.

Isleworth Town School Staff and sports teams 1939. Staff: from left: Miss Webb; Mr Brown; Mrs Nicolson; Miss Groves; Mr King; Mr Neal; Mr Pridham; Mr Thorpe; Mr Hunn; Mr Bevan; Miss Keene; Miss Pegg. Pauline Betts, back row of pupils, fourth from right, in front of Mr Hunn.

Ashton House School staff and pupils, 1945. Staff include Miss Lake (Principal), Miss Brizley, Miss Smith, Miss Waraman. Pupils include David Ledbetter, Elizabeth Livingstone, Barbara Reynolds, Carol Ann Chitty, Brenda Williams(on), Doris Seal, Ralph Bodilly, Gillian Martin, Jacqueline Watts, Shirley Rhodes, Gill Bird, Richard Redman, Robert Wilson, Jack Foster, Susan Allen, Jill Simpson, Gillian Gamber, Brenda Lamsten, Rodney Poulter, Christine Parsons, Rosemary Meredith,

Chapter Eleven

Literary Legacies

'Mansion House' polish used a cartoon portraying the adventures of a family of mice to advertise their product in a 1930s household magazine. At three years old I was too young to read, but would often lie under the sideboard and pore happily over these pictures, which were no doubt based upon 'Teddy Tail' of the Daily Mail, and showed the mice living in a house much like ours. This was my first conscious experience of becoming absorbed in a book on my own account.

Another early oddity was a scrap book of 'Pip, Squeak and Wilfred' cartoon strips, which Aunty Em had culled from the Daily Mirror and pasted in. The stories were read or explained to me, and as a result I extended my vocabulary to include the word 'Oinck!'. The other memorable thing about this book was the unique smell arising from some unidentified ingredient in the paste.

We had an accumulation of books, some of which were adult and some children's. Of the latter, Pauline's books were the best preserved, and these included Beatrix Potter's *Peter Rabbit* and *Jemina Puddleduck*, a storybook with a number of intricate pop-up pictures, and a colourfully illustrated 'Noah's Ark', in which the menfolk had straggly beards, ragged trousers and open-toed sandals, giving them a suspicious resemblance to hillbillies, as much to biblical characters. She also had an old annual with a distinctly Dutch flavour, windmills, clogs, speed skating on frozen dykes and so on, imbued

155

with a certain harshness, as exemplified by the fascinating cartoon story about a lazy boy with long, thick hair who ended up tied upside down to a wooden pole and being used as a mop.

The general stock included *Alice In Wonderland*, a black and white *Bonzo* book about four inches square and two inches thick, portraying the adventures of the popular 1930s cartoon dog, Charles Kingsley's *The Water Babies*, in which I had coloured the pictures with crayon, *Aesop's Fables*, a *Mickey Mouse* annual, *Budge and Betty at the North Pole* by Ernest Prothero, which contrived to mix the adventures of Prince Zoolog, Thickrug the bear and others with sound geography and interesting pictures of bighorn sheep in the Rocky Mountains, a rag nursery rhyme book made of soft but indestructible cloth and having a musty but long familiar smell, and a superb and very large book of nursery rhymes, with the Queen of Hearts on the blue hardback cover, well illustrated and containing all the best-known items.

Learning to read came quite easily, and I enjoyed finding out about new words. My ability developed, but I never wanted to let go of those books I had enjoyed, partly because they were not being replaced by enough new books, and partly because the pleasure in them continued, and so these resident favourites were picked up countless times and read or browsed, gazed at and dreamed over.

I drank in the stories, but the illustrations always made a big impression too. I had a large paperback book based on *Jack and the Beanstalk*, but featuring Mickey Mouse as Jack, with detailed drawings of the Giant in his domestic surroundings. His sprouting bristles and stubby fingers and toes with their too-short nails were outstanding features, and equally fascinating was the huge piece of Gorgonzola cheese riddle with holes in which Mickey hid. We never had Gorgonzola, usually Cheddar, which Father called 'mousetrap', but I developed an appetite for cheese just by looking at the pictures. The Thurlows gave me a 'Granpop' annual. Granpop was a 1930s cartoon orang-utan, and again there were wonderful pictures, notably those with details of Granpop's half eaten fruit, like carelessly discarded banana skins and nibbled apple cores, and a superbly colourful and atmospheric picture of a group of elves sitting on toadstools in a wood clearing, their backs towards me as they enjoyed a moment of silent reflection watching the huge red orb of the setting sun sinking below the tree line. It was captioned 'Supper Time'.

Pauline had compiled a decorative and interesting scrapbook from pre-war cards, crackers and magazine pictures, and occasionally, as a special treat, she would let me look at it. My favourite pictures were two glossily illustrated half-page jokes, one of the two Scots in a shop, the shopkeeper withholding the goods while the customer withheld his money, neither wishing to be the first to hand over, and the other being of the golfer searching for his invisible ball on a beach of golf-ball sized pebbles. I wasted a lot of time trying to spot the ball.

In Father's Daily Express, I followed the adventures of Mary Tortell's *Rupert Bear*, sometimes cutting out and collecting a whole adventure. I was given a number of the yellow hard-backed Rupert books as presents, and found the stories all quite believable as he encountered brigands, discovered mystery castles and built an autogiro, along with his pals Bill and Algy, and visitors from afar like Ping and Pong the pekinese.

Unlike a number of my classmates, I did not get a comic delivered weekly - there was no question of using scarce money in that way. Luckily, I did get given used comics, and gradually built up a collection, which I liked to browse through. I thus had copies of Dandy, Beano, Playbox, Radio Fun, Knockout, and especially enjoyed Korky the Kat, Pansy Potter (the strong man's 'dotter'), Dennis the Menace, Desperate Dan, with his stubbly chin and huge appetite for cow pie, and Lord Snooty and his Pals. I found most of the characters amusing, and they and their doings were often the subject of discussion at school, although I was never up to date. Around 1945 a quantity of American comics appeared and were circulated, but they seemed to be aimed not so much at children as at childish grown-ups, and I found them far less entertaining than ours.

When I was away from school for a short time, recovering from some ailment at the age of ten, I was given the Puffin book *Worzel Gummidge*. I really enjoyed it, and it conveyed lasting images of farm and country in autumn, with muddy yards, falling leaves, thinning hedgerows, flapping rooks above windswept trees and cosy farm kitchens, creating an unquenchable appetite for such characteristically English surroundings.

Miniature books appeared during the war, to combat the paper shortage. They ranged upwards from about two inches square, some on thin paper, others with cloth covers, but all illustrated and in colour. On the way home from school, Jean Redford showed me the first 'flicker' book I had seen, where flicking the pages made the images appear to move, but this one was special, because you had to wear cardboard spectacles with tinted cellophane lenses to get colour and a sort of three-dimensional effect.

The Thurlows passed on to me a book called *The Book of Railways*, which became a firm favourite. It was a mixture of facts concerning actual railways and trains, and the adventures of some children in connection with the railways. The illustrations of railway scenes with named engines gave some impetus to my contemporary hobby of trainspotting.

At Christmas 1944, Dennis gave me *True Tales of Sail and Steam*, by Shalimar. Although apparently an ideal boys' book, and therefore a possible step out of the nursery literature, it proved way beyond my grasp at nine. In later years, it was interesting to discover that it was still heavy going with its laboriously detailed account of otherwise dramatic incidents at sea.

My breakthrough into boys' stories really happened towards the end of 1945, when I read Conan Doyle's *Rodney Stone* from the shelf in the top class at the Town School. However, although by that time I had either read or listened to many of the classic tales - Johann Wyss's *Swiss Family Robinson*, RL Stevenson's *Treasure Island*, Daniel Defoe's *Robinson Crusoe* - I had almost no good boys' books of my own at home, and when my pals offered to exchange, I could still only produce the children's books that had served all along.

It was not until I was nearly eleven that this was rectified when I received from Aunt Rose a collection of cousin Peter's annuals and adventure books, as he was by then long past such fiction and serving in the Royal Navy. There were books published by Blackie, and Herbert Strang's *Omnibus*, and various *Bumper* and *Champion* books, all being filled with stirring tales of Red Indians, the

Mounties, Scotland Yard detectives, spies, racing car drivers, sailing boats and smugglers, polar treks, jungle journeys, grizzly bears, and boarding school bullies and heroes. There was also a large edition of Robin Hood. They were all illustrated - I would gaze for long periods at a very striking and stirring colour picture of a Pawnee Brave on horseback - and at last I had a stock of something to read that my classmates were interested in.

Mrs Harris, at number forty nine, was personal assistant to Professor AM Low, pre-war president of the Interplanetary Society, and she gave me a book he had written for boys, entitled 'Adrift in the Stratosphere'. It had been published about 1939, and was an early science fiction adventure, in which three boys find a rocket in a barn, get inside it, and accidentally set it off. It takes them into space, where they encounter Martians and other extraordinary things before returning safely. This was a whole new area, and after discussing it with Mike ('Muss') Hayward from down the road, he showed me a short story on similar lines in one of his boys' adventure books. We enthused over the concepts, and speculated long over what might be found on the planets and in distant galaxies.

I struggled through Fenimore Cooper's *Last of the Mohicans* - both Peter Cooper and I had been given copies for Christmas - but it was hard going, and I had more enjoyment from *Peril on the Amazon*, a cracking adventure by Douglas Duff. *The Bats of St Bede's* (B. de Guerin) was another present that I could not put down. It was a story of St Bede's school, and to become a 'Bat', a member of the school's secret society, the boys passed an initiation test by swinging from one beam to another in the dead of night, holding onto the clapper of the huge bell in the belfry. Of course, as the school was near the sea, they just happened to spot a German submarine signalling to shore, and were instrumental in capturing the enemy and the local traitors, which fuelled my interest in spies and detective work, as well as secret societies.

Around 1942, Dennis, Pauline and Phil Harris formed a local 'Spitfire Library'. This entailed pooling the adult books that resided in our houses, and loaning them out to neighbours and friends for a fee which was donated to the Spitfire Fund to help build more fighters. For their efforts they each received a silver-coloured metal

Spitfire lapel badge. The stock in our house, most of which I was to read eventually, was mainly of the romantic thriller or adventure genre, plus a few oddities. It included books by Sax Roehmer (*Fu Manchu*), Joseph Conrad, Sapper (*Bulldog Drummond*), Leslie Charteris (*The Saint*), Damon Runyon, Peter Cheyney's wonderful *Sinister Errand*, and such other titles as *A Century of Thrillers* (*Poe to Arlen*), *The Buffalo Hunters*, Swift's *Gulliver's Travels*, Edgar Wallace's *The Four Just Men* and *Sanders of the River* (which later got referred to as 'Ay-ee-o-ko, yea-ga-tare', following the film with Paul Robeson), *The Blue Lagoon*, *David Copperfield*, *Jane Eyre*, *Three Men in a Boat*, the anonymous *War Birds - Diary of an Unknown Aviator*, *Secret of the Creek* (Victor Bridges), and *Boy Woodburn* (Alfred Ollivant). Oddities included Cole's *Fun Doctor* (humour compiled by EW Cole), *Dr Brewer's Guide to Science* (c1860), *A Humorous Reciter* (more humour, compiled by Ernest Pertwee), *Aircraft and the Air* (Eric Sargent), *The Dunlop Book - Motorist's Guide, Counsellor and Friend* (c1920), and *Dr Jaeger's Health Culture* (advocating that all clothing should be made of wool, even handkerchiefs!)

Dennis belonged to the public library and, around 1945, he took me along to both Isleworth and Osterley where I joined the junior section. My first borrowed books were stories of wild mustangs in the Wild West, a taste which was in part prompted by my own storybooks, and partly by the fact that both Father and Dennis often borrowed westerns by Zane Grey and others.

I discovered *Tarzan* at Osterley library, and went on to read all of Edgar Rice Burroughs. It was at this time that I paid a routine visit there with Mike ('Muss') Hayward, during which he unintentionally but unquestionably left his mark upon things. We were queuing to get our books stamped, with Mike in front. After stamping, you passed through a waist-high, polished wooden door, but only if the librarian released it with the hidden push-button. Mike, inspired by some of his more athletic book heroes, decided not to wait for me or the button, and vaulted the gate. Unfortunately, he had calculated without his raincoat, which caught on the top, and amid the hitherto hushed and hallowed atmosphere, broken only by the occasional cough, the rustle of a newspaper, the flick of a page and the subdued thump of the rubber stamp, he crashed to the ground beyond the barrier like a felled oak. In the pin-drop silence that followed, and while Mike sucked in air, one could feel the score or more of Osterley-conservative-and-tennis-club eyes turning doorwards, and then the prim bespectacled lady librarian, bristling with outrage and shock, looked down at his ticket, peered over the top of the counter at the tangle of legs, coat, books and arms on the floor, and said in a strangled voice, 'Michael Hayward - don't you ever, ever do that again!' The faces that had turned towards us, registering disappointment at what they may well have considered an anti-climax after witnessing the cardinal sin of a Huge Noise, went back to their browsing, and Mike, keeping low to the floor, made a hastily scrambled exit through the swing door, while the now crimson librarian stamped my books inaccurately and with unseemly vehemence.

That episode had something in common with Richmal Crompton's *William*, and at eleven I was at last able to enjoy these stories, as did Mike Curwen. We both picked up the language and the ideas, and when we set off to the park, we spent time looking for William's kind of adventure and imagining his reactions.

At eleven or twelve, I was reading the school stories, including classics like *From Pillar to Post* by Gunby Hadath, and there were many less well-known examples on the shelves then. They were ripping tales of sporting heroes and 'good eggs' who became head boy, who defeated and reformed bullies, exposed local criminal gangs, and were incidentally successful academically, while being more enthusiastic over rugby, cricket, boxing or soccer. Boarding school was made to seem the breeding ground for true British bulldogs, and the 'dorm', study, quad, close and tuck shop were a manly and almost cosy substitute for the comforts of home. I was very taken with the whole scene, as long as it remained an imaginary one - the reality would have been unthinkable.

Among the more educational books at home, I had a partial set of Arthur Mee's 'Children's Encyclopedia' magazines, passed on by Mrs Harris, and some excellent books bought from Woolworths, each dealing with a period of English history. Each page had a score or so of small black and white drawings reflecting an aspect of the contemporary life, showing weapons, dress, produce, transport and so on. As well as the unbound magazines comprising Wilson's 'The Great War', Father also owned a set of *Harmsworth History of the World* in proper book form, but although it was illustrated, by comparison with the Woolworths' paperback histories, Harmsworth was all rather dry.

I had two fascinating Victorian school books, although nobody seemed to know where they came from. One was a 'science' book, and the other a 'nature' book, and between them they covered and illustrated stimulating topics like the history of fossil discovery, the great blizzard of 1881, and the mystery of the devil's three-toed footprints that appeared in the snow on roads and rooftops throughout south-west England during a single night.

A treat I was at last given, if only for a short while, was to be allowed to have 'The Champion' comic delivered each week from Baxter's. I was, for once, able to share up-to-the-minute adventures with school pals, and to swap for equivalent comics like the 'Wizard', or the 'Hotspur'. In the 'Champion', I particularly liked the exploits of 'Rockfist Rogan', an invincible and very English pilot and boxer who would be in action in the air at one moment, and then knocking out a German on the ground the next. Wilson the super athlete was another favourite, who in one story was actually running at fifteen miles an hour - unheard of and considered unachievable at that time.

The finest magazines I had were 'Modern Wonder', given me by Lennie Hills, and the 'Meccano' magazines given me by Phil Harris. 'Modern Wonder' was published every Wednesday in the 1930s, and although only a weekly paper comic-style magazine, it was large, with colour covers and centrepiece, and bursting with enthusiasm. It featured (pre-war) advances in science and technology with such stirring headlines as 'I flew at 400 miles an hour - and I thought I was dying!' (a flight in a Rolls Royce Kestrel with designer FG Miles). The centrepieces illustrated subjects like the equipment of The Royal Navy, detailing all the flags, badges, ship silhouettes, lights, ranks and signals, or detailed illustrations of the workings of a dam, or of famous locomotives, or special aircraft, and one notable spread was of a crowded underwater scene depicting the 'wonders of the deep'. There was motor racing coverage by TH Wisdom, mentioning great names of the time like Mercedes, Auto Union, ERA and Mays, Dobson, Nuvolari and Caracciola, and there were science articles about almost any subject, from optics, blind flying using the American invention 'Air Track', solar eruptions, model aircraft, natural history, the automatic pilot, naval gunnery, television, amphibious vehicles and stratospheric balloons, to lie detectors and Westinghouse's atom-smashing gun. There were great science-orientated adventure stories too, by Clifford Cameron, LT Driver, W Stanton Hope, Peter Barr, the unlikely-sounding Sheikh A. Abdullah, and my favourite tale, 'The Lost Kingdom' (Atlantis) by Ralph Stranger and G Bowman, with its underwater secrets, huge serpent and the mystical door that opened automatically when the moon shone on it.

The pre-war monthly 'Meccano Magazines' that I had were thick and glossy, and largely factual, with articles about Hornby trains, wagons, ancillary equipment and layouts, Meccano construction and modelling, stamp collecting, photography, descriptions of the workings of locomotives and aircraft, book reviews, competitions, and news from the Meccano Guild, the Hornby Company and from the worlds of engineering, science, manufacturing and transport.

There was always a page of jokes included, under the heading of 'Fireside Fun', mostly of the good old sort:

Detective: 'Got away, has he? Did you guard all the exits?'

Village Policeman: 'Yes, but we think he must have slipped through one of the entrances'

and some which I found hilarious, especially the word or language-based ones, like 'The Sleeper' ('asleep in a sleeper which travelled over the sleeper', etc), and 'The Recipe', in which the listener, wanting to write down a recipe, heard his early morning radio programme on cookery get mixed up with another station broadcasting a programme on keeping fit ('break three eggs ... over the head and rub briskly with a rough towel ... add pepper and salt and garnish ... with a pair of old plimsolls' etc).

Keeping the best till last, I always ended up browsing the many pages of advertisements, which were an Aladdin's cave of what seemed to be the most desirable and ingenious toys ever invented, once upon a time available for those who could afford them, from the legendary London toy shops like Hamleys', Gilberts', Gamages' and Bonds', or Lucas's in Liverpool, but of course largely vanished in my time owing to the war. I pored over penknives, pogo sticks, periscopes, pedal cars, clockwork cars, steerable cars, yachts and boats, roller skates, gyro cycles, gyroscopes, kaleidoscopes, telescopes, microscopes, magnifying glasses, night glasses, signalling lamps, sleuthing sets, archery sets, catapults, carpentry sets, and stock for stamp collectors. Major mouth-watering advertisements included Brock's Fireworks, Lott's Bricks (building construction), Lott's and Beck's Chemistry Sets, Harbutt's Plasticine, Hobbies Fretwork Sets, Hornby Railway Sets and Rolling Stock, Meccano Models and Constructor Outfits, Frog Model Aircraft, Dinky Toys and Dinky Builder Sets, Daisy Air Guns, Berwick's Wembley Miniature Football, and the intriguing Ernest Sewell Conjuring Cabinet. Even the less relevant seemed desirable - Drydex Batteries, Miller Dynamos, Pifco Meters, and good old Seccotine Adhesive.

Only one rare item came my way - a 'Seebackroscope', handed on by a neighbour but still in its box. The advertisement for it showed with a dotted line how this amazing device, clenched in your eye like a monocle, enabled you to see who was behind you without your pursuer realising he had been spotted. Another indispensable aid for the sleuth and, indeed, I rarely travelled without it.

The greatest legacy of all was the two comic supplement magazines, one being dedicated to the world's strongest men and the other showing the methods of the world's greatest detectives.

The 'strong man' magazine, besides describing amazing and inspiring feats and world records, by people such as Eugene Sandow, and George Hackenschmidt, both of whom Father had much admired in his time, also showed the way to exercise in order to build a body like those heroes. I did my best to follow it through, but from the start there were certain problems. I had no money to buy barbells or chest expanders, I had nowhere to suspend the sack full of sand that I was to use as a punchbag and, surprisingly, I was not allowed to screw a chest-lift bar into the doorframe of my bedroom. I made do with the remaining exercises, but concluded that I must have been made incorrectly, because physically there was little to show for it, even after two weeks.

The 'detective' magazine was easier to live up to. It was all a matter of observation and deduction, with a few aids thrown in, like a magnifying glass and graphite powder for fingerprints, a retentive memory, a knowledge of tracking, a few secret codes, good map reading, a torch for searching and signalling, and the ability not to be noticed. It gave rise to a lot of fun, and I was able to share that with my friends.

At the age of eleven, my whole reading spectrum was changing and I began to realise that, in addition to the sheer pleasure it gave me, great ideas and the answers to many questions could be found in books.

CHAPTER TWELVE

THE JUNIOR SCHOOL:
EDUCATION, MEDICATION AND RECREATION

The dark days appeared likely to go on forever, but the months passed, and after a year we moved up into Class Five with Miss Groves. She seemed pleasant, which gave us some hope, although for me it was not until the following spring and the end of the war that the all-pervading gloom began to lift. Fortunately for us all, Miss Groves was an exceptionally good teacher, as we were to find out.

During our time in Class Five, owing to staff absences, we were sometimes 'farmed out' to other teachers - to Mrs Redgrove (formerly Miss Keen), who taught us English while we tested her patience ('a female shepherd is a shepherdess, but a female actor is not an actoress, but an actress, so what is a female conductor? No, no, no, boy, not a clippie!'); to Mr Palethorpe, who taught us more maths, and to Miss Enstice, who taught us about art. She showed me how to draw with the pencil laid across the palm and resting on the little finger, a technique that I never mastered, but I was quite lost gazing at her as she gave me her full and most gentle attention, speaking with what seemed to be a trace of American, and leaving me feeling pleasantly disturbed. Miss Enstice, who in due course married her soldier boyfriend and became Mrs Tucker, was diminutive and pretty, but it was Miss Webb who was the most glamorous teacher. She came to school on a new Sunbeam bicycle, and in contrast to the rather drab, sensible and hard-wearing dress style of many of the staff, she wore colourful and fashionable outfits in mauve, red or purple, with matching scarf and hat and stylish shoes, her properly made-up face framed by auburn hair, and her white hands, when not encased in fur gloves, were tipped with scarlet nails. But I thought she always looked serious and, as I was never in her class, I used to wonder what she was really like.

Miss Pegg was a popular teacher, and we had some lively lessons with her, and also with one or two lesser lights, including a new young lady with red hair who, at the same time and to our astonishment, entered and won a Carroll Levis 'Discoveries' programme on radio, singing 'Cherry Ripe' in a fine soprano voice. We were forewarned and duly listened with some pride to the performance of 'our teacher', but the mould had been broken, her brief term at our school was quickly over, and our star departed. Was it a domestic crisis, or did she decide that the life of a professional singer was actually preferable to facing us every morning?

In the classroom I was making average progress, always being somewhere in the top dozen or so, although never right at the top. Peter was usually above me, and there were some very bright sparks, like Bill Klesel, Brian Ritter, Ian Fowler, John Rumins, and Geoffrey Alderton, who could not be beaten. English and related subjects still came easily, but maths troubled me and then, while I was away ill for a week, the class was introduced to 'mathematical problems', and my difficulties increased tenfold, although I found it easy enough to laugh at the burlesque versions - 'if it takes a week to walk a fortnight, how many apples in a bunch of grapes?' I did not catch up again until I got extra tuition while preparing for the scholarship a year later, and in the meanwhile I spent many a miserable lesson trying to guess what the method was for solving those nightmare conundrums, and being annoyed that the answer would often appear obvious once it was revealed.

The joyless singing lessons continued, although by now I had learnt to reduce the attention by singing intermittently and mouthing the rest. We added more traditional ballads to our repertoire - 'Cockles and Mussels', 'The Ash Grove', 'The Raggle

Taggle Gypsies-O', and even I was impressed as we became quite polished when a special effort was made to learn the sung version of the 23rd psalm, 'The Lord's my Shepherd, I'll not want'. The carols at Christmas fortunately never lost their charm, but hymns seemed to add to the gloom in the Hall, giving an almost fraternal feeling for 'those in peril on the sea', and suggesting an unwelcome if imaginary familiarity with those 'dark satanic mills'.

The poorer children at the Town School were generally better clothed than they had been at the Marlborough. All wore shoes, plimsolls or boots, although these might be split or 'holey', like the socks, which often had 'potatoes' in the heel. At least most children had socks by then.

The girls wore long or ankle socks, cardigans or jumpers, dresses, pinafores or blouse and skirt, under which they wore pink, white or blue knickers, cotton vests, winceyette petticoats, and in the cold weather, fleecy lined 'liberty bodices', which were a source of amusement to their brothers.

Some boys wore caps habitually while others, like me, wore them at times to protect against the rain or snow. Knitted balaclavas were worn by some, and Terry Tidy had a black leather hat with ear muffs and a strap under the chin.

There was a school badge bearing the white gothic cross taken from the Heston and Isleworth insignia. Some had it on their cap, but only a few had a jacket badge.

I wore long socks kept up by elastic garters, white cotton pants and vest in summer, and beige woollens in winter, and a grey or white shirt and grey trousers. In winter I also had a pullover and jacket and usually wore a tie, and if it was cold or wet I wore a raincoat and a home-knitted scarf, and perhaps home-knitted gloves too.

My clothes, if I did not outgrow them completely, were sometimes old and worn out from new, but often they were second-hand. New clothes were relatively rare and special, and any we had bore the utility label of 'two cut cheeses', but whether new or second-hand, all clothes were liable to get lost, torn or stained, and I was frequently in trouble at home for scuffed shoes. It was due to playing football with a tennis ball, but as I was always accused of kicking stones, I was able to protest my innocence.

At one time, I was made to wear a pair of second-hand shoes that had obviously belonged to a girl, because they had pierced hole patterns in the upper, but Father insisted nobody would know. He was wrong, of course, and I tried desperately to keep the holes filled in with blacking or mud, and kicked the shoes out as quickly as I could.

My baby teeth had long since become loose and fallen out one by one. Some were optimistically placed under the pillow, but only produced a sixpence on those occasions when such action was pre-arranged, confirmed and budgeted for. Once, while in Amhurst Gardens on my way to school, Eddie Baker threw a stone with such accuracy that it knocked out my relatively new centre-front-lower without damaging the lip. I must have been wearing a broad grin at the time.

Teeth, eyes and hair were regularly inspected and occasionally treated by the Busch Corner Clinic and their roving staff. The Clinic, where we also went for our inoculation and vaccination, was nearly a mile from the Town School. It was adjacent to Busch House 'Open Air School', which was presided over by Miss Burridge, and dedicated to disabled, delicate and convalescent children.

Nobody liked going to the dentist, even though it meant time off school. Mother had to come too, to ensure the victim did not escape, and there was always a queue, with babies and young children squalling and crying, a smell of mouthwash, ether and cloves, and an atmosphere of foreboding. My extractions were by gas - there were no gum injections - but apart from the panic at being smothered, the succeeding oblivion was merciful. A frosty nurse called your name, you were steered into the chair and then, before you could begin to socialise, you were peering into the dentist's nostrils, suffocating under the hissing mask, descending into blackness, and then blinking in the recovery room. Fillings were something else. With senses unimpaired by anaesthetic, the slow action drill seemed as shatteringly heavy as a road mender's, and the noise, vibration, and smell of burning molars was certainly not forgotten by the next visit. When you could wobble out of the recovery room, if you had been 'good' you got a sweet from the nurses, and started the whole rotten cycle off again.

It was through a junior school inspection by the Clinic that my defective vision was revealed. I was given further tests at Busch Corner, fitted with small, black metal rimmed glasses and ordered to wear them at all times - or go blind. I found them uncomfortable, unsightly and a nuisance, and throughout my schooldays I rarely wore them, although from time to time I got re-tested and issued with replacements, largely because I outgrew the frames. Old Sid Conquest, Father's optician, later established that the condition was hereditary, Father having an identical fault, and my sight changed little over the years, but I did not take to wearing glasses until, in my twenties, the proprietor of the Spring Grove Driving School, Pauline's school chum Trevor Cullum, pointed out that it was obligatory to read a number plate at seventy five yards for my driving test

At the regular hair inspections, the hapless few were singled out for treatment to frighten off lice or nits, but I escaped all that, although I suffered from dandruff, for which there was then no treatment. Mother rubbed in olive oil, but that did little except to darken the lining of my cap.

While at the infants' school, I had had chicken pox as well as German measles, but otherwise I appeared quite well, except for being hard hit by colds and sore throats, and disabling headaches. In a one-off broader physical examination, the Clinic doctors decided I was undernourished, and prescribed cod liver oil and malt. I could take cod liver oil quite happily, but the addition of malt turned it into a sweet substance of suffocating stickiness which glued my mouth and throat together and just would not go down, so I dramatically gagged my way free of that unpleasantness. This brings to mind the contrasting pleasure of the lip-smacking 'brimstone and treacle' (sulphur and syrup), which Mother dosed us with each spring 'to clear out the system'.

The visiting medical team also told me my ankles and insteps were collapsing, and after another visit to Busch Corner, I had to do daily exercises at home, walking on the outside rim of my bare feet, and picking up a pencil with my toes. Beneficial though this undoubtedly was, I had other hobbies that were far more interesting, and the days were too short to fit everything in. Besides, I could run and jump as well as anybody.

The playground was the focal point of our school social life. We entered it first thing in the morning, after returning from lunch, and occupied it during the morning and afternoon breaks.

Main features of the playground included the two front entrances flanking the caretaker's house, of which I always used the easternmost, nearest to Amhurst Gardens. The corner alongside this entrance was boarded up with huge hoardings, too close to the frowning authority of the school for us to follow our instincts and investigate what lay behind. On the opposite side, next to the western entrance, there was Lawn Lodge, an old house with a high dividing brick wall, and in the playground under the shadow of this wall ran 'the bushes', from the gate up to the large brick barn-like building known as 'the hut' or 'the shelter', which was meant to give us somewhere to go if it rained. Fortunately there never seemed to be an occasion when all six hundred scholars required shelter at the same time.

At the back of this shelter, a bench ran along the wall. It was rarely used for sitting on, but was the concourse for 'bench fighting'. The combatants would stand on the bench facing each other with the arm and leg nearest the wall advanced and raised ready to grapple, lever, shove or kick the opponent off the bench. Some champions, like Peter Naish, were very adept, and there would be Peter on one side and a queue of challengers building up on the other side to face him, one at a time.

The inner walls of the shelter were sometimes used by the girls to play 'donkey', forming a queue to throw a tennis ball against the wall and jump over the returning bounce, without being hit, which would put you out, and then running round to rejoin the queue. They also juggled two or three balls against the wall, in time to a chant that preserved a military incident which was somehow overlooked in our history books :

> 'Oliver Cromwell lost his shoe,
> At the battle of Waterloo,
> Left, right,

Left, right,
Attention, halt,
One, two.'

Further along the school wall and beyond the shelter was the brick built coke store, which was strictly out of bounds, although some brave souls raided it for missiles or to retrieve a lost tennis ball, and then came the outside toilets, where we were not expected to loiter. In front of the coke store was the flagpole, and on Empire Day, which was also my birthday, after a morning of lessons and stories concerning the Empire, the school would assemble facing the pole. Then, with the Union Jack flying, we would have a short ceremony, with a prayer, and a thought for our British and Empire troops, after which we were dismissed and away, running for the gate and freedom to enjoy a precious half day's holiday.

Some children living in the vicinity of St John's Road and the Woodlands would use the back gate. These huge gates were behind the school at the western end, and led via Smallberry Avenue into Linkfield Road and St John's. Occasionally I went that way for a change, or to accompany a friend, and then I always lingered over the railings by the Duke of Northumberland's River, to watch the ducks. This was a common enough distraction for passing children, but I was drawn in part because my sister often sang the 'Ducks' Ditty' from *Wind in the Willows*, and the words became associated with that spot:

'All along the backwater,
Through the rushes tall,
Ducks are a-dabbling,
Up tails all!',

'Slushy green undergrowth,
Where the roach swim,
Here we keep our larder,
Cool and full and dim!'

The other treat on that journey was to inhale the rich scent of hops from Isleworth Brewery, and to loiter round their gates and see the drays and huge kegs, and watch the women clattering across the cobbled yard in their clogs, until they started to call out to us, and then we would be off before they carried out their good-humoured threats to 'have us for dinner' or worse!

With up to six hundred children playing, the playground must have looked chaotic, and yet within that there were many small groups engaged in organised games of football, catch, 'he', marbles, cigarette cards, skipping and all the other traditional pursuits, and there were social circles. We knew where we belonged.

The closest circle was comprised of a few 'best' friends, which was often the result of living near to each other and sharing some mutual respect. Then there was a looser group consisting of those who were from nearby roads and who took the same route home. Those who sat near us in class might be best friends, but not necessarily - remember Rose!

The next closest group would consist of the rest of our class, and perhaps other acquaintances within the school. Then there was the rest of the school, and those you spoke to and those you avoided. We knew many of our own age and above by name, but paid little heed to anybody younger, unless they were related. In my case, outside of my classmates, all my friends were older than I was, but at that time no younger person latched on to me or my group.

On entering the playground we made for our close circle first, but failing that, we worked outwards until we found somebody to talk or play with. My own immediate circle comprised Peter Cooper, the leader, from Hartham Road, Brian Bidgood from the London Road opposite Pears, John Rumins from the London Road near Teesdale Gardens, and Tony Carter and Bernard Francis from Hartham Road. In my first year there, some of my older friends were in the top class, like Mike Curwen, Bert Hole and Ray Plowman.

It was Bert who originally uttered the title of this book, and Bert also had a great imagination. On one occasion, while walking to school, I told him about the little book I had, published by Colman's Mustard, which described the magical island a small boy discovered in the middle of the pond in his back garden. Bert then told me that in his garden they too had a pond with an island, and that he and his older brother Ernie had various electrically controlled boats and submarines which patrolled the waters and berthed in secret harbours and caves on the island. We both knew it was not true, but it was a kind of game to explore the wish, and it did not have to be prefaced by 'Wouldn't it be good if we had. . .'

The playground was generally ruled by one or two tough characters, who each had their close circle of mates, supporters and hangers-on. I learnt that the wise thing was to keep away from them, because they were liable to pick on anyone and make life even more miserable, just for something as trivial as eye contact, which would be challenged with 'Who are you looking at?', 'Am I wearing some of your clothes?', 'Do I owe you money?', or 'Having a good look then?', to be followed by encirclement and some form of prolonged taunting and possibly assault. If the ritual was interrupted, then the threat of 'I'll get you!' might keep the victim on the run for days. Ray Folly was one older boy that nobody wanted to upset, but when I first arrived, the real top dog was Roy Varley, and for the girls it was his sister, Joan.

There were plenty of ordinary fights, usually interrupted by a teacher, with the combatants hauled off for punishment. In an exceptional case, Bobbie Minnis and George Basley fought each other to a standstill, undetected. Even I was involved in one dispute with Billy Klesel, just over a matter of opinion, but it got no further than the customary initial shoulder-barging and the articulate...

'Yeah?'

'Yeah!'

'Yeah?'

'Yeah!'

before somebody shouted a warning and we all melted into the background.

Soon after I arrived at the school, there was a boxing tournament held in the hall which we all attended. The competitors, who were mostly boys in the top year, apparently stayed on one night each week for training, and I was especially impressed with the boxing of Mick Roberts from Syon Park Gardens, who won his bout decisively.

Some children were well known or popular for reasons other than their fighting ability - being particularly tall, or very small, for example. Freddie Peake was very small, but what made him better known was that as a very talented football player, on one occasion he was seen to dribble the ball straight through the legs of a tall opponent and out the other side, still in possession and running. Children with some sort of disability were popular and usually protected from bullying or too much taunting, although a little bit of poking fun was expected, and weaknesses were inevitably brought up as ammunition in the event of an argument. One child with hydrocephalus was sometimes brought to visit the school, and there was always an instant crowd of children round the pushchair, eager to be involved. Ginger Knapp was another boy with a large following. He had stepped off the pavement into the path of a trolleybus, and lost one leg. With his ginger hair and freckles, great spirit and fiery temper, he attracted a circle of helpers and admirers. They would play games and tease him a little, and then flee as he hurled his crutch at them like a javelin, occasionally succeeding in catching one in the back and 'downing' him. The helpers would rush to recover the crutch, and Ginger would be acclaimed top of the heap again.

Games in the playground were many and varied, although we could not carry anything much in the way of toys that could not be pocketed. The tennis ball was a firm favourite, and there were great games of football, or kickabouts, and throwing to catch, or we might play 'kingy', which meant that whoever was 'kingy' had to throw the ball hard to hit one of the others anywhere below the neck, although fists could be used to punch the ball away. 'Kingy' was a 'travelling' game and so could be played on the way home as an alternative to the casual heading, kicking and throwing. Stationary games like 'queenie' could only be played in the playground or in the road where you lived. This was more a game for the girls, or perhaps for a mixed crowd, in which queenie threw the tennis ball backwards over her head and, when ordered to turn round, she had to guess who had it. A correct guess meant swapping places. 'Piggy in the middle', with two people throwing a ball that the third person in between tries to catch, was a stationary game that was by and large relegated to the situation in which one had to amuse or tease somebody much younger, although it could be used in a rougher more knockabout fashion.

Another girls' game was 'O'Grady says', otherwise known as 'Do this, do that', in which O'Grady called out 'do this!' in accompaniment to poses which the crowd had to copy, but not if she called 'do that'. Speed was of the essence, and if you got caught out and moved on 'do that', you became O'Grady.

The girls also used a loop of string or wool to make string figures such as 'cat's cradle', and get someone to use finger and thumb to 'take off' and produce other designs like 'London Bridge', 'parachute', and 'witch's hat'. The ideas for this were brought originally from China by our sailors, and at one time their figures all had stories woven about them. The girls would also clasp their hands to show:

> 'Here's the church, and here's the steeple,
> Look inside and see the people.'

There were games of 'it' or 'he', and 'release-i-o', at the height of which you could get a moment's respite by calling 'fainites!' and pretending to tie up a shoelace, but 'hide and seek', popular at home or in the street, was not very feasible in the playground because we were not allowed in the bushes or the coke store, and there were few other hiding places. A few played 'fivestones', which was not strongly in vogue at that particular time, but there were other traditional games, like 'bung the barrel'. This entailed a boy bending down with hands outstretched to the fence, and a string of bent boys behind him, each clasping the waist of the boy in front. Then there was a queue of boys to take a run at the line and leap frog as far as possible along the backs to make room for those to come. The outcome was usually that the weight of the straddling boys became too much for the 'backs', and the whole lot collapsed on the floor.

The autumn brought conkers, and everybody had their strings

and engaged in battles to claim supremacy for their polished brown 'gladiators'. We tried all ways to toughen them up for the conquest - boiling, baking, soaking in salt water or vinegar, but despite all that they were liable to just give up and split at any time, and we all knew that those who claimed to have 'fifteeners' and 'twentiers' were fooling nobody.

Another seasonal game was making a slide, in the ice that formed around the drains in the middle of the playground. Surprisingly, it was usually tolerated by the teachers, perhaps because it was easily seen and avoided. If it really got going after being developed for a couple of days, there would be spectacular performances by those skilled enough to keep their balance on the glass-like stretch that might run for fifteen feet or so. There would be a permanent queue to 'keep the pot a-boiling', and the onlookers would shout encouragement to the best, and enjoy a good laugh and a jeer at those who were less skilled but equally entertaining in the sitting or fully recumbent posture.

Of course, if it snowed we played snowballs and got pelted or rubbed in it by older boys, and did rather better against our own age or younger. Coming home one darkening afternoon on such a day in the winter of 1944, Father let me in at the front door, but he had not noticed that water was running down the hall wall. He was not as pleased as I expected when I pointed out my discovery to him. A pipe in the loft had burst, a not unusual event in those unlagged times, and for a day or two the household was several degrees colder in a chaotic turmoil of rags, towels, ladders, buckets and blowlamps.

One of our main playground games was 'flicking' cigarette cards from a given line, either to 'cover' the opponent's card and take it, or to knock down one that had been stood against the fence, and so to win all those flicked unsuccessfully so far. I had a winning card with a magpie on it (Birds and their Young) and another magpie card stuck to its underside, thus making it a heavy and accurate but illegal 'flicker'. I was however, honest, and always declared it after the throw, so it was just a 'joker'.

Paper aeroplanes were a popular and simple pleasure. Providing you could get a good type of paper, and exercise book paper was the best, not newspaper or brown paper, then it was a matter of accurate folding and smoothing into the right gently curved shape to achieve the best flight. The planes were much more satisfying than the paper darts, which tended to have a single loop or straight flight. If, as sometimes happened, a good plane got caught up in a gentle air current, then it could fly for a surprisingly long time at around twelve feet off the ground, which was a thrill many of us enjoyed. We also made parachutes by tying a piece of thread to each corner of a linen handkerchief and tying the four ends of the thread round a lead soldier or a small stone. We then rolled it up and threw it as high as we could, and it would unfurl and float to earth just like the real thing - hopefully landing where we could recover it without it falling into the wrong hands.

One morning, when the playground was teeming with life as usual, shouts went up over by the shrubbery. As we all ran across, we saw coins flying towards us over the high wall of 'Lawn Lodge', seemingly by the handful, and moving progressively towards the shelter. The bushes may have been out of bounds, but they were soon alive with two hundred pint-sized paupers on hands and knees scooping up this amazing disowned treasure from the sky. The joy was short-lived. Teachers appeared from nowhere, rounded up everybody, and caused all pockets to be emptied. The loot was later handed to a policeman who came on the scene. As usual, we did not get an explanation, but the rumour was that a thief was being chased out of the house and was throwing the heavy coins over the wall to lighten his load and distract his pursuers. It made little sense, as the major distraction occurred away from the action, on our side of the eight foot wall, and it would have been a lot easier for the thief to simply drop the coins, but it was a good topic of conversation for a while.

We did not often play marbles in the playground, because of the difficulty of keeping the feet of the multitudes out of the way, and because we preferred the more rugged terrain of kerb and pavement. So instead we frequently played on the way to and from school, and although we were careful not to be late to school, we were often home an hour after we were expected. Marbles got chipped and worn in these games, so we tended to withhold those with the finest colour patterns, and we did not play much with the larger ones, called 'alleys'. The best looking marbles were semi-transparent with different coloured inner whirls, and I had a very special one with shades of golden brown and an overall smokey appearance. The small marbles were singles (larger ones being two-ers, or even sixers), and to win an opponent's marble, one had to make the equivalent number of strikes. There was some custom and jargon involved - 'bombs' being an extreme penalty where you claimed the right to compensate for your opponent's offence by standing over his marble to drop yours onto it, and 'Bags I go lardy' was a usefully confusing claim that some thought meant 'go last' and others said meant 'go first'.

So, there were arguments, but Pete and I played to the simplest of rules, and we were quite dedicated, often to be found in the gutters up and down Amhurst Gardens, or in Wood Lane, or along the London Road past Frazer Nash's, and past Rimmers, the newsagent where Peter's mum ordered his Dandy and Beano annuals, and so along to Brian Bidgood's house. Late on winter afternoons, unwilling to give in to the darkness, we must have been seen as strangely animated bobbing and flitting kerb-side shadows, and in the seclusion provided by a gathering yellow fog, we would all but vanish into that world of our own.

Hoppity and I came to the parting of the ways. He remained attractive and interesting, but the novelty had gone, leaving the labour and the strong smell, and I did resent the fact that far from showing gratitude whenever I took him out of the hutch for his time in the garden, he would flip his rear end and succeed in spraying me with urine, no matter how I held him. By mere chance, in chatting to Brian Bidgood about him, it turned out that he was keen to take over, so Hoppity moved house.

Brian lived opposite Pears' Soap factory, and the area was often permeated by the sweet smell of their finer products. Peter Cooper's dad, Dick, worked there and Peter told me of the unusual way his parents met. His mother, Dora, worked in a factory in Mansfield making decorative tinware packaging, some of which was destined for Pears. She and some of the other girls, for a bit of fun, wrote notes, including their names and addresses, and put them in with the packaging in the knowledge that they would be found by workers at Pears. Peter's dad replied, made the trip up to Nottingham and eventually they were married and lived happily ever after.

Peter's mum had a Nottingham accent and he used to tease her in front of us by getting her to say 'pup', which she did, laughing and in good part, pronouncing it 'poop' - a rude word in our southerners' circle.

Peter's house in Hartham Road was novel for me in that, like Brian's, it backed onto the railway, and somehow the proximity of passing trains and their passengers seemed more interesting and less impersonal with this private viewing. I was not a fan of felines, but because Peter had a cat called Smokey and his sister Jean had one called 'Whisky', I was able to see and understand his admiration of their aloof detachment. The house was gas only, so lamps had to be lit by match and the radio ran off an 'accumulator' battery, which Peter had to regularly take to Stella's cycle shop in Linkfield Road and exchange for a charged up one. I often accompanied him on this novel errand.

When he was ten, Peter had a birthday party, mostly for his school friends, and we had a jelly and cake tea. In addition to 'blind man's buff' and guessing whose lap you were sitting on with a cushion, one of the games we played was 'Going to the dentist'. In this, we were all sent out into the hall to await the summons. Peter's older sister Jean came out and said 'Next!', then blindfolded the patient and led him into the room and shut the door. The patient was helped into the dreaded chair, where Peter's mum asked 'Gas or cocaine?' I said 'Gas' and was told to open my mouth, whereupon, to my relief, a toffee was placed therein (cocaine was an acid drop), and it was all over for me. I had no idea what to expect, so the surprise was complete and that was typical of the undemanding level of amusement we enjoyed when among friends.

Peter was a keen, knowledgeable and adventurous sweet eater who introduced us to Horlicks tablets as a good substitute for the scarce treats, and one day he discovered Baxter's new line was giant glucose tablets, the size of a cartwheel penny. That morning at school, Peter ate several, and on the way home at lunch time he had to travel faster and faster, but in the end he knew he could not get to his house in time. I stood guard while he dashed into the old, wooden, outside toilets at the back of the 'Rising Sun', which normally we instinctively kept away from. He eventually emerged, greatly relieved but still short of his usual cheery smile, and walking awkwardly. There was never any toilet paper in those places.

One or two friends just outside my circle, like Billy Klesel and Malcolm Champion, were in the Wolf Cubs, and after conversing with them and picking up their enthusiasm, I persuaded Mother to let me join. The big item to buy was the green jersey, but surprisingly I was taken to get one from Abernethie's in Hounslow, and then the rest of the outfit was easier to come by second-hand - the brown scarf, green cap, green sock tabs, and brother Dennis's 'woggle'. Dennis had been in the 6th Osterley scouts a few years before, and his souvenir scout hat and woggle had remained in the bedroom. Around 1936 he had been to camp at Littlehampton, where Pauline had been taken on the train to visit him, and he could still tie a reef knot, a sheep shank, or a running bowline, and from the wisdom of some unknown comedian, asserted that 'boy scouts are nifty'. The biggest help for me came from his old 'Boy Scout's Diary', which had hints on basic woodcraft, first aid and signalling, as well as knots.

The venue was St Francis Church hall, with meetings once a week, and in addition to the payment of 'subs', the price included attending Sunday school and a church parade once a month. The parade was but a short march and bugle blast from the assembly point, with a line-up before and after church. I found this ceremony more easily assimilable than Sunday school, which I did not really take in or enjoy, although I came away with a few religious stick-in or transfer pictures and a palm leaf cross.

The weekly session in the hall was novel and good fun. We went through the rituals, and I was prepared for investiture under the guidance of 'Akela', one of the Miss Bailey's who lived on the corner of Albury Avenue and who had an interesting fish pond in her front garden. We split up into groups for training in various crafts and skills, from darning socks and sewing on buttons, to first aid and semaphore, and also to study for our badges. Then we played games, like 'piggy back fighting', and the vigorous 'British Bulldog', where one cub within the circle had to try and shoulder barge his way out through the ranks. I did not take part in a 'gang show', but I did attend a well-supported one, and enjoyed the sketches, however shaky the punch lines:

(A boy walks past another who is fishing from a bridge): 'How many have you caught?' (Boy who is 'fishing' pulls line out of the water to reveal a cooled bottle of drink on the end) 'You're the fourth today!'

(A group of boys playing cricket, dominated by one who insists on having it all his own way) 'My bat, my ball, my stumps, I'm bowling.' The same goes for fielding and then batting, but when he hits the ball over the fence and breaks a window, the chorus is: 'Your bat, your ball, your stumps, you pay!'

I got my 'Collector's Badge' by handing over my stamp collection to Billy Klesel's father, who kept it overnight for inspection, then got Billy to return it next day with the message that I had passed. I was presented with the badge, which was blue with a magnifying glass emblem, and Mother sewed it on my sleeve. I also had the pack badge sewn on, and a little gold-coloured wolf's head lapel badge.

Bob-a-job week came round, and I offered my services to the neighbours. I was lucky to get several tasks: chopping firewood, weeding a border, going to the shops, but the most generous response was from Mrs Webb over the road. It was quite a privilege to be in her house, and I cleaned her lower windows, inside and out, while she chatted away to teenage daughters Jessie and Sylvia. When I had finished, she said what a marvellous job I had done, and gave me half a crown. This was exceedingly generous, and when combined with the other jobs I had netted seven shillings and sixpence, which I duly handed over to Akela. I was then embarrassed to receive a special mention in front of the pack, while the rest were admonished for not doing so well.

I was fortunate enough to qualify, by cub meeting and Sunday school attendance, for a double-decker bus outing to Chessington Zoo. Although zoos during the war were not well stocked with animals, there were plenty of swings, slides and other distractions, and with glorious sunshine and our home-made picnic lunch it proved a good and exhausting day. My wolf cub days did not long survive the fading memory of the summer treat, however, and I allowed my membership to lapse.

Had I been anything of a singer, I might have been cajoled into joining the choir at St Francis Church, because the choirboys actually got paid. I was not recruited, however, thereby sparing two hundred parishioners the need to change their religion, and I only heard second-hand the tales of peas in the organ pipe, pump failure and other mischievous pranks perpetrated upon organist and congregation.

Mike Curwen had a birthday party, and we had the traditional tea, then games, which to me were quite advanced. These included pinning the tail on a large picture of a donkey while blindfolded, being blindfolded again and trying by feel to guess the objects on a tray, where I was defeated by what I thought was a wooden toadstool, never before having encountered a stocking darner. We had a 'beetle drive', in which we were paired off with opponents and had to throw dice to match the beetle's numbered body parts, the winner moving on to try and be first to complete the circuit, and then we went outside for a competitive round of clock golf on the back lawn, organised by Mike's dad, who also took some photos. I was a year or two younger than the rest, who included Jill Bardell, Jean Beer, Ray Plowman, and Jimmy Girling - all near neighbours. There were prizes for each of the games, and Mike's mum, ever fair, ensured that we all left with something.

I had a great affection for Mike's mother. She had been a primary school teacher, specialising in English and music, and was a genteel, gracious and tolerant lady who seemed to know just how to treat and speak to young children. I was always pleased to go to their house, although being boys, we did not always do the approved thing when nobody was about, as for instance when we investigated the practicality of descending from the bedroom window by climbing down the washing line tied to the leg of Mike's parents' double bed. Our weight and stress calculations went awry, and to our surprise and horror the bed leg cracked ('Must have been a cheap ol' bed, that's all I can say,' we concluded), but we tidied up as best we could and, despite anxious hours while Mike waited for an ear-splitting crash during the night, the damage was never brought to light in our time.

Mike had a small pond, set in the paved area at the bottom of his garden, and in it were a few goldfish, while on the surface floated lilies and a quantity of green weed. Mike told me in confidence, that at the bottom, which could not be seen through the murky water, they kept a number of large man-eating oysters, to guard it. So when one afternoon, while trying to see the bottom, I fell in, I could think only of being trapped by the weeds while those great snapping oysters went for my dangling legs. I catapulted myself out like a leaping salmon, festooned with weed, and Mrs Curwen had to give me a hot bath, a change of clothes, a hot drink and a soothing talk to calm things down.

Two nieces of Mrs Harris came to stay with her at number forty nine. They were Beryl, a year older than I was, and her younger sister Marion, from Leicester. They would knock at our door and say, in what to me was a very unfamiliar accent, 'Can ya koom?' I did and we played happily, mainly in the road or in my back garden. At that time, there was an old mattress folded up in our shed awaiting disposal. We clambered upon it and Beryl, who had a recent back injury, slipped backwards over the top and became painfully stuck. I helped her straighten up and sportingly she told nobody, but I daresay it slowed her recovery, and as they almost immediately returned to Leicester, it left me with a nagging concern for evermore.

While living in Shepherds Bush, Mother had been befriended by Mrs Hawkins, a refined and well-spoken lady of similar age but in rather better circumstances, whose husband was 'something in the City' and whose son John was destined to become an accountant. Although Mother with her larger family was fairly housebound, Mrs Hawkins never gave up on the friendship, and made the long bus journey from Surbiton at least once a year, just to stay for lunch. She was very knowledgeable on cookery and things nutritional, and she it was who said we had to chew each mouthful thirty two times, even milk. Such news came hard at a time when I could not wait to leave the table and return to more interesting pursuits, and would in any case rather swallow whole the greens and fatty meat I did not like. I got over these dislikes by pretending I was an outlaw or caveman, and the food was venison or dinosaur I had just killed, and had to eat ravenously before the rest of the tribe arrived.

Our milk was delivered by the milkman from Clifford's Dairy in Cross Lances Road, Hounslow. His seemed an interesting job and not too difficult, so I offered to help him on his local round, and after a trial run he agreed. No price was fixed, but at the end of the week I got between sixpence and one shilling and sixpence, depending upon the takings, and as much milk as I wanted to drink. I helped at weekends and during the holidays, and he told my Mother I was 'the most intelligent lad he had ever had', which may not say a great deal for the other helpers, but it was good enough to ensure Mother's support and my continued employment.

The milk delivery was by horse-drawn cart, and one of two horses would be used, a brown one called Tommy and a grey which since I was much younger I had always called Whiteler, although the origin of that remains obscure and I have forgotten his real name. Whiteler was a bit of a character and inclined to threaten, so I used to throw our carrot tops down on the pavement for him and watch from behind our front fence as he munched and watched me. He had a habit of turning to put his hooves up on the pavement, thereby cutting off the escape of unwary pedestrians, especially little boys, and he would toss his head and look down with a baleful eye, daring you to walk past

I liked the smell of the horse and harness, especially close to, and I accepted its unselfconscious rude habits, while always remaining curious about them. The only thing I did not like about it was when I was told to run out into the road with the clanking enamel bucket and coal shovel and beat any competitors to scoop up the fresh pile of manure that was adjudged to be 'so good for the roses' yet nobody else in our house was prepared to go and get it.

The responsibilities of helping the milkman suited me and I enjoyed the contact with customers - coming unexpectedly face to

185

face with curlers and dressing gown at the front door, being recalled for an extra pint by an uncombed head and waving hand, or having a more civilised exchange about the weather when collecting the money on a Friday. I was in due course allowed to take the reins and drive the cart, and got quite a boost if I then saw someone I knew. I had already seen how careful one had to be round the cart, because some time before, while we were playing in the street, the milkman drove off unexpectedly and the rubber-tyred back wheel went over Valerie Blanchard's foot, to everybody's consternation. She seemed to recover well enough, but it shocked us into being circumspect.

We delivered in all roads on the estate, from Harewood Road to Syon Lane, with occasional breaks for a drink from the bottle - 'not so much a break, more breakages,' the milkman would say. While delivering to a downstairs flat in Redesdale Gardens, I saw through the window two men squaring up to each other in true boxing stance. Each was wearing a singlet but one had on a sailor's hat, and behind but between them stood a glamorous young lady with long fair hair wearing a dressing gown. I always wondered if they were play-acting, posing for a picture or getting ready to fight for the lady's hand.

When we reached the top of Redesdale Gardens, the milkman would 'park' the horse and cart and take me over the Great West Road to the Better 'Ole cafe for a cup of tea. The cafe was always busy with civvy and army lorry drivers, crews from buses, roundsmen, and workmen from the factories, as it was a very convenient location for a snack, and was famed for its marmalade toast (most often without butter, as it was rationed). There was also a shortage of cutlery, but the milkman claimed that he stirred our tea with his oft-licked behind-the-ear pencil because it gave it a better flavour. The crowning glory there was the jukebox, a rarity then, and I was really taken with the hit song 'Cow Cow Boogie', by the 'Squadronnaires' RAF Dance Orchestra with vocal by Sid Colin, because of the catchy horse-riding cowboy rhythm and the intriguing jargon.

In the summer of 1944, the milkman was replaced by a milklady, and she inherited me and my services. We got on well, although I was a little disappointed that she did not frequent the Better 'Ole. Another difference was that whereas the milkman had ignored the horse's inclination for uninhibited splashy relief and rude draughts and droppings, she and I would complain and laugh about it. She too allowed me to take the reins, but there were a couple of occasions when her instinct for self-preservation overcame her supervisory role, and it taught me a bit more about people.

The first incident happened at the top of Campion Road. The milklady was sitting beside me, and I was holding the reins as we prepared to move off down the hill. The horse suddenly took fright at something, reared up, kicked the cart with its hind legs and started to plunge forward as if bolting. I held the reins fast and luckily the brake was still on, so the moment passed and he soon calmed down. It was then that I realised I was quite alone in the cab, at which moment the milklady's head rose up from the pavement at the far side of the cart, and she said, 'If he ever does that you want to get off quick!'

The second occurrence was on a fine summer's morning when we were outside my house. The siren went and we almost immediately heard the crackling buzz of a doodlebug coming towards us from somewhere as close as Albury Avenue round the corner. 'Get under the cart!' she shouted, and dived between the wheels. I looked down and there was plainly no room for me. I looked up and saw the stark, black shape of the awful machine overhead, with its motor crackling and exhaust flaming, and seconds later the motor stopped. The danger to us was in fact past, because by then the thing had moved away to the west, and actually landed as far away as Hounslow. Furthermore, in a moment's reflection, it did seem to me that the wooden cart with its load of bottles was more hazard than protection, with the added risk that the brake may not have held back the cart if the horse had bolted. However, although no harm was done, I had experienced a moment's fear for the second time during the war. It had the effect of making me even more enthusiastic about mapping the progress of our troops through France and hearing about our planes bombing the Germans.

We had a number of scares from doodlebugs passing overhead, and Peter Cooper had his windows blown out by one that landed in Syon Park, but there was one bigger fright to come. On the morning of 21st March 1945, while I was at the Town School, we heard an explosion, and when we went out to the playground for the morning break, we could see a column of smoke rising from what I thought was the direction of my home. I found Miss Groves and surprisingly (for a ten year old) got permission to go home on my own and find out if all was well. I ran all the way and found everything still standing, but even from Northumberland Avenue it was apparent that something had happened on the Great West Road where Dennis was at work.

Dennis came home in due course, after helping where he could, and it was a great relief to find out that he was unharmed. We learnt that a V2 rocket had fallen on Packard's factory, and that there were many casualties. Dennis's description remained terse and not very informative, but Phil Harris, who worked at Napier's in Acton, said they were told over the tannoy that people who lived near the Great West Road should go home. He cycled home at speed, and saw the damaged Packard and Pyrene factories, with the grass verge and cycle track outside littered with some of the five hundred casualties on stretchers. Dennis's colleague and friend John Mundell said that in the Institute of Automobile Engineers, separated from the disaster by just two factories, Coty's and Lincoln, they knew nothing until the building suddenly shook and glass started falling, so everyone dived under workbenches, and then they heard the explosion. He too saw the many casualties, some of whom were ferried to West Middlesex Hospital in open lorries because the ambulances were fully engaged. Thirty two people died.

Waiting for Mr Pollard - with Dennis too!.

The Citroen - Father and Uncle Harry in front.

"Chauffeurs' Rest" - The George, Henfield.

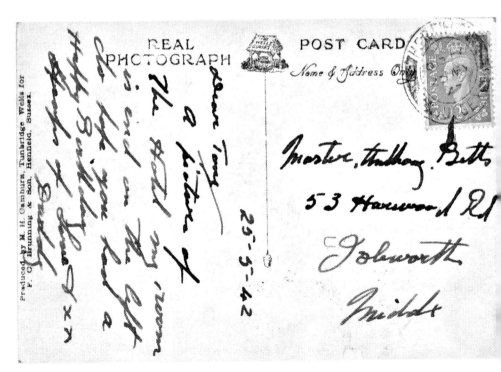

A break in wartime security.

Woods Mill House Henfield - side view.

Woods Mill House - front view.

The Maids - Florrie Bartlett and 'Evvie' Evans outside Woods Mill
with Mother, Father and Sylvia.

Phil Harris (on bike) and Dennis - 1946.

Dennis (centre rear) and 'the lads' - 1946. John Mundell, middle row, far left.

The Thurlows, with Mother and Father.

Mike Curwen's party, 1945. (Rear left to right) Jean Beer, Ray Plowman, Jimmy Girling, Jill Bardell. (Front) Mike and me.

Brenda and Robin Morrison.

Mike Curwen with Mum and Dad.

A tantalising glimpse of Olive Jukes, aged nine,
hiding behind her cousins.

Chapter Thirteen

Entertainment

The naked body of the man hung grotesquely three feet off the floor, suspended by an iron hook through the stomach. Quite how I got into the Chamber of Horrors so young I do not know, but the obligatory, illicit peep behind the curtains at this shocking exhibit became an essential part of the itinerary of any visit to Madame Tussauds, and despite the fact that it made one spend the night shrinking from thinking, it seriously rivalled the fun of loitering by the distorting mirrors in the exhibition's entrance hall.

Family outings were fairly rare. This was partly because of the cost, partly because it meant going by bus and carrying everything, and partly because of the restrictions upon travel during the war.

We did go to Epsom Downs by bus and to Windsor Park and Chertsey, and after the war, to Marlow, Arundel and Littlehampton by borrowed car. There were also occasional trips to Kew Gardens, where we raced round path and pond, gazed at flora and fauna, inhaled the dank steaminess of the greenhouses, stared at the dangerously derelict pagoda, and looked with some regret at the tarpaulins covering the forlorn and abandoned funfair by Kew Green. We went to Richmond Park, to Gunnersbury Park, and to London, where we looked at the mighty Thames, picnicked in Regent's Park, Hyde Park or St James's Park, and at different times visited the zoo, the Tower,

Madam Tussauds and the museums, of which the Natural History with its dinosaurs and huge whale was my favourite.

In the summer of 1940, Father learnt that Salter's pleasure steamers were still running up the Thames from Windsor. We went on the Green Line bus to Windsor, and duly embarked for my first river boat trip.

There were not many passengers, and the atmosphere was friendly but rather hushed as we travelled up river, the 'captain', resplendent in blue peaked cap, pointing out various places of interest, including Cliveden, and we all expressed envy of those who lived in large houses with lawns sloping gently down to the river bank.

Suddenly there was a distraction, and it was not the riverside scenery that people were looking at but the sky, as a stray German bomber appeared, probably navigating by following the river. Our captain did not panic. He changed course and steered the boat towards the shore, where by good fortune there was a small but serviceable private landing stage that reached out just far enough. We were ordered ashore and scrambled off the boat to run up the boards and make for the cover of some large trees that were near the water's edge. By the time we had arrived there, got our breath and peered out from beneath the foliage, the plane was well on its way past and rapidly disappearing down river. If he were not so far from home, the pilot may well have laughed at our undignified dash for cover, but he may equally have cursed at not having anything to throw at us.

Visits to the theatre were a huge treat, but unfortunately rare. Early in the war we went to the Stoll Theatre, where we sat very high up in seats that seemed to have an almost sheer drop to the stage, but that was soon forgotten as we were convulsed by Will Hay and his pupils in 'Ask A Policeman'. At the Chiswick and Shepherds Bush Empires, in various variety shows we saw Norman Evans in 'Over the Garden Wall', Wilson, Keppel and Betty in 'Cleopatra's Nightmare', Troise and his Mandoliers, Teddy Brown, the enormous man who played the xylophone so brilliantly, and Albert Whelan, who whistled his delightful signature tune 'The Jolly Brothers', while taking off or putting on his hat, coat and gloves. Mother had seen quite a few of the stars in their heyday, including Little Tich, but Father used to frequent the Metropolitan Edgeware Road before the First World War and had seen just about all, from Marie Lloyd, Eugene Stratton and Chirgwin, to Harry Champion, Vesta Tilley and Florrie Forde.

One Christmas we went to see the pantomime 'Jack and the Beanstalk', and at Christmas in 1943 we went to the Q Theatre to see 'Claudius the Bee', which captured my imagination because the scenery was scaled up to give a bee's viewpoint, and in addition to a good representation of the roots of huge grasses and weeds, they had a giant white 'aspirin' for a prop to suggest scale.

Locally, I went to St John's Hall when the Green School put on Arthur Wing Pinero's 'Trelawney of the Wells', and a couple of years after the war, to the Marlborough Senior School, when a local company called 'The Thespians' put on comedy-thriller plays, including 'Night Must Fall' and 'An Inspector Calls'. We went to these with the Thurlows, and setting off along Northumberland Avenue in the otherwise silent darkness of evening, I once more became aware of the shuffling of hundreds of feet, as we were joined by people from Campion Road, Northumberland Avenue, Albury Avenue and Roxborough Avenue, because so many went to see such entertainment and everybody walked. On the way home on each occasion, all agreed that the play was excellent and that leading actress Jean Cooper, Peter's elder sister, had stolen the show.

At St Francis Church, we enjoyed some entertaining shows put on by our local Air Raid Wardens, who called themselves the F3-sians, after their official unit number. Mrs Curwen, Mike's mother, played the piano and arranged the music, and we had song, sketch and dance from the various members, including Darcy Curwen, Winifred Bailey, Gordon Vinton and Dickie Bird from Harewood Road, and Brenda Kapper, the hairdresser from Syon Lane. One of their best numbers, and Mrs Curwen's favourite, was the 'Whiffenpoof Song' from Yale ('We're three little lambs who've lost our way'), but the big hit on their final concert, which was as late as 1946, was Dickie Bird singing 'I'm Dangerous Dickie MacBird', a gunslinging parody to the tune of 'The Green Cockatoo'.

The cinema was cheaper and more convenient than the theatre, and we could walk to the Odeon on the London Road in ten minutes, or to the Dominion on Tudor Parade at a pinch. Even the other Hounslow cinemas came within walking distance as I got older - the Empire halfway up the High Street, and the Regal and Alcazar up past The Bell, on the Staines Road. Some folk went regularly and often, and as everybody walked, you could almost set your clock and calendar by the passing of some, like Mike and Peter Tomlin, and Ernie and Bert Hole.

The Odeon was 'modern', a classic nineteen thirties' design, and nicely kept. It was where my schoolmates went to Saturday morning pictures and joined the Saturday Morning Club. I went with them a couple of times and saw George Formby and Gene Autry, but I did not have the money to go regularly.

It was Father or Dennis who took me if we went to see the current feature film, which was usually on for six days of the week. The programme usually consisted of a short or 'B' picture, the newsreel, a few advertisements, an interval in which the lights went up, then the main feature, the whole lasting two hours or so, which was good value for ninepence, or even one and ninepence. On Sundays, there would be a special one day showing of a film that had already done the rounds, with the doors opening at about four o'clock, enabling us to see a film again, or catch one that had been missed the first time round - or if it was not one that we wanted to see, to complain that there was nothing to do on Sundays!

Among those films I saw during the war were 'Hellzapoppin' ' which was supposed to be funny, but I remembered it more for the tremendous lindyhop dancing; 'The Road to Morocco' with the super dixie-style title song and the hugely romantic 'Moonlight Becomes You', both of which Dennis bought on record; the exciting 'Typhoon'; various 'Tarzan' adventures; 'Hoppity Goes to Town', the rabbit cartoon that made me want a pet rabbit; 'The Life and Death of Colonel Blimp', an epic that gave me a headache; 'Forever and a Day', the sad story of a house built to last forever but finally bombed in the blitz; 'One of Our Aircraft is Missing', a super film about the boys in blue; the Ministry of Information film 'Target for Tonight', about how our boys were tackling the bombing of Germany; 'Song of the South' (Disney's Uncle Remus); 'Buffalo Bill Cody' (Father had seen the real Bill Cody); 'Can't Help Singing' which gave us the taste for Deanna Durbin's beautiful voice; 'Incendiary Blonde', the life of Texas Guinan starring Betty Hutton, 'the blonde bombshell', from which I came away with no appetite whatever for her frenzied style; and inevitably various westerns and other adventures. One of these was 'Salty O'Rourke', a tale of the turf starring Alan Ladd. In keeping with the fad at the time, I sent off to Hollywood for his autograph. I was amazed to actually receive a short letter in reply, accompanied by an autographed photograph.

One Christmas, Dennis took me to the Regal on the 'down' day after Boxing Day to see Errol Flynn's version of 'Robin Hood' - it was as good as a visit to the pantomime, and always a privilege to go out with big brother - or so he said! We invariably had a good laugh when we were together, despite the ten year age gap.

When 'The Overlanders' came round, we all enjoyed it, as the first film we had seen from 'down under', and being a sort of Australian western, it helped maintain their rugged image.

Naturally Dennis, who was now out at work, went more often to the pictures than the rest of us. This was one of the reasons why, when he started taking an interest in piano playing, he also bought the shilling and sixpenny wartime economy sheet music for the featured hit songs, like 'On the Atchison Topeka and the Santa Fe' from 'The Harvey Girls', 'Cow Cow Boogie' from 'Swing Symphony' and 'Reveille with Beverley', 'The Way To The Stars' from the film title, 'Accentuate the Positive' from 'Here Come the Waves', and 'Swinging on a Star' from 'Going My Way'.

The most readily available entertainment and a great influence upon our lives and language was the radio. The degree to which it was heard varied in different households. Some made their own music or entertained visitors, or habitually went out, or had pursuits that required a quiet atmosphere, but in our house the radio was on a great deal, for Mother during the day, for the children at tea time, and for the whole family during the evening.

I remember hearing the theme song of 'The Ovaltinies', which Pauline listened to until it was discontinued in 1939, but I was too young to take in the programme itself, and in similar vein I only vaguely recall 'Bandwagon', although the character 'Nausea Bagwash' and Sid Walker's catchphrase 'What would you do, chums?' remained in the family language.

Certainly throughout the war we relied upon the BBC programmes, and when they got into their stride, we felt they really provided a lot of first class entertainment and information. Most people like us listened whenever possible to the news, which was hourly through the day, and especially to the evening news at six and nine o'clock. It was often grim, but there was encouragement too, especially when 'Winnie' Churchill spoke and exhorted us to 'carry on' at home, and to support our troops abroad.

There seemed to be a surfeit of organ music during the day, but although I was never keen on the instrument, Reginald Foort's programmes and Sandy Macpherson's 'Half Hour' and 'Post Bag' usually had some favourite tunes in the selections. Mother especially welcomed 'Music while You Work', mid-morning and mid-afternoon, with its cheery signature tune 'Calling All Workers' and a quarter of an hour of intentionally lively music played by a good band. 'Desert Island Discs' was listened to because of the human interest and because we liked a variety of music, especially with the possibility of a pleasant surprise. However, we did not care much for opera, nor religious music, and were not great fans of classical music, except for the more popular melodies and some of the piano music. We all liked 'the old songs', and the better popular songs and dance music, but Dennis veered towards jazz and swing and took Pauline and me with him. We thus developed a taste for The Inkspots, the Mills Brothers, Fats Waller, The Skyrockets, The Squadronnaires, Harry Parry, and of course the American bands like Dorsey, Miller and Goodman, and the dance music of Victor Silvester.

Father was united with us by his liking for Bing Crosby, but his special taste was for one of the older songs by a good tenor or perhaps a duet by Anne Ziegler and Webster Booth, and he was not averse to spending Sunday evenings with The Palm Court Orchestra at the Grand Hotel, a regular offering which he alone enjoyed, and which we put on a show of enduring with silent suffering. Mother especially liked Charlie Kunz' piano medleys, but her favourite item of the week was 'Those Were the Days', a programme of old time dance music quite acceptable to all, and played every Saturday evening by Harry Davidson and his Orchestra, with the evocative background noise of real dancers enjoying 'the lancers', 'the barn dance', the 'two step', 'the gay gordons', the 'veleta', a 'Viennese' or 'St Bernard's waltz', while step instructions were called out from the bandstand.

We soaked up the sentimental songs in 'Forces Favourites' and Vera Lynn's 'Sincerely Yours', and became absolutely absorbed in the drama of Paul Temple, with Vivian Ellis's exhilarating 'Coronation Scot' signature tune, (and I developed a soft spot for the warm voice of Marjorie Westbury's 'Steve'), and we revelled in the excitement of Dick Barton, spurred on by the frenetic 'Devil's Gallop'.

I rather shied away from Wilfred Pickles' 'Have A Go' quiz, with Violet Carson at the piano and the 'Give 'em the money Barney' catchphrase and philosophy - its wholesome down-to-earth approach seemed so obvious and unsophisticated, and definitely designed for 'old people'. Father enjoyed it, and found he was on his own again! On the other hand, we all got something out of 'Monday Night At Eight', with its varied content of Ronnie Waldman's 'Puzzle Corner', the mystery series entitled 'Meet Dr Morell', and Barbara Mullen's tales of leprechauns in 'The Story of Miss Paddy O'Toole', which used the hit song 'Let Him Go Let Him Tarry'.

'Workers' Playtime' on three days a week accompanied our dinner, which was in the middle of the day because it suited the children's needs, and Father conveniently had his main meal at J Lyons - and where better! The standard of performance on 'Workers' Playtime' was very variable, but it was good brisk variety, and did include many recognised turns, like Two Tun Tessie O'Shea, Harry Hemsley and his fictional family, Suzette Tarri who had adopted our treasured 'Red Sails In The Sunset' as her signature tune, and Cardew 'The Cad' Robinson. We really looked forward to any variety show, and there were many, like 'Variety Bandbox', 'Ack Ack, Beer Beer', and 'Music Hall' on Saturday night, with turns like the monologues of Robb Wilton ('The day war broke out, my missus said to me') and Gillie Potter ('Good evening England, this is Gillie Potter speaking to you in English'), the 'Odd Odes' of Cyril Fletcher ('This is the tale of Christine Crump, who thought her figure was too plump, and used to cry 'It is a sin, I bulge out where I should go in!'), and his 'soppy date' delivery of Edgar Wallace's 'Dreaming of Thee', the cosy chatting of Elsie and Doris Waters (Jack Warner's sisters, known as the Waters of England), and the humour of Stanelli, Sirdani ('Don't be fright!'), Nosmo King, Nat Mills and Bobbie ('Wait a minute, wait a minute!'), Sandy Powell ('Can you hear me, mother?'), Revnell and West ('the long and the short of it'), Vic Oliver and the Western Brothers ('Good evening cads and cadesses'). 'Garrison Theatre' was a similar favourite, although I was too young to stay up for it except as a treat, but we all picked up on Jack Warner's 'bruvver Sid', the 'ruleway laines', his 'blue pencil' this or that, and his 'occupational monologues' about the 'bunger up of rat 'oles', the 'caster up of alabaster plaster', or the 'fumper and flattener of feathers'.

Comedy series began to become a habit, with 'Hi Gang', which involved Vic Oliver with the Lyons family, and 'Danger Men at Work', with 'Mrs Ponsonby' and 'Nicholas Ridikoulos'.

On Sundays we listened to Mr Middleton's advisory talks 'In Your Garden', and to Big Bill Campbell's cowboy music on 'Rocky Mountain Rhythm', with Peggy Bailey, 'the sweet voice of the west', and the singing ranch hands, like Norman Harper 'the yodelling buckaroo' and his horse 'Starlight', and we agreed with Big Bill that it was all 'mighty fine'.

Saturday nights featured the unmissable 'In Town Tonight', a variety of people being interviewed and sometimes performing. It was heralded by the rumble of traffic and Eric Coates' 'Knightsbridge', then the announcer's dramatic 'Stop! - and as we stop the mighty roar of London's traffic ...' , and then at the close, the call to 'Carry on London!', followed by the voice of Emma Baker, one of the long since vanished flowersellers of Piccadilly, calling 'Violets, sweet violets, lovely roses'. This all fired the imagination, and conjured up images of our bustling, colourful and beloved metropolis.

'Cut fut sut decents and minerals' - this inexplicable and absurd parody which in our house, followed in the wake of Leslie Sarony's song 'Teas, Light Refreshments and Minerals', goes some way to illustrate our fondness for comic language and expressions, and perhaps helps to explain why many radio shows with their funny names and catchphrases were so popular with us. We liked our tongue-twisters - 'Red leather, yellow leather, red leather, yellow leather' seemed to get everybody going - and our silly jokes:

> 'Vy didn't the viper vipe 'er nose?'
> 'Because the adder 'ad 'er 'andkerchief!'
> 'Why did the owl 'owl?'
> 'Because the woodpecker would peck 'er!'

- and we just liked to try and induce each other to laugh, or create a little fun to offset the grimmer reality outside.

The biggest radio hit was of course 'ITMA'. I was soon asking to be allowed to stay up and listen, as it was on from eight thirty to nine o'clock at night and, initially at least, past my bedtime. We waited for each character to make his entrance, and for each catchphrase to be delivered. Our own conversations were liable to be peppered with the sayings and with imitations of the familiar characters: Colonel Chinstrap's 'I don't mind if I do', Ali-oop's 'I go - I come back ', Signor So-So's 'No likey? Oh, crikey', Mark Time's 'I'll have to ask me Dad!', Sam Scram's 'Boss, Boss, sump'n terrible's happened!', Lefty's 'It's me noives', Mona Lott's 'It's being so cheerful as keeps me going ', Norman the Doorman's 'Vicky verky', Lola Tickle's 'I always do my best for all my gentlemen', and many more, not forgetting Mrs Mopp and her 'Can I do yer now, Sir?' and 'TTFN'. It was probably this cult of the catchphrase that caused us to enjoy mimic's, like 'The Voice Of Them All - Peter Cavanagh'.

Father had always had his catchphrases and lingo, taken from variety or the music hall or other sources. He used a bit of rhyming slang, like apples and pears (stairs), lump of lead (head), bath bun (sun), plates of meat (feet), but when he got a good fire blazing in the hearth he would refer to it as the 'Rory O'More' or the 'old

Rory', which was a deliberate misuse born out of the noise the fire made, because 'the Rory' was actually the floor. He used Harry Tate's 'Ooh, I don't kno-ow!', and 'Good-By-ee!', and would refer to me as 'Stainless', from Stainless Stephen the 'punctuation' comic, and he would encourage with 'Come on Steve!', from the Daily Express cartoon horse. Asked how long or far something was, he might say 'As long as a piece of string', which was followed by 'And how long is that?' 'Ooh, that and a bit more!', or asked how big something was, it would be 'A yard foot and a thick wide'. Asked how he was, he might take a line from George Formby Senior and say:

'It's me chest, me left lung's proper poorly' - then, in a stentorian Harry Tate boom: 'BUT MY RIGHT LUNG'S AS SOUND AS A BELL!'

He professed to have learnt French and German in France during the Great War, and so, in addition to expressions like 'Allay, oop!' and 'Pardon, messeu!', perhaps for the benefit of a young visitor the routine was:

'You speak French, Dad?'
'Wee Messeu - tray bon - un peu, see vous play'
'Go on, say something in French, then.'
'Ah pah de!'
'What's that mean?'
'Half past two!'
'Now say something in German'
'Verken mit de scoop'
'And what's that?'
'Working with a shovel!'

It was in this vein that Phil Harris introduced us to an infectiously rhythmic trifle in 'Chinese' lingo:

'Rah, rah, chickerah pooh-lee,
Om pom pooh-lee,
Gulla wulla weeza,
 Chinese pom pom!'

198

- origin obscure, but probably no further east than Stratford.

Another foreign-sounding and rhythmic 'chant' Dennis and I picked up on our walks was the stomping war cry of the Borough Road College 'Bees' rugby team:

'Hi-diddy zum-ba,
Zum-ba, zum-ba,
Hi-diddy zum-ba,
Zum-ba zee!'

Dennis contributed little gems from time to time:

'What's a twack?'
'Dunno - what's a twack?'
'It's what a twain wuns on!'

'What's the difference between a duck?'
'Dunno - what d'you mean?'
'One leg's the same!'

The Forces' comedy shows provided more names and expressions to conjure with, and were also well liked. 'Mediterranean Merry-go-round' had a different show for each of the three services. It led to the Army's 'Stand Easy', and we absorbed master criminal 'Wippit Kwick', 'Ray Ling' the Chinese fence, 'Stabu' the elephant boy, but Mother frowned upon the greeting 'Wotcher Tish!' 'Wotcher Tosh!' as being just too common. From the Navy's 'HMS. Waterlogged' we had 'Steady, Barker!', and Flying Officer Kite's 'I say, I rather care for that!', and the Air Force had 'Much Binding in the Marsh', with a more genteel humour, as in 'Not a word to Bessie!' and 'Read any good books lately?'

More generally and subtly service jargon was picked up. Aided by Dennis's entry into the Royal Air Force for National Service, we greeted with 'What ho!', if there was nothing doing we 'stooged around' and 'got browned off', and sometimes things were 'wizard', but we 'took a pretty poor view' if they were 'a bit ropey', and if life was easy it was 'a piece of cake'.

Naturally, the best programme of the day for me was the BBC Children's Hour. Like many children, I derived comfort from Uncle Mac's voice, and some sense of order and continuity in time of turmoil from the reliable regularity of the programme - it was something to look forward to and to hold on to at the end of each day, and it provided a complete distraction from the day's events.

Because it was between five and six o'clock, it was associated absolutely with tea time, always a thoroughly appetising meal with toast being made on a toasting fork over the fire, and spread with dripping or jam, or we might have bread and paste, rissoles or Welsh rarebit, sprats or herrings, to be followed by one of Mother's rock cakes or a slice of her larger cake, which Father irreverently referred to as "obnail'.

The more factual children's programmes like Nature Parliament, Farming, the Zoo Man, were interesting, with a bit of added excitement for the competitive element in Regional Round quiz. Slightly better for me were the more imaginative country features like 'Cowleaze Farm' with Ralph Whitlock, and Bramwell Evans's 'Out With Romany'.

I was always a good listener to stories, and on Children's Hour they were read so well, from AA Milne's *Winnie the Pooh* and Anna Sewell's *Black Beauty*, to Kipling's *Just So Stories*, and from *Mary Plain* the bear to Kathleen Hale's *Orlando the Marmalade Cat*.

Best of all were the plays and serials. The dramatisation was excellent, and my imagination worked overtime in conjuring up the scenes and almost participating in the action. The music and sound effects helped too.

Parade of the Tin Soldiers introduced *Toytown*, with the very familiar characters of Larry the Lamb and Dennis the Dachshund, Mr Grouser and Ernest the Policeman. There was the immortal *Wind in the Willows* by Kenneth Grahame, with Richard Goolden's 'Mole', Freddie Burtwell's 'Toad' and Fraser-Simson's haunting music; Noel Streatfield's 'Ballet Shoes', which was graced with 'The Jewel Song' from 'The Madonna' by Wolf-Ferrari; and the entertaining commentary of Mompty the Cat (Vivienne Chatterton) and Peckham the Dog (Ernest Jay) upon their human household in

Martin Armstrong's 'Said the Cat to the Dog', with its catchy signature tune 'Popular Song', from 'Facade' by William Walton.

Anthony Buckeridge's 'Jennings' and his pal Darbishire gave us good schoolboy stuff, and 'Gosh Fishooks!', and Anthony Wilson's 'Norman and Henry Bones' furthered my sleuthing interests with their mystery adventures in Norfolk, and made the chiming church clock and hooting owl an essential ingredient in establishing a scene at 'dead of night'.

Most evocative of all was the pre-Christmas atmosphere created by John Masefield's fantasy adventure 'The Box of Delights', combined as it was with the 'Noel' section from Hely-Hutchinson's 'Carol Symphony', with its insistent and stirring counter melody, redolent of snowy Christmas Eves , and putting us in a frame of mind to really believe 'the wolves were running'!

Jersey Gardens, the dividing alley.

Jersey Gardens (west) - the Daisy Lawn.

Jersey Gardens (east) - the Field, with St. Mary's Church spire in the distance, and under the trees, the low bank that is the remains of the public air raid shelter.

Wood Lane, from Jersey Road.

Osterley Park, Osterley Lane - towards Wyke Green.

Osterley Park - 'the Home Guard field', showing the firing range target.

Osterley Park - the 'High Lake'.

Osterley Park - the 'Low Lake' and woods.

Osterley Lane, Osterley Park, beyond the lakes.

Osterley Park - remains of 'the Newt Pond' and the leaning tree.

Me, aged eleven - "boyhood at last."

CHAPTER FOURTEEN

A PASTORAL PARADISE

Father's one excursion into car ownership was when he and his brother Harry had briefly shared a 1925 disc-wheeled Citröen Tourer (XX8288), but he had to surrender this luxury when he took on the expense of buying the house. He was, however, a much respected driver of other people's cars.

His skill, competence and reliability as a driver/mechanic provided him with good references from the Great War and earlier days, and he was later awarded many 'accident free' diplomas by the National Safety First Association under the London Safety First Council. Consequently, as a chauffeur with J Lyons and Company, he had a fairly secure job from 1920 right through to his retirement in 1958, although his wage remained very low. For the Company, he drove mainly large cars: Daimler, Bentley, Humber, Armstrong Siddeley, Austin Shearline, but we saw little of this as he rarely brought one home, except when, during the war, he could not get any public transport. On those occasions, because he was not keen on parking a large, showy car outside our house, he used to leave it overnight round the corner in Musgrave Road. The reaction of those residents is not recorded!

He worked five days a week, although sometimes with extended hours, and he went away with his employer as required, and also on every third weekend. He would normally collect his car in Hammersmith from Cadby Hall or Normand Garages, and take his orders for the day. He not only drove people, but also went on special pick-ups and deliveries, and of course there was a lot of waiting about, sometimes in difficult situations, especially during the war. The wartime connection with the Ministry of Food also meant special journeys to unfamiliar places, some of which were quite demanding and hazardous, what with the blackout, and no road signs.

He drove Mr George Pollard, a director of Lyons, throughout the 1920s and most of the 1930s, and that meant driving the family as well, which included Mrs Ashburner, and Mrs Hayward and young Vivienne. When, after nearly twenty years, Mr Pollard's health deteriorated, and he headed for retirement, Father was transferred to drive Major Monty Gluckstein, and his family as required, which included Miss Mavis (Mrs Robinson), and Mr Kenneth. Major Monty was destined to become Chairman, and then President.

The Glucksteins stayed in Town, but they also had a country house at Henfield, near the Sussex Downs, which was permanently staffed in readiness for their visits.

No doubt as a result of his good record and service, Father and his family were looked upon with some kindness by his employers, and so when I was ten, they invited Father to bring me along to spend a week at Henfield. My sister Pauline had already been to stay there, and in due course Sylvia went too. For me, it was the first of several visits, the last being in 1948, and I found it an exciting and very happy experience.

Accompanying Father in the big car, I was able to see at first hand just how well he knew London. He used to say you could never get lost if you kept in your mind a picture of the main roads as they ran roughly parallel or at right angles to The Thames, but he also knew his way through all the minor roads or 'back doubles', even though he did not always know their names. Of course, there were few one-way streets then, and he was able to park at will outside Lyons Corner Houses, The Cumberland Hotel, The Strand Palace Hotel, The Trocadero in Shaftesbury Avenue, or Harrods in Knightsbridge.

On one trip, we first picked up Mrs Gluckstein, or 'Mrs Monty' as she was known, it being the custom to give Madame her husband's first name. She wanted a book to read, so Father stopped outside Harrods, with a nod to the commissionaire, and I was invited to accompany Mrs Monty inside. I was most interested to discover that my visits to our library were much more to my liking, as half the fun for me was browsing the shelves and the 'recently returned', whereas Mrs Monty and I were shown to a seat in the library department, where the librarian was asked to recommend a couple of books. This he did with the utmost consideration, deference and aplomb, and after two had been selected from the half dozen, we were escorted all the way out. I was surprised to note that no money changed hands.

Major Monty usually came on the trip, but not always. He was a large, bluff man, of typical military appearance and manner, and did not waste words. Nevertheless I found both he and Mrs Monty to be very considerate and courteous, and of course we all felt it was generous and kind of them to treat us to a holiday, when there had been no chance of our going anywhere, even if we could afford it, at least while the war was on.

The journey to Henfield seemed long, although I sometimes sat in the front, where the scenery was easier to take in. Once, when Father and I went down alone, the journey was considerably enlivened because Father was never happier than when driving somebody for pleasure, especially his family, and when free of the conventions of his role, he liked to talk and to break into snatches of song. I wondered what the reaction of the Glucksteins would have been to a sudden outburst of 'Has anybody here seen Kelly?', or 'Ginger, you're barmy!'.

We travelled through Leatherhead, Dorking and Horsham, then turned off to Cowfold, and finally, at last, to Henfield, past 'The George' where the chauffeurs traditionally stayed, and on down the lane to Beeding. The lane was bordered by woods and hedges, almost to Small Dole, and then at last we were turning into the gravelled drive, past the distinctive entrance feature of a group of huge pampas grasses and shrubs.

'Woods Mill House' was then quite modern in appearance, and very attractive with its mixture of brick, dark woodwork, red tiles, and whitewashed rendering. The Major and Madame were always admitted through the front door, and Father and I would take the side path to the kitchen, which was round the back.

The kitchen was the hub of life in the house. Not only was the food provided from there, but it was the meeting place and refuge for the staff, and they took their meals and breaks round the large kitchen table. There, too, was where they ended their day with a drink and a gossip before retiring to bed or departing for home or lodgings.

Miss Johnston was the cook, and a very capable and talented one at that, as one might expect in the service of the head of a major food company. Her skills transcended her disabilities of deafness and a speech impediment, and although she was wont to get into a flap and mutter to herself at times, these eccentricities were accepted by all and she was liked and respected.

Miss Johnston's sister came to visit her. She was a sergeant in the ATS, and her slow moving bulk and earthy humour were in complete contrast to cook's slim, self-conscious, distracted flutterings and absent-minded responses. Sergeant Johnston prodded and quizzed me good-humouredly in front of everybody, as part of the show:

'Do you swear?'

'No'

'I'll bet you do!'

'No, I don't'

'Go on, what words do you use?'

'I don't use any'

'I'll bet you do, when the teacher's not there!'

Uncanny perception or not, I was not about to let anything slip in front of Father and the rest

The ladies' maid was 'Evvie', Miss Evans. She was tall and thin, and hailed originally from Wales. A very practical and experienced and good-humoured person, as was 'Florrie', Miss Bartlett the parlourmaid.

The other mainstay was 'old Akers', the gardener. He kept the grounds in good shape, and ensured a constant supply of salad, vegetables and seasonal fruit. His lean, stooped figure in boots, grey cap, trousers and 'weskitt', was as much part of the landscape as the trees and shrubs, and his gnarled old hands working alongside nature achieved wonders. Although he came fairly frequently into the kitchen and sat down for his breaks, and talked of the weather and the soil, I never took in much he said, because I was so fascinated by the strong Sussex burr that I just switched off and let it soothe the mind, like music.

Cook and the maids slept in the house, but Akers lived at home in Small Dole, while Father, and his colleagues, stayed at The George in Henfield, otherwise known as The Chauffeurs' Rest. This suited him, because he was then able to ensure his daily pint, although he would have much preferred to be at home with his family.

I always had the guest room that overlooked the garden at the side of the house. The room was above the loggia, and in the middle of the lawn that extended away from the house on that side was a monkey puzzle tree - a name which I never understood, as there was little to puzzle over, and certainly no monkeys.

It was usually still light when I went to bed, and as the room was very tastefully furnished and the bed sumptuously soft, I would gradually slip into my sleep while looking round and trying to take in the luxury of it all.

One night, while in this euphoric state, I heard a scratching noise over by the open window. It was intermittent, but I knew it was some creature that had come to share my retreat. As it was still light, I watched and waited, listening to the rather menacing noise. I tracked it down to the curtains, and taking my life in my hands I tiptoed across to the window.

There, sure enough, halfway up the heavy curtains by the open window, was a huge hairy black spider, which looked to me about the size of a saucer, its legs scratching on the curtain material. I had no idea how to get rid of it, and could not think of disturbing Florence or Evvie, so I got back into bed and with one watchful eye over the covers, drifted into a fitful and dream-laden sleep.

When Florrie appeared in the morning to give me my usual call, I told her about the unwelcome visitor. She went to the curtain, where it was still clinging, and with a deft shake launched the monster out of the window and down into the garden below.

I realised at that moment that she must have had to deal with all sorts of tricky and distasteful situations whilst in service, and it increased my respect.

During the day, all I had to do was to amuse myself, and come in for meals, and elevenses, when called. Beyond the house was the vegetable garden, at the edge of which an offshoot of the front driveway led to a large garage. Inside was a table tennis table, intended as a diversion for the staff, or the children, and we did manage an occasional game, but generally they were all too busy or too tired. There were also a few bicycles, and an autocycle upon which the chauffeurs could travel to and from Henfield village, as an alternative to the car.

Father showed me how to operate the autocycle, and took me for a few rides, but I was not quite big enough to go solo, and had to be content with running the engine whilst it was on its stand. I had a few bicycle rides round the local area, with Evvie and Florrie, when they had the energy, and sometimes we would go for walks across the fields or into the woods. Once I visited in early spring, and Evvie took Father and me to the woods beyond the field at the back of the house to hear how they echoed with bird song and to see how they were carpeted with primroses.

Usually my visits were in summer, sometimes for a week, and sometimes for a long weekend. One summer I was introduced to a relative of Mr Akers, a boy of my own age, from Small Dole. He took me to the woods near his home, and he showed me pathways through the trees, and the place where woodmen were working, and we played by the stream and shared his secret hiding places - gifts as generous as any that one young lad can give another.

There was plenty for me to look at all round the garden, and from certain vantage points I could gaze into the distance and see the Downs, and the trees of Chanctonbury Ring. Beyond the garden was a field that belonged to the house, and this became the place I always made for when alone. I loved getting 'lost' in the long grass, or playing with the cut hay that lay drying in the sun. At the far side of the field in one corner was a stile that led towards the nearby woods, and further along that hedgerow towards the back lane were some derelict pig styes and a small, empty barn - always quiet, as any deserted country spot is - and I would keep perfectly still and try to detect the stirrings of mice and other small creatures, and watch the movement of birds and insects, and listen to their song.

While walking in carefree fashion through the long grass of the field on a hot sunny day, lost in the pleasure of it all, I startled a hare, which leapt up in the air from underneath my feet and bolted for the hedge. I ran back to the kitchen with the news, my heart still thumping, and old Akers rumbled 'You should've caught'n for your supper!', and ever after I got my 'townie' leg pulled for failing to bag a natural country prize.

In the evening, when the work was done, and we had our final drink, which for me was hot cocoa or milk, Florrie, Evvie, Father and I would sit round the kitchen table playing cards. The stakes were in pence, the game usually rummy or sevens, and either by luck or manipulation I won more times than I should - and when they had all finally retired, and occasionally met up with my folks to reminisce, that was what they always recalled of my visits there. That, and the hare!

Chapter Fifteen

The Junior School:
Celebration, Humiliation and Graduation

The Allies were advancing on Germany, and at home we listened joyfully to the good news on BBC radio and kept track with our flags on the wall map, but as the threat of bombs and rockets faded and victory seemed assured, everybody began to relax a little.

The end finally came and the long awaited VE day was announced, at last, as Tuesday 8th May, which was declared a public holiday, and in fact we got two days off school. Red, white and blue bunting and Union Jack flags decorated the outside of every house, including ours, although we were unable to make use of two large national flags of undisclosed origin that had resided in Mother's wardrobe for many years, one being Belgian and not very relevant, and the other the setting sun of the hated Japanese Empire! Their usefulness was reconsidered, and they were both 'lost' after VE day. Phil Harris lived up to his reputation as a 'wizz' by constructing an electrified metal box to hang in their porch and continually flash the victory signal, 'V . . . .' (vee dot dot dot dash). It was so impressive I brought various school friends to see it.

Like most areas, we had a street party. Fortunately it was a sunny day, and chairs and tables occupied the side of the road with each house contributing towards a selection of sandwiches, cakes, jelly, tea and sundry other drinks. There was music and a bit of singing and dancing, and a small bonfire which scorched and then melted the road surface. Fireworks had become available just in time for the celebrations, and we had a small but representative selection, mostly set off by adults, although Mike and I were trusted enough to have a few of our own to light. However, there was a Slight Misunderstanding, as our inexperience led us to put one of the rockets into an unsupported milk bottle. The result was that the blast knocked over the bottle, and the rocket shot up the road about six inches off the ground. Old Rusty, the canine car chaser who was standing some way off, minding his own business and idly dreaming about unrationed marrow bones, was not aware that he was in a flight path, until the rocket struck him in a tender spot, instantly transforming him into the world's fastest dog, and causing him to shoot off up the road in a blur of fur as if all the alley-cats in Isleworth were after him, and he was not seen again for three days. Mike and I got lost in the crowd.

VJ day, in August, was something of an anticlimax. There was no street party and we were already on holiday from school, so we gained very little. Mike and I and some other lads went round to the Borough Road College to see their bonfire and firework display. What made it memorable for me was that I got into a wrestling match with an older boy, and when we were on the ground, he got his feet on my shoulders and pulled on my neck until I had to give in. It took me a while to lose the symptoms of strain, and I always felt that the permanent discomfort in my neck started then, although I managed to obscure it later with more obvious damage by cycling into the back of a couple of vehicles.

At school we were asked if we would like to go swimming, so after due consultation with the circle of friends and at home, I got a costume and went along, thinking confidently enough that it would be good to be able to swim like Dennis, although I had never been to the baths, and had not been immersed in anything other than our bath since the Tankerton holiday.

We were walked from school to Isleworth baths, got changed with all the usual racket, went through the shower bath, and were directed to the shallow end. There awaiting us in his customary grey suit was the fearsome figure of Mr Hunn (affectionately and improbably known as 'Bunny' to his friends, apparently). We were greeted with 'Get in the water!' Some were jumping in, but I followed others to the steps, which gave rise to a Slight Misunderstanding. I thought that they went down only as far as they were visible, and that was where the bottom was, so I just stepped off the second rung, and plunged below the surface. I somehow found air and got myself the right way up, then I clambered out, gasping and a bit shaken. Mr Hunn was beside me in an instant. 'What's the matter, boy, not scared are you?' Then, to an older boy, 'Take him out on the rope'. Still slightly confused, I was propelled to the steps and a canvas belt was slipped over my head and under my arms. The belt was attached to a long rope, at the other end of which was Mr Hunn. The older boy helped me into the water, then swam with me up the middle of the baths to the deep end, where he trod water while I threshed about in something of a panic. In the distance, I heard Mr Hunn bellow 'Now swim, boy!' The older boy let go, I slipped under the surface and was hauled down the baths to the shallow end, to be pulled out and held up on my feet while Mr Hunn put his face into mine and boomed 'You're yellow, that's your trouble, boy. You're a coward!'

I did not go again with the Town School, and it was twenty years before I faced up to the problem and overcame it. The answer was fairly simple, and I was surprised that while being categorised and castigated as a 'nonswimmer' throughout the rest of my schooldays, no swimming coach had suggested it.

My Father had learned by diving in at the deep end with sufficient power to carry him underwater most of the way to the shallows. That was too heroic for me. I reasoned that since I was afraid of going under and being unable to breathe or find my feet, if I started off in the shallows with a deep breath, crouched under water on a safe footing, then swam for the other side, I had thus already overcome most of the anticipated difficulties. It worked, and with a little practice I was soon swimming on the surface, albeit within my depth. I was later able to enjoy swimming in the sea and even indulge in the luxury of floating on my back in the warm sun. A far cry from the panicky and unsuccessful struggles at Isleworth and Hounslow baths.

I struck up a friendship with Mike Hayward, who lived in the bottom half of Harewood Road. He was a year older, but we often walked to school together while he remained in the top year. We would discuss all the usual contemporary topics, and we had a mutual liking for the current hit tune 'Cossack Patrol', with its stirring evocation of Russian cavalry crossing the Steppes.

Mike was nicknamed 'Muss', which was an abbreviation of 'Musclebound', a soubriquet he had earned by a sterling performance in chopping up firewood at a recent 6th Osterley scout camp. His dad worked on the railways, and like most fathers, was rarely seen, but his mother was usually around to keep an eye on us, although this was not enough to keep us entirely free of trouble.

Muss had the first chemistry set I came across, and we had some fun experimenting. The copper sulphate invisible ink was as always the best product we could make, and as the paper had to be heated to make the message legible, we used a lighted candle standing on a saucer on his dining table. At the end of one such session, while Mrs Hayward sat in front of the fire doing a bit of sewing, we began clearing up, and noticing the accumulation of molten wax in the saucer, I reached across and emptied it into the open fire. This was a Slight Misunderstanding, and revealed an important deficiency in my knowledge of the properties of molten wax. It sent a sheet of flame out into the room, temporarily obscuring the fireplace while it licked the mantelpiece, and startled Mrs Hayward sufficiently to cause her to shriek and leap backward, thereby upsetting the chair and, of course, losing her place with the needle and thread. The flame subsided almost immediately, but it was some time before Mrs Hayward calmed down enough to start telling us off. In later private discussion however, Muss and I considered that as such things go for experimental chemists, it was not too bad, because apart from a few sooty marks and scorched eyebrows, you could hardly see that anything untoward had happened.

We were eventually forgiven, and shortly afterwards Mrs Hayward took us for a treat to see a memorable picture, 'The Adventures of

Tom Sawyer', at the Empire cinema in Hounslow, which we all voted one of the best films ever.

At school, Mr Taylor returned from the army to take up his old job of caretaker, which Mr Chennell had temporarily filled. Mrs Greig left, and Mr Bevan returned to teach once more, following his release from army service.

On moving on to Class one, Miss Groves had taken control of our lives, and her influence was growing, as she was educating us generally as well as preparing us for the scholarship. In appearance she was quite tall, with short cropped silver-grey hair; she wore no make-up but was of a ruddy complexion and usually dressed in jumper or blouse, with a tweed coat and skirt and brogue shoes. She had a well modulated voice, and strong well-manicured hands with long fingers, but if the whole sounds somewhat 'masculine', she was in fact distinctly female without being strongly feminine. Like a number of her colleagues, she cycled to school.

Miss Groves was actually proving to be not only a good teacher, but a fair and considerate person who was concerned with the welfare of all fifty of her charges. Peter Cooper got his shoes, socks and feet soaking wet one morning in a rainstorm (well, by walking through the puddles, actually), and she made him remove socks and shoes to spread them out on the warm radiator, dried his feet, and then sat him down with them encased in her large sheepskin mittens, to the amusement of all.

Outside of school, some of the boys found a large quantity of soap stored in a shed which had easy access and seemingly nobody interested in looking after it. Making the rather gross assumption that it did not belong to anybody, they took quantities of the soap home, whereupon the missing owners surfaced, the police rapidly tracked down the miscreants, and a court appearance and probation followed. Miss Groves addressed the class just before the culprits returned from court to school, and she told us they had learned a lesson, and we were never to mention the matter to those concerned. As far as I know, nobody did.

I sat next to Gwen Dalton for a while. She lived in St Johns Road, and I was attracted to her. Gwen, on the other hand, had no real interest in me, but she had a soft spot for Jeremy Fowler. Jeremy was a quiet, dark-complexioned curly-haired lad, and already an excellent football player, and we got on well. Like me, he had an older brother, and we discovered they both went to Vic Feldman's Jazz Club in Oxford Street. Jazz was in the air, as my favourite record at home was now 'Oh, Monah', featuring Nat Gonella, and Jeremy and I found we had a mutual liking for Louis Armstrong, whose record of 'Shadrach' had just become a hit. Even so, although I liked Jeremy, I still tried to talk Gwen into being interested in me, but to no avail, except that I tried so hard during lessons that Miss Groves got annoyed a couple of times and hauled me out to rap my knuckles with the ruler. Nothing put me off, and I just did not want to give up on Gwen, mainly because I liked her appearance so much. I even went so far as to pluck up courage and walk home with her, but it was all in vain - for her, the chemistry was just not there.

My English continued well, except that my ideas tended to tail off when creativity was required. We had a project to write a novel, or at least a longer essay, and I immediately thought up a good title - 'The Mystery of Beacon House' - a name I had remembered from a dwelling near the beach huts at Tankerton. I wrote a number of pages, and constructed hard red covers, with ribbon ties and the title in bold, flanked by a motif of flaming beacons - then the inspiration dried up, and although it was a disappointment, even to me, the story remained unfinished.

Mental arithmetic was not too difficult, but I was struggling with the 'problems' that required a logical or formulaic approach, and with the more complex sums, for instance those involving various mixed imperial measures, like chains, furlongs and acres, although I knew my tables well enough, and we were given little memory joggers, like 'a pint of water weighs a pound and a quarter'. Predictably, Miss Groves came to the rescue, and got me some special question papers which had both examples and tests, so every evening for some weeks I worked on these at home and she checked them for me the next day - and she did not neglect her other forty nine children either.

We were told that 'the film people' were visiting schools in our area, and across England, looking for someone to play the part of

Oliver in David Lean's 'Oliver Twist'. Mother expressed the fond view that I would be a likely candidate, being slight and fair-haired, although beginning to grow taller now, but no doubt the directors would have been looking for rather more than mere appearance. It fired everyone's imagination for a while, but nothing happened, and then we heard they had chosen someone. It was two years and a change of schools before the film was finally shown at the Odeon, too late, by then, to criticise the choice of John Howard Davies as Oliver.

We were asked, together with Class Two, if we would like to go to see the film 'Henry the Fifth', starring Laurence Olivier, which was coming to the Odeon. We duly brought in our sixpences and were marched up St Johns Road to the cinema for a special morning showing. It was long and the Shakespearian language was wordy and not all readily understood, but we easily followed the action, the battle scene was terrific and it was a unique outing for pleasure, away from school, so everyone enjoyed it immensely.

John Rumins had a birthday party at his house, and this time girls were more in evidence. In addition to our circle from school, there were the Crook brothers, Eric and George, and John's neighbouring friend, Alfie Thatcher. John's elder sister Pamela, who attended the Black and White school, was there, and so was their cousin, Maggie Sandford, who was about the same age as Pamela. Maggie was, in looks, the epitome of an English rose, with a pretty face and curly auburn hair. I was immediately taken by her appearance, and as quickly shaken by her manner when, in my first ever game of 'postman's knock', she rejected my attempted kiss in the hall in no uncertain terms. I was completely disillusioned with girls - I thought then, forever.

It was John who came up with the Final Solution, the answer to The Big Question - where do babies come from? Not that we ever gave it much thought, and it was never mentioned at home, but it cropped up every now and then in relation to 'rude' jokes or pictures, and 'rude' parts of the body. John had asked his dad, and got a straight answer - the child was the result of physical contact and intercourse between a man and a woman, it grew in the woman's belly, and after nine months it came out where she spent a penny -

and that was that. No more theories about belly button births, storks or gooseberry bushes, and we never doubted his word.

Public interest in professional football revived somewhat about this time, as the better players were relieved of their wartime commitments. Peter's dad, a fine footballer in his day and recently released from the Royal Army Service Corps, supported Brentford, and he took me along regularly with Peter to watch the home games. We would catch the 657 trolleybus to the Ealing Road and then walk the rest of the way up to the ground, and here, once more, I was aware of that intriguing sound of hundreds of feet, this time giving a background to the hubbub of voices, getting louder as supporters of both teams met and joined with a similar stream coming down Windmill Road and Ealing Road to converge on Griffin Park. We stood on the side terraces - it was ninepence for the privilege - and cheered our stalwarts with 'Come on the Bees!" and 'Up the Bees!' - the check-capped Crozier in goal, bald Gorman at right back, Smith at centre half, Townsend centre forward, and the rest made up of Munro, McAulay, Paterson, Hopkins, Stewart, Wilkins and Girling. Sadly, it was not a winning combination, and despite our support they slid into relegation at the end of that season. On those autumn Saturdays, the weather was often sunny to start with, but seemed to get gloomy by half-time, and London fogs would often steal up from the nearby Thames and begin to shroud the stands in the late afternoon. This could add to the interest, as on one occasion, while the fog was swirling down the pitch, the players were sometimes visible and sometimes only audible, when suddenly a Brentford player emerged from a dense patch, running towards the opposing goal with the ball in his arms. A great roar went up from the crowd, delight from the Bee's fans, anger from the visitors, and he dropped the ball and dribbled on, undetected by linesman or referee.

I had been steadily losing favour within my own circle. I could not understand and did not know the reason at the time, but it was most likely just the usual recipe of frustration, irritation and envy on a bed of boredom with a dash of contempt.

It seemed petty, but I was increasingly taunted over the books I read and possessed - those at home were still mainly of the ilk of

Rupert Bear, Alice in Wonderland, The Water Babies - young children's adventures, and not 'proper' boys' stories such as the rest were starting to accumulate. Most had comics delivered, and they were given comic and adventure annuals - like the one Peter lent me which, in among the thrilling stories, contained Alfred Noyes' great and stirring descriptive poem 'The Highwayman'. It was illustrated with a super colour print of the moonlit scene with his girl Bess, of the tumbling dark tresses and scarlet ribbon, waiting for the highwayman at the window of the old inn. I got carried away by the whole notion, and it remains inextricably entwined with my later knowledge of Hounslow Heath and of Colnbrook. Nevertheless, however much I would have liked to, I could do nothing about my stock of books, apart from mention my wishes at home, as I was entirely dependent upon what I was given at Christmas and birthdays.

I was also taunted with being 'spoon fed' - which apparently was something to do with my Dad's job, and something to do with what things I had at home, although they did not seem to rate those very highly - and I was accused of being a 'snob', which they explained meant that I was 'too reserved', and obviously therefore thought myself better than anybody else. The latter problem arose from a form of shyness, which meant that I got on well with one or two companions, but I was lost for words in a crowd, or indeed, if separated even by a slight distance from somebody I was acquainted with, which no doubt made it look as though I was not sociable, or inclined to ignore people.

This whole unpleasant trend worried me a lot and undermined what pleasure there had been in going to school, or playing on the journey. I eventually told Mother, but after thinking about it, she simply advised me not to take any notice of it.

Things eventually came to a head. One afternoon on the way home from school, I was surrounded by the others and forced to go to an alleyway off Hartham Road, where in a mock trial I was accused of all those things. One boy acted as prosecutor, others gave evidence and one acted as judge, but when he said 'I will now put on the black cap to pronounce sentence', my patience gave out

218

and I pushed them aside and stalked off home, hearing Peter call out, 'Has he gone mad?'

Strangely enough, normal relations were resumed almost immediately after that, but it subsequently served to identify and firm up for me both the close and the cool connections within the group.

In class, I discovered on the shelf the book *Rodney Stone* by Conan Doyle. It was a stirring story of a blacksmith's son who is strong in body and spirit, fights and beats the bullies and becomes a great pugilist, and I found it to be a good antidote to the less pleasant realities. In addition, it was quite advanced reading of real boys' stuff, and what was more, none of the others had read it. It gave me an edge, and for once I did not hesitate to tell them about it.

It was at about this time that Auntie Rose gave me the boys' adventure books and annuals that cousin Peter no longer wanted, and so my stock deficiency at home, and thus my credibility, were at last corrected. I also got through Fenimore Cooper's *The Last of the Mohicans*, which Dennis gave me: a none too easy read that put me on a par with the rest of our group, who were also battling through it, its popularity being due to the fact that the film had recently been released and shown at the Odeon. I did become aware that some boys were even more advanced in their reading matter, like Ian Fowler, who was reading a history book describing the time of Henry the Eighth. He told me of the lurid description of the fascinating incident when Henry's corpse was resting overnight at Syon House. The stomach exploded and the dogs were eating it and had to be driven off. It seemed that not all history books were dull.

The interest in reading was general and quite widespread at school, and when news came that there were cheap books in the newsagents at Tudor Parade, just before The Coach & Horses, I walked there with a little of my precious savings in my pocket. What I found was that because of the paper shortage they were selling miniature books, about four inches square, each containing one story and costing only a few pennies. Over a short period I bought several, and they proved to be surprisingly good reading, some being adventures and some moving more towards the adult romantic, which began to strike chords of interest. The two best stories I had were a motor racing tale, based at Brooklands and full of ruffians, swindlers and car chases, with our hero getting to the starting line just in time and winning the race, and a touching wartime romance concerning a fighter pilot and his sweetheart, called *Home's Where the Heart Is*.

Peter then discovered a second-hand bookshop just past The Bell, on the north side of the Staines Road, and we made an expedition there, penetrating the gloomy but encitingly overladen depths of the shop and coming away with some very cheap books and a collection of 1920s 'Boy's Own' magazines containing cracking adventure stories set in far-off lands.

While at work in Town, Father had found a blue Boat Race rosette, which he gave me. The 1946 race was imminent, and as I had no particular loyalties, I went along with the colour of the rosette and became a Cambridge supporter. This proved to be a Slight Misunderstanding. There had been no race during the war years, so this was the first since 1939, yet oddly enough it transpired that most people in our group supported Oxford. The race was won by Oxford and I was rightly put down, but only after that was it pointed out that my rosette was not in fact the Cambridge blue, but that of Oxford. Finding that my public display of support had been thus compromised, I did the only honourable thing and returned to my former state of indifference.

Father was admitted into Hammersmith Hospital for an operation to remove warts from the bladder. I was taken to visit him and did not much enjoy seeing him down, as he was a mainstay of our lives; nor did I like being in the hospital surroundings. While he was in there, Miss Groves was adding a touch of realism to a nature lesson by relating to us how, while travelling abroad in a car before the war, they had driven over a snake and, upon going back to it, had found its insides squashed out on the road, but the snake still alive. Somehow it all got tied in with Father and his operation - everything went black for me and I slid to the floor. I came to and she sat me down and forced my head between my knees; then, when I was recovering, she took me with a chair to the open door at the end of the corridor and made me sit there in the fresh air until I was able to rejoin the class. Of course, everybody wanted to know what had happened to me - they had never seen anything like it before, and I was none too pleased to be the centre of attention in such an incident.

We sat the scholarship at last, and I managed the Mental Arithmetic and English well enough, and the General Paper, and battled away with the dreaded Maths paper to find I was arriving at answers more readily than I expected. Afterwards, I tried to avoid discussing my conclusions with the others. I was not confident enough, and the outcome seemed so important that I did not want to face the doubts and worries that could arise from hearing that what I had done was wrong.

From home, I was wandering further afield, sometimes in company, sometimes alone. I was friendly with Jimmy Girling, who lived 'at the bottom of our garden'. He was a little older and already at the County School, but we often chatted over the back fence, out of range of the houses, where he would climb up his tree and I would sit on my swing. We went several times to play by the Grand Junction Canal. We would walk down the Great West Road, past the factories, under the railway bridge, and there, on the south side, was a field, or rather an expanse of waste ground covered with grass and bushes, which we crossed to arrive at the towpath. There was a fair amount of canal traffic, with men leading horses that pulled the barges, often loaded with cement from the Blue Circle premises on the opposite bank. We sometimes stood out in the open and exchanged a greeting with the bargees, and sometimes hid in the shrubbery, pretending to spy on the movement of enemy forces. We did not stray very far along the towpath - the field was a pleasant place to be, a peaceful backwater in the hot sunshine, overlooked only by the captive figure of the diving girl in a bathing costume, advertising Jantzen swimwear, high on a wall beyond the Blue Circle. It seemed the bees and grasshoppers were making more noise than the distant road traffic, and the greatest disturbance came from the soft thud of hooves as the big horses plodded from time to time along the towpath.

Jimmy, Muss Hayward, Mike Curwen and I formed a small secret society with an interest in sleuthing and undercover work. We studied my paper magazine on the subject, 'How to be a Great Detective', and we devised passwords and initiation tests, and codes using the alphabet and numbers, we kept magnifying glasses handy, and test tubes full of graphite powder for detecting fingerprints, and we agreed secret hiding places where we could leave messages for each other. Jimmy rigged up a Meccano 'cable car' which could be loaded with a paper message (like the overhead railway system in Treble's shop) and ran on cord in the back garden from his tree to one of ours, which worked quite well, although rain and rust were an unforeseen problem. We learnt Morse code, and torches had become commonplace as a result of the blackout, so by arrangement at night, as both Jimmy and I slept in the back bedrooms, we would signal to each other in Morse. This tended to fall apart, and recriminations would follow the next day, when all too often one of us forgot to give the 'sending message' or the 'signing off' signal.

Jimmy was of an age to be interested in girls, and we both liked to go through our collections of film star cigarette cards and pick out our favourite lady of the moment. A recent big hit song on the radio was Rodgers and Hammerstein's 'It Might As Well Be Spring', sung by Luanne Hogan in the film 'State Fair', and its wistful words and tune tugged gently at me and struck a lasting chord: 'I'm as restless as a willow in a windstorm ...' We even went for walks in the light early evening after tea, looking for girls along the Great West Road, still warm in its exposure to the late sunshine, and in Jersey Gardens, with its enticing mixture of sunny lawns, shadowy paths and convenient huts, and once or twice we were lucky and got talking to a couple. I was conscious that here was a new aspect of life, but just for the moment I remained on the threshold.

As a member of the St Mary's Sports Club, whose grounds were round the corner in Musgrave Road, Jimmy encouraged me to join, saying what fun it was to play tennis, and to use the field and attend the various sporting activities during the year. The snag was it cost ten shillings just for the basic membership, which meant tennis and the clubhouse was extra - a huge sum by our standards. Nevertheless I was excited by the idea, and got up the courage to work on Mother and Father, until at last Dad capitulated. It was a big day when I went round to crusty old Mrs Berry who lived at the corner of Wood Lane and Musgrave Road, braved their snappy chow dog and handed over the subscription.

My early visits were indeed exciting. It was a new area to explore, with different people to meet, and for once I was on the inside, because it excluded those who did not belong. I soon found, however, that this supposed privilege had two sides, as there were not always agreeable companions to be found on the premises, and my other friends could not be admitted. I played tennis once with Jimmy, as his 'guest', but I found Dennis's racquet extremely heavy and virtually unmanageable, so that was not a success.

Some of the older hands among the boys showed me other games which had little to do with the Club's real purpose. On the far side of the field by the wall bordering the railway was an old oak tree, reputed to be the home of a barn owl, which we all climbed in order to investigate the hollow and to watch the trains go by. A new clubhouse had replaced the old pavilion backing on to College Road, and so while the lads playing football and cricket still used the old premises to change in, what little furnishings there were got treated with scant respect. That included a collection of 1920s gramophone records, and a game enjoyed by many was in taking these out into the field and 'skimming' them over huge distances down towards the bottom end.

Sadly, Jimmy and his parents were moving to distant Twyford that summer, and although I subsequently attended a few cricket and football matches at the Sports Club, and the bonfire and firework display on Guy Fawkes night, without a close companion the magic evaporated and my interests were taken up elsewhere.

With Mike Curwen, I had been making forays northwards up Wood Lane. In an early expedition, after passing the landmark of Bernard Sunley's 'Estate Office' on the corner, we stopped outside the ancient wall behind the Osterley Hotel. It surrounded a nursery garden which seemed to be derelict, and therefore fair game, although we did not know that it belonged to Wyke House. Mike had been told that if you threw a stone over the wall you could hear ('old') glass breaking - why that was always so fascinating I do not know - so we tried it, and found it to be true. Then, as was the way in those days, the largest policeman I had ever seen suddenly and silently materialised beside us, dwarfing his huge bicycle and startling us no end.

'Now then - what are you two up to?'

'Nothing, sir'

'Nothing, eh? Not throwing stones, I suppose? Over the wall perhaps?'

We took a calculated risk. 'No, sir'

'That's all right then, but don't let me catch you up to no good. We've had serious complaints about young lads like you up to no good round here, and I wouldn't like to be in your shoes if I catch you at it!'

'No, sir'

'All right - now, where d'you live?'

'Down that way, sir'

'Be off with you then!'

'Yes, sir'

It sometimes paid to bluff, and it always paid to be polite.

We roamed Jersey Gardens, sometimes meeting up with other friends there. All the paths and the valley had to be explored each time, and all three huts inspected. We had a ritual drink from the water fountain, the girls made daisy chains on the 'Daisy Lawn', we located the park keeper, 'Old Nosey', and when it was safe, made a raid on the cordoned off valley known as 'The Dell', where the water pump stood inside its iron railings, and then we would roost for a while in the hut up the hill, enjoying its separate compartments and its commanding view, and carving our initials into the wooden walls.

As we explored, we were constantly sidetracked, learning the landmarks, peering through hedges, trying out trees, delving into ditches, and we looked for anything of interest, and for the 'bounty of nature' that was such a feature of adventure stories. We picked up useful sticks, clamped acorn stem pipes in our mouths, threw burrs and grass head 'arrows' to stick on each other's clothing, blew 'squealers' with a blade of grass stretched between the thumbs, tasted rose hips and found them lacking, chewed the leaves of the may hedges, but learned they were not remotely like their 'bread and cheese' label, split 'milk stones' and were disappointed to discover that they were dry inside, but we found that dock leaves did relieve nettle stings, and served another purpose when we suffered an occasional unexpected 'looseness', and we also found that the sloes culled from the Borough Road College grounds were just tolerable to the palate.

Walking up Wood Lane, we spent time loitering by the sports field gates, and standing on the bridge to watch the tube trains go past, then looking over the stile across the field, with chickens and a goat where once cricket had been played, and where we discovered a surprise stock of lavatory pans and other builders' materials in the dusty pavilion, no doubt the property of Seccombe Brothers of Wyke Farm, although we did not make the connection at the time.

Further still we roamed, across the very rough, boggy, churned-up ground of Wyke Green, with its ruts, deep water-filled holes and narrow pathways, and so past the lodge gates into Osterley Park. Osterley House was closed to the public at that time, as were the grounds surrounding it, and also the whole of the land along the south side of Osterley Lane, which ran through the Park from Wyke to Norwood Green. The Lane was sandy, stoney, and badly potholed, but to us that just made the walk more interesting. In the first field on the left we saw the Nissen huts where the prisoners of war were held. On the right was the field with the massive concrete, sand-banked wall of the rifle range, where the Home Guard had trained.

We arrived at the spot where the road passed between the two lakes, ahead on the left the open water of the High Lake, with its iron railings and 'Keep Out' warning, and on the right the Low Lake, bordered by a tall wooden fence. Enticed at first by the massive oak with its low and accessible bough, just inside the Home Guard field, we climbed over the low railings, but hearing a commotion in the woods, we skirted the tree and approached the Low Lake. By the fence at the field's edge we hid and watched soldiers on manoeuvres, the woods full of running, diving figures in khaki, and echoing with rifle fire and shouted commands. When we set off for home on that occasion, we felt we had had a real adventure.

As I grew more familiar with the park, I even went there alone when there was nobody to play with. There were usually other boys there, and although there were tramps and other characters loitering, no harm was done. We never anticipated any real danger, but we were always wary.

The big wooden gates to the Low Lake were soon to be thrown permanently open, after all military activity had ceased, and we were always attracted to that area. We would follow the asphalt path right round one side, over the stream, and up to the high fence that prevented access to 'The Aviary', a house which at that time belonged to the American racing driver Whitney Straight. There were birds galore, the woods alive with their movement and song - from the tiny chattering wrens that abounded in the holly bushes, and the large, gravely silent grey heron, balancing on a tree trunk fallen half in the water and concentrating on his fishing, to the more elusive, brightly coloured woodpeckers, whose tapping echoed across the lake, and whose ringing laughter mocked us from the canopy of the many tall trees.

Following the asphalt path in the opposite direction brought us to the ruined wooden footbridge that led across the narrow neck of the lake to 'The Aviary', and from there we had a fine view of its lawned gardens, stretching down to the water's edge, where, in the centre, was the life-size classical statue of a nude lady.

Beyond the bridge was the reedy stream that topped the lake, but if we turned back and followed the circular path round to the right, we could stray from it to go over the stile, by the hollow tree where ducks nested, and into the field to play in the tumbledown hayloft, derelict but still full of sweet-smelling hay. Partridges ran in this meadow and the next, and each May, the joyous call of the elusive cuckoo echoed across the fields and round the lakes.

Once, when alone, I met an older boy by the Low Lake. We got talking because he had a spaniel, and he was carrying a stout staff, which aroused my curiosity. It transpired that he was a boy scout from Greenford, and the staff was his trusty ash scout pole. He demonstrated how he used it to vault the stream, and to defend himself. He let me practise vaulting with it, then he took me to where the stream went through the ancient culvert under Windmill Lane. He said it was an initiation test, to go through the low tunnel, come out in Bluebell Woods and then return. He went first, and I followed, straddling the water and finding a foothold on the sloping cobbles on either side, the spaniel running to and fro and splashing us both.

We emerged in Bluebell Woods, and close by was the 'camp' belonging to 'Old Moses' (sometimes called 'Old Rip'), whose appearance and outdoor life classified him as one of the old traditional tramps. His camp against a bank of earth by the stream was little more than a few bits of wood supporting a waterproof cover, with a scattering of old pots and pans and other discarded objects. He was always encased in a couple of layers of worn-out clothes of a uniformly grey colour, with a string round the waist of his overcoat, his ruddy wild-eyed face framed by a bushy grey beard and a mass of curly grey hair. However, he was not at home on that occasion, which was perhaps fortunate, as he was not a man one could comfortably converse with, being in fact somewhat irascible, and with a manner that suggested he was preoccupied with a fierce struggle in some other dimension. He was indeed often to be seen walking the local streets, even amidst the traffic along the London Road, pushing his barrow full of junk while shouting abuse at an audience that only he could see above the rooftops. We children were told to take no notice and not to stare, so we watched and listened surreptitiously as he passed by, quoting from the Bible and cursing God, Jesus and the church, a religious obsession which gave rise to his nickname.

I passed the tunnel test, and then it was time for me to go home. My new-found friend and his dog accompanied me to the Great West Road. Here we shook hands and agreed to meet again in the park, whereupon he presented me with his staff. I never saw him again, but the staff I treasured for years.

When we explored further along the Lane, we discovered the Newt Pond, just inside the fence, a little way past the Low Lake and on the same side. A typical watering place for the horses and cattle in the field, it was surrounded by a grassy, sandstone bank, but with a well-worn, trampled and hoof-marked slope leading down to the boggy drinking spot. There were two or three oak trees round the perimeter, sheltering the pool, and we became fond of roosting in one particular tree which leaned out over the water. It was an easy climb, and had comfortable branches from which one could get a good view of the Lane without being seen.

In the spring, there were newts galore in the pond, and I brought a jam jar and took some home. They lived and hibernated down the garden, in my 'secret place', in the cool, shady area around the tin bath full of sand, in which I maintained a pool of rain water and a supply of weed, worms and other delights.

I was in between bicycles at the age of eleven, having outgrown my little red cycle, but Mike had progressed from his blue bike to a full-sized black roadster, and I had to run or trail along as best I could.

We often used to chat to old Mr Titcombe, Mike's next door neighbour who was frequently to be found standing at his front gate, watching the world go by. He was a good old boy, dressed with waistcoat and fob watch, sporting a military moustache, and smoking a pipe, always with a twinkle in his eye and a joke for us. Hearing of my plight, he said I could borrow his bicycle as often as I liked!

Borrow it I did, and after a struggle, I was soon riding alongside Mike, around the local roads, and up to the Park. The reason for the struggle was that it was a roadster with a massive twenty eight inch wheel diameter - the normal size being twenty six inch - and at the age of eleven I was not yet man-size, but determination somehow made up for lack of reach.

Things were becoming steadily more pleasant in Class, largely due to Miss Groves. She tried to broaden our education by talking to us about worldly matters, for instance discussing the unfairness of allowing disapproval of gambling to overshadow the thrill of horse-racing, and we listened to the exciting live radio commentary as Airborne won The Derby. She read to us increasingly - from poetry, like Sir Henry Newbolt's 'Fighting Temeraire', and 'Vitai Lampada': 'There's a breathless hush in the close tonight, ten to make and the match to win' - stirring stuff, even if few of us knew the difference between a 'close' and a quadrangle - and she read from fiction like Ballantyne's *Coral Island*, and extracts from a volume of ghost stories, with a notably enthralling tale of mysterious deaths in a bedroom, solved when a nest of poisonous spiders was discovered in the trunk of the old tree that scraped its branches on the window.

Our coaching in English continued almost unnoticed. We were told to be proud of the finest language in the world, not to snigger at a word like lavatory, which only meant 'washing place', given advice such as the preferred way to pronounce 'controversy' with the accent on the second syllable, and given spelling tips like remembering that the word 'stationary' with an 'a' as in car referred to immobility. I was one of those chosen for our high standard of English to help the less able children in other classes learn to read. Most of my sessions were among the lower age groups, in classes which were the province of Mr Bevan, and Miss Treweek, who was near retirement. Miss Treweek was tall and thin, and she wore pince-nez and dark coloured dresses that might have been fashionable in the time of the Great War. She was very pleasant and well-liked, and worked tirelessly in the uphill struggle to help her less able scholars.

The results of the Scholarship came through and I had passed, as had about three quarters of the class - an astonishingly high number, and a just tribute to Miss Groves and to the system. In fact, the majority of Town School pupils at that time emerged with the ability to read, write, spell and calculate, and the decency to show respect and courtesy to other people.

I ran all the way home that lunchtime, and bumped into Mr Morrison at his front gate.

'Hello T for Tony, you're in a hurry today!'

I blurted out my good news, and he said:

'Well done! That calls for some recognition. Here ...'

Fishing in his pocket, he produced half a crown and pressed it into my hand - an extremely generous gesture. Mother had taught us that it was wrong to accept money from people outside, but I weighed up the circumstances and the spontaneous manner in which it had come about, and I was pleased to feel that I could justify it for once - and that it might even be churlish to refuse!

There was no school sports day as such, but an annual 'sports trials' day, in which various races were run, and the best picked to represent the school, as my sister Pauline had done, at the inter-schools competition held in Lampton Park. I won my race, which was little more than a dash from one end of the field to the other. I was told afterwards by a disgruntled competitor that I had only won because I ran with my elbows sticking out, preventing the others from getting past. In any event, I did not represent the school, as Mother could not buy me the necessary shorts, shirt and shoes to run in, and nothing less would do. Anyway, I did not much fancy going without the rest of the gang, and there were plenty of other things to occupy us.

In the fine sunny weather we went more frequently out onto the field and played rounders, or stool ball. The latter was a cricket-style game from Sussex that Miss Groves was fond of, and we all grew to enjoy. The 'wicket' consisted of a large square wooden board fixed to the top of a portable post The batsman stood in front to defend it and to try and score runs, using a solid but light wooden bat like an oversized table tennis bat, and he could be caught or bowled out, but would more often than not strike his own wicket, to howls of derision from all sides.

The first of two extraordinary things that happened to me in those summer months occurred when I formed a close relationship with Michael Jenkin, who was a late joiner, having moved in from Grove Road School in Hounslow. He was a sensible but tough, freckle-faced lad, with an open, friendly nature, who could run like the wind despite his boots, and he and I just suddenly got on well together. More than just a friend, he became my 'supporter', beside whom I felt I could face up to anybody or anything. This was an entirely new experience for me, and at a time when I was recovering from a really low level of self-confidence, it was a tonic that could not have been bettered.

The second extraordinary event concerned another relationship. A game of 'kiss chase' in the playground was 'developing', as it was wont to do when somebody favoured a partner outside the immediate circle, and suddenly I was confronted by Olive Jukes. She was perfectly proportioned and nicely dressed, wearing a black blazer over a blue check print dress, with black shoes and white ankle socks, her long, dark, curly hair framing a pale-skinned and lovely face - and everybody else in the playground just faded from my awareness.

Olive was another late joiner, having returned only the year before from evacuation to Bromwich. We were of the same age, although from different classrooms, and yet had never consciously seen or encountered each other, but now an instant bond was formed. If her looks were appealing - and I thought she compared favourably with Bess, the 'Highwayman's' sweetheart - they seemed equally matched by her combination of gentleness with fragrance, vitality with grace. The other lads called her 'sexy' and 'a smasher', and Michael, with exceptional manners for that age, neither competed nor derided, but encouraged and supported the liaison. The three of us spent time together at school, and suddenly life was good.

I called on Olive at her home in Mandeville Road, where I met her family, and when I was introduced to her mother, sensing it was a formal occasion, I gave my full name, 'Anthony', and it stuck. In the continuing fine summer weather, we went for walks up Wood Lane to Jersey Gardens and to Osterley Park. Olive did not have a bicycle, and when I occasionally borrowed old Mr Titcombe's, it proved too big for her to ride, but she was content to walk alongside, holding on to me. There seemed to be no barriers.

In consultation with schoolmates and parents, and following the strong recommendation of Jimmy Girling, my first choice of secondary grammar school had been Isleworth County, and I got accepted along with Peter and many of our chums. It was a big disappointment for me that Michael Jenkin was not coming too, but our influence over such decisions was slight when the real world brought other pressures to bear.

The final day of school came at last We did the rounds of the playground and classrooms, and following the fad of the time, collected and exchanged autographs, teachers' and pupils' alike. Michael and I said farewell, with no inkling that we would never meet again. Then we all 'broke up', and made the final journey home, chattering and carefree, until alone we each entered our gateways, the lucky ones still flushed with success, good wishes and optimism, already mentally discarding the dark days and buffing up the brighter ones.

With the long summer holidays stretching ahead, and the promise of our first post-war seaside holiday on the Isle of Wight, I was for the time being able to set aside any apprehensions about the future, and enjoy the luxury of the reassurance given by the prospect of eventually rejoining old friends at the secondary school of my choice,

Alas for our blossoming relationship, poor Olive suddenly seemed too often burdened with the company of a clutch of dependent children half our age, and I was as yet too half-baked to understand or even discuss it. I just stopped calling on her. To have been associated with such youngsters would have meant a loss of status among my peers, and despite the pleasant and easy-going connection, I became too embarrassed to cope with a situation which seemed to be a premature commitment to the grown-up world.

Nevertheless, although I had turned away from the problem, even the apparent clumsiness of my failure in this matter did not impede the overriding change that was in progress. I do not know how it was achieved, nor quite when it happened, nor could I have defined it, but somehow I had at last made the mysterious but essential transition to boyhood, and the doors of childhood were closing behind me.

* * * * * *

"WASSA MATTER MATE, SOMEBODY 'ITCHYER?"

A Suburban Childhood

TONY BETTS

Pen Press Publishers Ltd
London